FRIENDS IN HIGH PLACES

THE BECHTEL STORY:
THE MOST SECRET CORPORATION
AND HOW IT
ENGINEERED THE WORLD

▲

LATON McCARTNEY

SIMON AND SCHUSTER

NEW YORK   LONDON   TORONTO
SYDNEY   TOKYO

Copyright © 1988 by Laton McCartney
All rights reserved
including the right of reproduction
in whole or in part in any form
Published by Simon and Schuster
A Division of Simon & Schuster Inc.
Simon & Schuster Building
Rockefeller Center
1230 Avenue of the Americas
New York, New York 10020

SIMON AND SCHUSTER and colophon are registered trademarks
of Simon & Schuster Inc.

Designed by M.B. Kilkelly/Levavi & Levavi
Manufactured in the United States of America

10   9   8   7   6   5   4   3   2   1

Library of Congress Cataloging in Publication Data

McCartney, Laton.
Friends in high places / Laton McCartney.

p.   cm.
Bibliography: p.
Includes index.
1. Bechtel Group.   2. Bechtel, Stephen Davison, 1925-
3. Engineers—United States—Biography.   4. Businessmen—Unite
States—Biography.   I. Title.
TA217.B4M38 1988
338.8'87—dc19   87–34562
[B]   CIP

ISBN 0-671-47415-4

ACKNOWLEDGMENTS

Joni Evans, former president of Simon & Schuster, was the sponsor of this work. I cannot thank her enough for her unflagging graciousness, support and enthusiasm. John Ware, my agent and friend, also played a vital role in my undertaking and completing this project. To him also very special thanks are due. Others who provided invaluable assistance include Robert Sam Anson for support, editing and toughness that aided at every step; Van Metaxas for his diligent research, resourcefulness and good judgment; Nancy J. Balz for her research and support; Bill Berkowitz and his colleagues at the Data Center in Oakland, California, who always came through when needed; Mark Dowie for his generosity and encouragement; Tim Shorrock for his valuable assist; Marjorie Williams for her insights and suggestions; Paul Cane, Tom Flynn and Al Donner for having the courage to grant an outsider access and Mel Shestach, Larry Eno and Jerome Bakst.

Others at Simon & Schuster who deserve thanks are David Shipley and Henry Ferris.

Alice Mayhew, my editor at Simon and Schuster, worked diligently and offered her support and enthusiasm. Without her this project would never have been completed.

To Nancy

CONTENTS

▲

CHAPTER 1

THE GROVE

On the last weekend in July in the year 1982, a chauffeur-driven Cadillac arrived in the exclusive Nob Hill section of San Francisco to pick up a solitary passenger. His name was Stephen Davison Bechtel, Jr., and to the few who may have seen him that sunny morning as he emerged from his luxury condominium across from Grace Cathedral and briskly walked the few paces to his waiting car, there was nothing to suggest he was anything but another businessman on the way to a weekend outing. Certainly, there was nothing to indicate that this casually dressed lean, balding figure in his late 50s, so unremarkable in appearance, was the leader of one of the richest, most powerful companies in the world.

Which, as it happened, was how Stephen D. Bechtel, Jr., preferred it. The chairman of the Bechtel Group had a passion for anonymity, and he went to extraordinary lengths to preserve it. The details of his personal life were a carefully guarded secret. His condo and other residences, studded with state-of-the-art security devices designed to foil a would-be burglar or kidnapper, were listed not in his name, but in that of one of his company's numerous corporate entities and subsidiaries.

On all his trips, including the one he was making this morning, the route was planned by a former U.S. Army antiterrorism expert, who varied it every time.

While there was some good reason for the caution and secrecy—in the early 1970s, Bechtel's name had shown up on a Symbionese Liberation Army "hit list"[1]—to an even larger extent, this was Bechtel's style and a reflection of the values of the remarkable company he commanded.

Founded by his grandfather seventy-five years before, and owned and operated by the Bechtel family ever since, the Bechtel Group* was the largest engineering and construction company in the world, with interests and political connections stretching from Saudi Arabia to Indonesia and back again. It had built pipelines in Peru, copper mines in South Africa, synthetic-fuel plants in New Zealand, nuclear power stations in India, a subway system in Washington, factories in California, hospitals, hotels, airports and industrial structures the world over. In the Middle East, its refineries and pipelines had made the rise of OPEC possible. In Libya, where Bechtel had been among the last American companies to depart, its creations inadvertently had generated the revenues that would help finance the regime of Muhammar Qaddafi. In the United States, where it had been influencing presidents since Herbert Hoover, it had built many of the roads and bridges that had opened the West, and the dams, such as Boulder, that had brought it life. And the list stretched on, seemingly endless.

This year alone, Bechtel and its 42,000 employees were engaged in building in 20 countries a total of 101 megaprojects, each with a value of at least $50 million, including one—the Saudi Arabian industrial city of Jubail—with a larger budget than the entire U.S. space program. When the balance sheet for 1982 was finally figured, Bechtel would report revenues of $13.6 billion—sufficient, had the company been listed in the *Fortune 500*, to place it as the 20th largest corporation in America, above far more familiar names like Standard Oil, Western Electric, Eastman Kodak and Xerox.

But Bechtel was not listed in the *Fortune 500* or on any public exchange. It was a private company, one of the largest in the world; and that too was the way Steve Bechtel, Jr. preferred it. He had no patience for troublesome stockholders or filings with the SEC, and

---

* In 1979, the Bechtel Corporation changed its name to the Bechtel Group as part of a company reorganization.

even less for the prying scrutiny of the public and the press.* "There's no reason for the public to hear of us," he had once told a reporter. "We're not selling anything to the public."

Instead, Bechtel did its selling to companies and to governments, quietly and out of view: in boardrooms, on golf courses, in kings' palaces and prime ministers' residences, or at the site to which Steve Bechtel's chauffeur was now ferrying him—a secluded, 2,700-acre stand of redwoods 75 miles east of San Francisco. It was named the Bohemian Grove.

For Steve Bechtel and the power brokers like him, the Bohemian Grove, which is owned and operated by the Bohemian Club in San Francisco, was the grown-up equivalent of a summer camp, a retreat where, for a three-day weekend every July, the country's corporate, political and military elite could gather, immune from care (it was burned in effigy at the start of every Grove encampment to symbolize the elimination of worldly concerns) and ringing telephones (there was but one at The Grove, and it was for emergencies only). Here, shielded from intrusion by a chain-link fence and the forces of the California Highway Patrol, men like Justin W. Dart, William F. Buckley, George Bush, Edgar Kaiser, Jr., and Tom Watson could walk in the woods, skinny-dip in the Russian River, toast marshmallows over a fire, dress in drag for a "low jinks" dramatic production, and, for a few days at least, hew to The Grove's motto: "Spiders Weave Not Here." In this place, as many as 1,600 of the nation's business and political leaders gathered every July for the annual Bohemian Club encampment.

The Grove, however, was not all fun and games. Since its founding in 1872 by the essayist Ambrose Bierce and a handful of San Francisco journalists and artists, The Grove had always had a serious aspect as well. It was in a speech at The Grove, for instance, that an Army general named Dwight Eisenhower had warned of a coming conflict in a place called Korea. Later, after Eisenhower had become president, his director of Central Intelligence, Allen Dulles, warned Grove members of the threat of Communism—a refrain H-bomb "father"

* Stephen D. Bechtel, Jr.'s, reluctance to grant interviews has lessened considerably in the past few years, thanks in large part to George Shultz. At Bechtel, Shultz' responsibilities included supervising press relations. "George pressed us to be more open in dealing with the media," a former Bechtel colleague explains. "He really helped open up the company to the press and encouraged us to begin putting out an annual report." Bechtel now publishes its yearly revenues—something it never did in the past—and gives access to reporters it deems "responsible."

Edward Teller reiterated at The Grove a quarter-century later, this time in connection with the Persian Gulf. Through the years, The Grove, whose membership included numerous governors and senators, three former presidents and whole battalions of cabinet members, past and present, had also been the scene of considerable politicking—most notably in 1967, when Grove member Richard Nixon extracted a promise from fellow member Ronald Reagan that he would not be a candidate for the 1968 Republican presidential nomination.[2]

But the real business of The Grove, where a favorite pastime was figuring out the corporate connections and interlocking directorates of incoming members, was just that: business. Not business by contract or by deal—both of which were barred on The Grove's grounds—but business by sheer association, by men spending time with, getting to know and to like each other. "Once you've spent three days with someone in an informal situation," explained John D. Ehrlichman, who attended Grove encampments while a chief aide to Richard Nixon, "you have a relationship—a relationship that opens doors and makes it easier to pick up the phone."[3]

Few understood that better than Steve Bechtel, Jr., who, like his father before him, had been coming to The Grove all his adult life. Nothing could keep him from this annual encampment, for it was friends like those at The Grove—friends in high places—who, as much as anything, had made the Bechtel Group the master builder that it was. It was they who had provided the contacts and the contracts; they who had opened doors which, in turn, had opened other doors; they who had smoothed the way, recommended, endorsed—and on occasion, skirted the law. It was they—and the Bechtel organization's shrewd courtship of them—who had made everything possible: the power, the nearly $2 billion* family fortune, the entrée to the White House and the seats of foreign governments.

Because of those friends, anonymous Steve Bechtel was a presence at The Grove, a man whose very appearance generated awed and admiring whispers. Set on a hillside, Mandalay, the lodge to which he belonged, was the most esteemed of The Grove's 127 separate encampments. Its membership and guest list included Steve; his father, Stephen D. Bechtel, Sr.; Henry Kissinger; former Bechtel Group president and secretary of state designate George P. Shultz (who this year

---

* Knowledgeable family sources estimate that in 1982, Stephen D. Bechtel, Sr.'s, fortune amounted to $1 billion and Stephen D. Bechtel, Jr.'s, wealth totaled between $600 million and $700 million.

was bringing West German Chancellor Helmut Schmidt as his personal guest); former IBM chairman and U.S. Ambassador to the Soviet Union Thomas J. Watson; former CIA director John A. McCone; Attorney General William French Smith; industrialist Edgar F. Kaiser, Jr.; former Nixon political aide Peter M. Flanigan; Pan American World Airways' onetime boss Najeeb Halaby; Wells Fargo Bank chairman Richard P. Cooley; former General Electric chairman Philip D. Reed; Southern California Edison chairman J. K. "Jack" Horton; Utah International Chairman Edmund W. Littlefield; Dillon Read's former boss Nicholas F. Brady, who was serving as an interim senator from New Jersey and, like Peter Flanigan, was Steve junior's guest; tire and rubber heir Leonard K. Firestone and, not least, Gerald R. Ford, the former president of the United States.

In addition, this year's encampment would feature such notables as former secretary of State Alexander Haig; FBI Director William Webster; computer magnate (and former deputy Defense secretary) David Packard; Chief of Naval Operations Thomas Hayward; Eastern Airlines president Frank Borman; Federal Reserve Bank chairman Paul Volcker; World Bank president Alden W. Clausen; Union Oil chairman Fred L. Hartley; Atlantic Richfield chairman Robert O. Anderson; publishing czar William Randolph Hearst, Jr.; Southern Pacific Railroad president Alan C. Furth; show-business personalities Charlton Heston, Art Linkletter and Dennis Day; and including, among various other pooh-bahs, the presidents of Dean Witter Reynolds, the Bank of America and United Airlines.

Among such men, Steve Bechtel, Jr., could unwind, for he was a friend and business associate of nearly all of them. John McCone, for instance, had been his father's business partner, while Edgar Kaiser's father, the legendary Henry J. Kaiser, had teamed with Bechtel to build Boulder Dam. When Nick Brady's interim term as U.S. senator was complete, he would be returning to the chairmanship of Dillon, Read, the Wall Street brokerage house in which Bechtel had a controlling interest. Peter Flanigan, another Dillon, Read senior executive, had, while serving in the Nixon White House, helped clear the way for Bechtel to construct a $3 billion coal-slurry pipeline. Philip D. Reed's former company, General Electric, had joined with Bechtel to build many of the world's nuclear plants. Southern Pacific Railroad, where Alan Furth was president, had given Bechtel some of its earliest business, while Pan Am under its patriarch Juan Trippe had tapped the company to build the bulk of its Inter-Continental Hotels. In Canada,

Bechtel had laid pipelines for Atlantic Richfield and Union Oil; in the United States, it had built many power plants for Pacific Gas & Electric and Jack Horton's Southern California Edison. IBM had given the Bechtel Group work as well, and Stephen Bechtel, Jr., was a member of its board. Gerald Ford had also lent a hand, as Richard Nixon had before him, and Ronald Reagan after him, by trying to give Bechtel commercial access to the nation's most secret nuclear technology. Overseas, the Bechtel Group had returned the favor by carrying out diplomatic missions for various secretaries of State, and more clandestinely, by providing "cover" and intelligence for the CIA.

Given everything, there was ample reason for Steve Bechtel, Jr., to make the long annual drive from San Francisco, and the reason had never been better this year. This year especially Steve Bechtel needed to be among friends, because this year the Bechtel Group was in trouble.

It was not a difficulty that showed up on a balance sheet—at least, not yet. Rather, it was something more elusive, an unease, a sense of the ground moving underfoot. Slowly, almost imperceptibly, the world in which Bechtel had done business so long and so profitably was changing. Nuclear power, an industry Bechtel had helped pioneer, and from which it had derived millions in revenues, was on the wane, driven back by skyrocketing plant-construction costs and environmental fears. Oil too was taking a pounding, and with it, the refineries and pipelines that had been a traditional mainstay of Bechtel's business. At the same time, European, Japanese and Korean builders were becoming increasingly competitive, and as a result, the foreign customers who'd come automatically to Bechtel and other big American construction firms for roads and airports, factories and bridges, dams and mines were turning more and more to non-U.S. contractors.

At home Bechtel was experiencing difficulties as well, not only with the environmentalists who had been the *bête noire* of its existence, but with its so-called "sweetheart" customers, the big industrial and energy concerns whose projects had for decades filled the giant construction and engineering firm's coffers. Confronted with a recession, declining oil prices and stiffer competition from abroad, Bechtel's major U.S. customers had begun cutting back on their expansion and developmental efforts, and those megaprojects which remained were getting harder to come by. It was, in short, the beginning of a lean time, one that for the foreseeable future, at least, promised only to get leaner.

There had been other such times for Bechtel, and with the help of its friends, the company had always survived them—sometimes narrowly, sometimes questionably, but, in the end, always successfully. The current times, however, were different. The stakes were greater, the potential loss more devastating. And there was one thing more: Bechtel was no longer an unknown. Its privacy had been shattered.

The veils had begun to fall away two years before when the company's general counsel, Caspar W. Weinberger, had been named Ronald Reagan's secretary of Defense. Weinberger's appointment had prompted questions about Bechtel and its methods of doing business, and as more Bechtel executives joined the administration, the questions had intensified. How was it, people were asking, that a private company could enjoy such close links to the government that was supposed to regulate it? How was it, too, that Bechtel did the bidding of the CIA on the one hand and the likes of Colonel Qaddafi on the other? Just what was the Bechtel Group? How and why had it become so powerful?

Now more strongly than ever, those questions were being raised again. Three weeks before, in a move that had staggered Steve Bechtel, Ronald Reagan had tapped the Bechtel Group's president, George Shultz, to be his new secretary of State. Already, Steve Bechtel's company was being probed and denounced in Congress. The press was gearing up investigations, interest groups readying dossiers, company enemies honing their spears. All at once, Bechtel was news, and its chairman did not like it.

In The Grove, where Shultz was waiting for him, Steve Bechtel could begin readying his defense. In The Grove, surrounded by old friends and allies, there would be quiet and respite, time to reflect on the past and prepare for an uncertain future.

CHAPTER 2

DAD

W hen they spoke of him in later years, his sons, the people who knew him and the men who worked for him would describe Warren A. Bechtel as a bear of a man, brash, bold, booming-voiced. "An American original," they would call him; a self-made, rough-around-the-edges figure who did big things because he dreamed big dreams. There were few like him, they would say, in tones of awe, respect and not a little fear, and when it came to building, none at all.

He was born September 12, 1872, in Freeport, Illinois, the first of six children. Both his parents, Elizabeth and John Moyer Bechtel, were descendants of German immigrants who'd originally settled in Pennsylvania.* They migrated west after their marriage, settling first in Illinois and then in 1884, when Warren was 12, moving to Peabody, Kansas. There John Bechtel, a former county road commissioner, acquired a farm and a grocery store.

As a youth, Warren was a restless sort, bustling, energetic, bored

* There is a town of Bechtelsville located in Berks County in the southwest corner of the state.

with school—which he attended sporadically when his various farm chores allowed—seemingly anxious to outgrow adolescence and get on with life. The one thing that could hold him was the slide trombone, which he played incessantly, both at home and at neighboring ranches, where he earned pocket money tending cattle and mending fences. Out on the open range, miles from the nearest farmhouse or fellow human, he'd play his beloved trombone for hours as, in the distance, coyotes yelped in accompaniment.

At the age of 19, Warren graduated from high school and, to the chagrin of his strict Methodist parents, joined up with a largely female dance band. The "Ladies Band," as it was dubbed, toured through the Midwest, though without much success. After less than a year on the road, the band broke up, leaving Warren stranded and almost penniless in downstate Illinois. Wired train fare home by his father, he returned to Kansas chastened and embarrassed, and determined, or so he promised his parents, to remain on the family farm.

For five years, Warren made good on his pledge. Then, in 1897, he met a woman—a slim, handsome 20-year-old from Aurora, Indiana, named Clara Alice West. In the company of her parents, Clara had come to Kansas to visit relatives. It was Warren, though, who caught her eye. The two began seeing each other, and after a brief courtship, Warren proposed marriage—a prospect that did not sit well with Clara's parents, her father especially. A prosperous merchant back in Indiana, he worried about this improbable young man, so long on ideas, so short on cash. How, he bluntly asked, did Warren intend to support his bride?

Warren, who had been giving the subject a lot of thought, had a ready answer: cattle. Cattle from Arizona, he explained, were shipped north to the stockyards of Wichita for marketing. But before they could be sold, they had to be fattened. With ambition and some borrowed cash, a man could buy a farm, grow corn, feed the cattle and, in a trice, make a fortune. Such, at least, was Warren's plan, and with the consent of Clara's still skeptical parents, the two were soon married. Not long thereafter, Warren borrowed the requisite cash, bought his farm, sowed his corn and, with the arrival of the first shipment of steers, prepared for the profits to come rolling in. They didn't. For in drawing up his scheme, Warren had forgotten one crucial variable: price. That year, prices for both corn and beef dropped to their lowest levels in memory, and before twelve months had passed, Warren was bankrupt. Forced to sell off the farm, he and Clara were left with only their personal possessions and a mule team Warren had managed to keep out of his creditors' hands.

But Warren wasn't one to despair. From homesteaders heading south for the Oklahoma land rush, he learned that the Chicago, Rock Island and Pacific Railroad Company was extending its lines westward into what was then still Indian Territory. A man with his own mule team could, he was told, almost surely find work grading track beds and hauling rails. Moreover, the pay was good: $2.75 per day.

With Clara; his firstborn son, Warren junior; his mule team and his trusty slide trombone, Bechtel set out for Indian Territory, spending more than a year grading track beds and living in a railroad-camp tent. After a brief respite in Indiana, where, on September 14, 1900, a second son, Stephen Davison, was born, the Bechtels were on the move again, following the railroads to Iowa, Minnesota, Wyoming, Oregon and Nevada. It was a harsh, nomadic existence, and house-keeping was primitive; often the Bechtels had to make do living in a boxcar. But with Clara holding the family together, and Warren working sunrise to sunset scratching out track bed, the Bechtels endured, and in time, Warren had made enough to pay off his creditors back in Peabody.

His first real chance for advancement came during the winter of 1902–1903, when a contractor's agent promised him a job on a construction site in the high desert country east of Reno. Eager for better pay, Warren arrived with Clara and the boys during an especially cold winter, only to discover that the agent had reneged on the job. Short of money—Bechtel later told the company biographer, "I landed in Reno with a wife, two babies, a slide trombone and a ten-dollar bill"[1]—Warren wandered the area looking for work, and one day hitched a ride on a buckboard driven by a Southern Pacific supervising engineer named A. J. Barkley. Something about Bechtel—a spark, a willingness to learn and work hard—impressed Barkley, and by the time the ride was over, he had offered to help get him a job on the Southern Pacific.

Bechtel signed on for $55 a month. It was less than he had been making on his own; but the work was steady, and Barkley had promised that there would be a chance for advancement. After a series of increasingly responsible jobs that gave him a solid grounding in all phases of the construction business, he was promoted and dispatched to Wadsworth, Nevada, as an estimator, gauging costs and quantities of material needed to complete a project. From there he moved on to Lovelock, where, among other tasks, he supervised a large stone-quarrying operation, whose most notable feature was the employment of the recently introduced steam shovel. Many of the old-timers were reluctant to have anything to do with the big, belching mechanized monsters, but Bechtel put them to immediate—and profitable—use. Coordinating the shovels, his manpower and his horse-drawn freight wagons, he proved himself a natural engineer and skillful manager. "'Beck' was always what I thought an engineer should be," his mentor A. J. Barkley recalled years later. "A man who understands what has to be done, knows how to do it, and finishes the job economically."[2]

By 1903, Bechtel's abilities had brought him to the attention of Silas Palmer, an inspector for E. B. and A. L. Stone, an Oakland, California–based construction company. Impressed by Bechtel's grasp of detail and his experience employing heavy equipment, Palmer urged him to come to California, where the Stone company was building the Richmond Belt Railroad and extending the Santa Fe line into Oakland, both projects badly in need of seasoned managerial help.

With Clara pregnant again—she would give birth to a third son, Kenneth, in July 1904–Bechtel accepted, and they arrived in a region poised for explosive growth. Already, the San Francisco–Oakland area had a population of 342,000, and there were many who were predicting it would soon become the fastest-growing community in the country. In San Francisco, William Randolph Hearst had just hired Ambrose Bierce as the "Prattle" columnist for his upstart *Examiner,* and his acidic attacks on politicians and other pooh-bahs were the talk of the town. In North Beach, Jack London was in the midst of an extraordinarily prolific phase—he would write four books in the next two years, among them *The Sea Wolf* and *The Call of the Wild.* Downtown, the 750-room Palace Hotel, with its teak and rosewood furniture and its sumptuous French carpeting, was the showplace of San Francisco, and the even more opulent Fairmont was scheduled to open in May 1906.

After years on the road, Warren was eager to put down roots. He moved his family into a modest house in a middle-class area of Oakland and for the next few years, limited his work to Northern California, completing railroad projects for Stone and taking on landfill and road-grading jobs of his own. He was far from getting rich—at one point, his funds were so low that a business associate had to guarantee his account with a wholesale grocer—but at least his family had a home.

However, not for long. Shortly thereafter, the Bechtels took up temporary quarters in Placerville, 60 miles east of San Francisco, where Warren briefly ran a slate quarry. On the evening of April 18, Warren, as was his custom, was taking his two eldest sons on a postprandial stroll. They climbed a hill near the quarry and saw to the west that the entire sky was aglow. That morning, San Francisco had been devastated by an earthquake. The glow they were witnessing was from the fire that would burn the next three days and nights, ravaging block after city block. By the time it was extinguished, four square miles of the city would be destroyed and nearly seven hundred people would lie dead.

The Great San Francisco Earthquake marked a turning point in many lives, including Bechtel's. Returning to Oakland later that year, he quit his job with Stone, and after quickly amassing a small stake building yet another railroad and digging an irrigation canal in the Sacramento Valley, purchased a steam shovel—one of the big Model 20 Marions, originally developed to dig the Panama Canal. Ignoring the fact that he was yet to be incorporated, Warren splashed a "W. A. BECHTEL CO." across the cab and proclaimed himself in business. He was 34 years old, and ready to strike out on his own.

As a builder, Bechtel was very much in the hands-on mold. An imposing man with a powerful voice that could be heard over the din of a construction site, he didn't stand by and watch work progress, but ran the jobs himself, operating the steam shovel and driving the wagon teams. Even years later, after he had become one of the most successful construction bosses in the country, he delighted in stripping off his suit jacket and climbing onto one of the big shovels, beaming like a schoolboy as he operated the levers that set the giant machinery in motion.

Besides his mechanical talents, Bechtel also showed himself to be a shrewd judge of character, and gradually began to surround himself with the team that would later dominate the Bechtel Corporation. One of his first hires was George S. Cooley, a gregarious, freewheeling contractor whom he'd first met in Nevada, and whose son George junior would later become a senior Bechtel vice-president and director, as well as the closest friend of Warren's own son Steve. Another early recruit was Earle G. Lloyd, a former insurance agent from Nebraska and a topflight administrator and purchasing agent. Eventually, Lloyd would go on to become a leading manager of the Bechtel Corporation's finances and Warren's most intimate confidant. An unapologetic partisan of family advancement, Warren also hired his younger brother Arthur, a happy-go-lucky "crane jockey" who prided himself on his ability to operate and maintain his brother's growing mechanical fleet. "That first Marion shovel we bought was my own baby," Arthur was to boast years later. "There wasn't another shovel-runner along the whole line I had to take my hat off to when it came to pitching dirt."[3]

As the business expanded, Bechtel sought out more and more work, particularly railroad construction west of the Rockies. This, in turn, brought him to a pair of cantankerous Utah brothers named William H. and E. O. Wattis. Elderly Mormons, the Wattises ran Utah Construction and, many believed, the State of Utah as well. Earlier, Bechtel had subcontracted work from them in Oregon; he now began badgering them for more. After months of entreaties, the Wattises, who were none too keen on working with non-Mormon "gentiles," finally relented. "Might as well have him in," as W. H. put it to his brother, "as to have him bitin' our feet."[4]

They offered Warren a major subcontracting job: the building of a large irrigation project outside Oakdale, California. There was, however, a catch. To get the work, Bechtel had to agree to take on as a partner E. O.'s son Ray.

Eager to ally himself with a powerful company, Bechtel agreed, and almost immediately began having second thoughts. One problem was that the job turned out to be far more difficult than he had imagined. For in digging, Bechtel and his new young associate soon ran into a massive ledge of blue diorite, an igneous rock nearly as hard as steel. Conventional hand drills barely dented it, and the fate of the project hung in the balance. The job was saved when Bechtel, who kept close track of new developments in construction technology, brought in a recently developed motor-driven drill that proved powerful enough to cut through the diorite. Because of the additional expense, however, Bechtel's profits were all but wiped out. Moreover, Warren also had problems working with Ray Wattis, who proved as headstrong as his father and uncle. The two men quarreled frequently, invariably over the money Wattis was spending on new machinery, and after a number of disputes, the partnership dissolved.

Despite the rupture, Utah Construction continued subcontracting work to Bechtel, including what was to be the company's biggest project to date: the building of a large section of the Northwestern Pacific Line through Northern California.

Working under a tight deadline, Warren replaced the traditional horse- and mule-drawn freight wagons with oversized gasoline-powered chain-driven trucks fitted with special aluminum dumping bodies, able to hold tons of earth and rock. They were among the first dump trucks employed in America. The trucks, however, were no match for the weather. On many days, the heavy, seemingly unending north-coast rains created knee-deep mud that made work—and getting in supplies —all but impossible. Fortunately, Bechtel had enough cement to continue working on the railroad line's concrete structures until spring. Other items, though—notably rubber boots and spaghetti for the largely Italian crew—were in short supply, and the workers were talking of walking off the job. Then, just when it seemed that a strike was imminent, a Parcel Post mule train arrived from San Francisco. Earle Lloyd recalled: "It was a sight to watch those pack trains of Parcel Post mules come in, thirty to a string, covered with mud and piled high with spaghetti and boots."[5]

Two years later, in 1914, Bechtel completed the last 106-mile stretch of the line, and received his final check from the Wattises. Including a generous bonus, it totaled, by one estimate, nearly $500,000. Warren was delighted. He confided to an associate, "I never expected to have so much money in my entire life."[6]

Suddenly well off, Warren and Clara acquired a two-story house on Perry Street in Oakland, where in 1912, their last child and first daughter, Alice Elizabeth, was born. As bigger jobs and even larger checks came in, they bought an even grander place in nearby San Leandro. The grounds featured a tennis court, a kitchen garden and a small open field, where Warren, still the farmer and ever the proponent of self-reliance, insisted that the boys grow tomatoes to sell at market. Clara, meanwhile, busied herself remodeling the house, adorning its gleaming oak floors with rare Oriental rugs recently purchased at the Panama Pacific Exposition in San Francisco. Warren himself began taking time off from work. At the prodding of Warren junior, he even took up flying. Togged out in aviator goggles and a leather helmet, he soared over the Northern California countryside already being transformed by the roads and railways he had helped build.

A formal family portrait from 1915 shows the Bechtels in the first flower of their newfound prosperity. The males wear suits, ties and high, rounded starched collars. Clara and 3-year-old Alice are dressed in their Sunday best. The little girl, a towhead with a big floppy ribbon in her hair and a doll in her arms, sits in her father's lap, looking loved and slightly spoiled. Ken, also fair-haired, seems bemused, as though he knows some marvelous secret the photographer can never share.

DAD

The older boys, both of whom will soon be going off to war in France, look off into the distance, as if trying to gauge the future. Standing alongside them, hands behind her back, Clara seems distracted, wondering, perhaps, about her family's uncertain deportment. Finally, in the center of the frame, staring directly into the camera, there is Warren—43, round-faced and, from the smile stretched across his face, clearly quite pleased with himself. He has a right to be. He has spent the last seventeen years working toward a dream, and it has at last been fulfilled.

But in the years immediately ahead, there would be trouble for Warren Bechtel, brought on in large measure by his very contentment. Satisfied that his business was running smoothly, and still fancying himself the wheeler-dealer of his youth, Bechtel allowed his attention to wander, and he indulged himself in several questionable enterprises.

The first was a placer gold mine outside Port Orford, Oregon. Invited to invest by the machine-gun-making Browning family of Ogden, Utah, Warren sank tens of thousands of dollars into the mine, only to have the local dairy farmers raise havoc over the silt and debris it was depositing into the nearby Sixes River. In what would be the first of many clashes the Bechtels would have with environmentalists, the farmers sued and eventually secured a permanent injunction which, to all intents and purposes, shut down the mine.

Embittered but undaunted, Warren invested several hundred thousand dollars more in the Sanifold Manufacturing Company of New York. The company had developed a toothbrush that claimed to be both sanitary—it came with a cap that covered the bristles—and handy—when folded, it fitted neatly into a vest pocket or purse. Warren, who had been brought up to know the value of personal hygiene and had spent half his life in camps where one cleansed one's teeth with one's finger if at all, thought that the product had the makings of a fortune. Excitedly, he announced to Clara, "Every camper and traveler in the country will want one of these toothbrushes."[7] They didn't, and the company folded.

He had better luck financially with a copper mine he bought in Arizona; better still, with an insurance company called Industrial Indemnity he cofounded in 1920 in San Francisco and, best of all, with several large tracts of real estate he purchased in downtown Oakland and San Francisco. In time, all three ventures would account for a substantial portion of the Bechtel family fortune.

Now, however, Warren's attention was turning back to building.

Thanks to Henry Ford and his Model T, Americans were embarked on a love affair with the automobile. Even Alice, who was barely big enough to see over the dashboard, was whining for a car of her own. Cars, Warren realized, needed roads to travel on—hundreds and hundreds of miles of new ones. For the W. A. Bechtel Company, this spelled fresh opportunity.

With Henry Hoey, a colleague from his days working for the Southern Pacific, Warren convinced the U.S. Bureau of Public Roads that with his wealth of related experience, he was eminently qualified as a road builder. Desperate to get under way, the Bureau, in 1919, awarded him the first federal public-road contract let in California: the building of the Klamath River Highway near the Oregon border. All went well with that project, and the following year, Bechtel and Hoey put down another federal highway, this one in Los Angeles County.

As his road-building work continued, Bechtel began to grasp the significance of the third factor in the automotive equation: oil. If more cars meant more new highways, they also meant the rapid, large-scale development of the West's oil and gas resources. Once the oil was drilled, it would have to be refined, and after refining, transported, which would require the building of pipelines stretching across the country. A boom was coming, and Bechtel meant to be part of it.

Before he could get under way, though, Bechtel needed help, a partner who could share both his work load and his enthusiasm for the opportunities he saw emerging in the postwar West. It had always been his intention that one day his sons would fill that role; but with Warren junior and Steve pursuing their studies at the University of California at Berkeley and Ken still in high school, that day was still some years off. Bechtel had to have a partner now, an experienced builder he could rely on completely. He found his man in the summer of 1921. His name was Henry J. Kaiser.

Ten years Bechtel's junior, and at least his equal in optimism and salesmanship, Kaiser had a self-made background not unlike Warren's own. He had begun his career at the age of 12, when, with $5 borrowed from a sister, he left his home in Whitesboro, New York, and set out to make his fortune. After a miscellaneous series of low-paying jobs, he bought a photographic studio and supply store and, by the time he was 21, owned a chain of them up and down the East Coast. But like Bechtel, Kaiser was restless. Selling off his business in 1906, he headed west with his family (like Bechtel, he had three sons) to start over again, winding up in Spokane, Washington, where he worked as a salesman for a gravel-and-cement company. From there he drifted to Vancouver, British Columbia, where he found employment as a road contractor. Living out of an automobile, Kaiser scrambled from job to job, underbidding the competition merely to get work. Kaiser's low-balling tactics did not endear him to his rivals, and by the time he reached California, where another low bid had won him a contract to build a 30-mile stretch of highway between Redding and Red Bluff, he was regarded as something of a pariah by most of the construction industry.

Bechtel, however, was intrigued. Whatever Kaiser's methods, there was no disputing his doggedness, nor his burbling effervescence. He was a born promoter and instinctive, near-habitual risk-taker. "They tell me I go out on a limb too often," he said of himself years later, when he had become one of the country's leading industrialists. "Well, that's where I like to be." Bechtel, who had gone out on a limb or two himself, could appreciate that outlook. Moreover, Kaiser possessed the same sort of driving ambition. "I always have to dream against the stars," as he put it. "If I don't dream I'll make it, I'll never get close."[8]

Increasingly curious, and prompted further by instructions from the San Francisco chapter of the Association of General Contractors, a construction-trade group of which he was then president, Bechtel dropped in on Kaiser's work site unannounced and asked if he could look around. "Be my guest," Kaiser said with a shrug, wondering who this big, self-assured visitor was. When he finished his inspection, Bechtel, who prided himself on the tidiness of his own work sites, congratulated Kaiser on his housekeeping. They began talking and found they had much in common. Bechtel was impressed with the newcomer. On his return home, he told his sons he had found the ideal partner. "This Kaiser fellow is a hard worker," he said. "He's enthusiastic, and he has a lot of ingenious ideas."[9]

Within a few months the two men had concluded a partnership deal. The terms were simple—a straight 50/50 split—and informal, concluded by no more than a handshake. "There are two principles he [Bechtel] followed," Kaiser said later. "He hated to sign papers, on the theory that if you couldn't trust a man's word, you couldn't trust his signature. And his usual condition for entering any proposition was a 50/50 division. [He] had no patience with 51/49 arrangements. He used to say, 'No man with a sense of self-respect wants to be controlled on that kind of percentage.'"[10]

Together, Kaiser and Bechtel were to build many of the major roadways up and down the West Coast. At first, though, Kaiser was un-characteristically cautious about his friend's notion of entering the pipeline business. Warren would go through his by now well-practiced spiel about how big pipelining was going to be, and Henry J., who was short-necked and fat, would nod his glistening pate and agree that pipelining would be a lucrative enterprise, but someday, not now. For the present, there was money to be made quarrying rock and building roads.

When seized, though, by an idea, Bechtel was not an easy man to put off, and ultimately his arguments won out. As a result, Bechtel and Kaiser were among the first contractors in the United States to tackle major pipeline projects, first for Standard Oil, then for Continental Gas. By 1928, when Kaiser departed to take up a new venture, the two men had built thousands of miles of pipeline together.

The lines, which were electrically welded in the field with a process invented by a Bechtel engineer, were set down so quickly and effi-ciently that the rest of the oil industry soon took notice. As more and more contracts followed, the relationship between Bechtel and Big Oil forged into an alliance, one that in the years to come would have a profound impact not only on Bechtel Construction, but on the Middle East and the course of American foreign policy.

By the end of the 1920s, that process had already made the W. A. Bechtel Company one of the largest construction companies in Amer-ica, and provided its founder with a fortune approaching $30 million. Nearing his 60th year, and not in the best of health, Warren Bechtel— "Dad," as his men called him, in affectionate mimicry of his sons— could, if he chose, spend the rest of his years enjoying himself in the luxurious high-rise apartment building he and Clara had lately bought for themselves and their offspring on Oakland's Lake Merritt. But for Bechtel and Henry Kaiser there was one more challenge still ahead. It was Boulder Dam.

CHAPTER 3

BOULDER

T he weather was hot; the air moist and sticky; the jobsite, deep in
the jungles of Cuba, remote as any could be. But if the conditions bothered Henry J. Kaiser, he did not show it. Seated on a camp-
stool, arms waving, voice booming, round body fairly bursting with
enthusiasm and effervescence, he was describing to his friend Dad
Bechtel what he called "the mightiest project of them all."

It was two years since the two men had seen each other. Kaiser had
accepted in 1928 a $20 million contract to build 200 miles of roadway
through the interior of Cuba. And yet during the months he had been
working on the project, which involved the employment of 6,000 people and the erection of no fewer than 500 bridges, Kaiser had been
obsessed by one extraordinary notion concerning the American West:
the building of a dam across the raging Colorado River. "I lay awake
nights thinking about it," he would say later. "I lay in my sweltering
tent and dreamed it over and over."[1]

Kaiser was not the first to have had such thoughts. Engineers had
been talking for more than twenty years of damming the Colorado,
harnessing its power to produce electricity and irrigate the West. But

though studies had been made and plans drawn up, nothing had come of them. Nothing, that is, until 1930, when a former engineer from California named Herbert Hoover decided, as president, that it was worth a go. Under his aegis, funds for the project had been allocated, and the U.S. Department of Reclamation had announced that it would soon be accepting construction bids. It was then that Kaiser had summoned Bechtel to Cuba.

As he heard Kaiser reveal his plans, though, Bechtel was less than optimistic. Unlike his sometime partner, whose dam-building experience was limited to a pair of small projects, Bechtel knew at first hand how demanding an undertaking like Boulder could be. For while Kaiser was building roads in Cuba, the W. A. Bechtel Company had, among its other endeavors, put up Bowman Dam, the second-largest rock-fill dam in the world. The work, managed by Dad's oldest son, Warren junior, had proved enormously taxing, not least because of the dam's location, high in the Sierra Nevada. Cut off from the rest of the world for almost half the year by deep mountain snows, the site had required the Bechtels to import a large herd of beef cattle simply to feed the crew. A complete hospital had also been necessary, along with a slaughterhouse and self-contained work camp. Hellish as building Bowman had been, Bechtel knew it was nothing compared with what would be required to erect Boulder. When at last Kaiser paused for breath, Bechtel allowed cautiously, "It sounds a little ambitious."[2]

Kaiser merely smiled. "Dad," he said, "problems are only opportunities in work clothes."

As the days went on, and Kaiser kept talking, Bechtel found himself gradually being swayed. Building Boulder would be the capstone to his career. More important, it would expose his sons to an endeavor beside which everything else would pale. In his ebullient fashion, Kaiser had told him that people someday would view Boulder as they did the pyramids of Egypt or the Great Wall of China, and that the dedication plaque at its base would list the W. A. Bechtel Company as one of its builders. Kaiser didn't have to say anything more. Dad was in.

With the decision made, the two men hurried back to the United States—Kaiser heading east to begin raising additional capital, Bechtel returning to California to sniff out what other bids were being made. He soon discovered that more than a few other builders were interested in Boulder as well, chief among them an old competitor from Boise, Idaho, named Harry J. Morrison.

A tall, sparely built man with a fondness for singing cowboy songs beside construction-site campfires, Morrison was the boss of the Boise-based Morrison-Knudsen Construction Company, and a most formidable rival. He had already come to California in quest of financial backing from Leland Cutler, a prominent San Francisco banker and an old friend and schoolmate of Herbert Hoover's. Cutler declined to put up any cash, and he told Morrison that whoever obtained the Boulder contract would be required to put up a $5 million surety bond. It was a staggering sum, especially in the midst of an economic depression, and Cutler had suggested that Morrison consider bringing in partners. As a possibility, he mentioned another builder who had expressed an interest in Boulder, Felix Kahn of San Francisco's MacDonald and Kahn.

Since that conversation, Morrison had been busily trying to round up backers. In addition to $500,000 of his own, he had one important lure: the participation of Frank T. Crowe, a whipcord-tough former Department of Reclamation superintendent, who was then counted as the premier dam-builder in the country. Twenty years before, as a young engineer fresh out of the University of Maine, Crowe had drawn up the original estimates for Boulder, and the dam had loomed large in his imagination ever since. "I was wild to build this dam," he told a reporter, years after Boulder's completion. "I had spent my life in the river bottoms and Boulder meant a wonderful climax—the biggest dam built by anyone anywhere."[3]

With Crowe's help, Morrison made his first approach to the Wattis brothers of Utah Construction, a firm with which both he and Bechtel had worked in the past. W. H. Wattis was 76, and his hand shook so badly he could barely hold a pen; but both he and his ill and sour-tempered brother, E. O., were enthusiastic about Morrison's proposal. The Wattises' problem was lack of cash. Though they could match Morrison's $500,000, they could not handle the entire surety bond on their own, much less the $40 million they estimated that Boulder would eventually cost. Moreover, they were not happy at the prospect of taking in partners. "If we can't do it on our own," W. H. griped, "the hell with it."[4] Morrison managed to mollify them, but only after promising them that any outsiders brought in would be "our kind"—if not other Mormons, then clean-living Christian folk.

Returning to San Francisco, Morrison went next to Charles A. Shea, a fiercely independent 47-year-old Irish-American with the build of a bantamweight boxer and a disposition to match. Though not precisely the sort of clean-cut associate the Wattises had had in mind, Shea had a reputation as the best tunnel-builder in the Bay area. Also, he was rich, as evidenced by the permanent suite he kept in the Palace Hotel. As Morrison made his pitch, Shea paced the room, hands thrust deep in his pockets, a cigar stuck in the corner of his mouth. When Morrison finished, Shea not only agreed to come in for $500,000, but to bring along his friends at Pacific Bridge for an equal amount.

The next candidate on Morrison's list was the builder Cutler had suggested: Felix Kahn. A rabbi's son and a University of Michigan graduate, Kahn was one of five brothers, all of whom were highly successful engineers. His partner was Alan MacDonald, a hot-tempered, outspoken Scottish Kentuckian with mechanical and electrical engineering degrees and a penchant for antagonizing bosses. Prior to teaming up with Kahn, he had been fired from fifteen consecutive jobs.

This odd couple were one of San Francisco's most successful building concerns and had put up a number of the city's largest structures, including the Mark Hopkins Hotel. When Morrison approached them, they quickly agreed to ante up $1 million—a sum more than sufficient to dispel any concern the Wattises might have had about working with a fiery Scot and a Jew. "That $1 million," Kahn wryly noted, "made me one of the family right away."[5]

On the East Coast, meanwhile, Kaiser had gotten Warren Brothers, the Boston construction company from which he'd subcontracted the Cuban work, to put up $500,000. He and Bechtel also were prepared to write checks for half a million dollars each, but, even so, they fell far short of the funding needed for the surety bond. Consequently, Bechtel suggested joining up with Morrison, the Wattises and their associates. When Kaiser agreed, Bechtel went to see the elder Wattis, who had recently learned he had hip cancer and was becoming increasingly concerned that he would die before Boulder was completed. Worried at the prospect of leaving his ailing brother to shoulder the entire financial load, and respectful of Bechtel's abilities—not to mention the $1.5 million he, Kaiser and Warren Brothers were offering—W. H. proved happy to have them. All that remained was sorting out the details of the partnerships and coming up with an acceptable bid.

On a mid-February morning in 1931, just two weeks before the deadline for submission of bids to the Department of Reclamation's Denver office, the contractors and their coterie of lawyers, accountants and engineers convened at the Engineers Club in San Francisco. Until the last moment, the participation of a number of the builders had been in doubt. Hospitalized now, W. H. had lately been threatening to pull out, while Morrison had had to scramble to borrow funds to meet his $500,000 pledge. Pacific Bridge, which Shea had brought in, had also found itself short, and was able to participate only after its president, Gorrill Swinert, sold 40 percent of the company's stock to the firm's attorney. Warren Brothers, once one of the most successful builders in the country, was in even tougher shape. Owing to the Depression, the company was teetering on bankruptcy, and had asked Bechtel and Kaiser to come up with its promised $500,000 ante. This meant that Bechtel and Kaiser, having between them contributed $1.5 million, had nearly 30 percent equity in the consortium, more than any other member of the group.

As Kaiser mounted the podium and called the meeting to order, the air was charged with a special electricity. Collectively, those present had done much to change the face of the American West; and until this moment, most had never met. Kaiser quickly got them down to business. The first order was comparing various estimates of Boulder's costs. Morrison and Crowe stood by their projection of $40 million, a vast sum in the Depression era. Remarkably, given the magnitude of the project and the host of variables involved, two of the other companies present came in with estimates within $700,000 of that figure.

Next the consortium turned to the task of naming itself. Someone suggested "Continental Construction" or "Western Construction," neither of which elicited much enthusiasm. Then Kahn had an inspiration. Why not, he suggested, "Six Companies"? Though there were actually eight companies in the room, his idea won enthusiastic approval. Six Companies, as the Californians present were well aware, was the name of the council the Chinese tongs in San Francisco used to arbitrate their differences. If Six Companies was good enough for the tongs, Kahn joked, it was good enough for this group.

Once the name was chosen, Kaiser proposed that the organization be run along military lines, under the control of one commander-in-chief—presumably himself. His notion was voted down almost as soon as it was voiced. The builders were an independent lot and not at all willing to take orders from any individual. Instead, it was decided that Six Companies would function under a board of directors. By the time the group adjourned to the Palace Hotel for a working lunch, an organizational chart had been drawn up. W. H. Wattis, who was fading fast and couldn't be present,* was named president, Dad Bechtel first

---

* Notably absent from the Engineers Club meeting, the brothers Wattis were both

vice-president and E. O. Wattis second vice-president. Charlie Shea was put in charge of field construction, working closely with Harry Morrison, while Felix Kahn was designated to handle finances. To no one's surprise, Frank Crowe was the unanimous choice for general superintendent.

One crucial piece of business—exactly how much to bid on Boulder—was put off until later. The construction business was a tight-knit, competitive, gossipy fraternity, ever alert for intelligence on upcoming projects. One offhand remark by anyone about Six Companies' bid could, conceivably, doom the entire project. Accordingly, it was not until forty-eight hours before the bid deadline that the builders met to settle on a final figure.

Gathering at the hospital bedside of W. H. Wattis, Bechtel, Kaiser and the other builders listened as Frank Crowe, who had built a scale model of the dam for the occasion, reviewed each phase of the project and its attendant costs. When he had finished, the partners totaled the numbers, then added 25 percent. If all went well, this would be their profit. As soon as the decision was reached, Crowe bolted from the room and rushed to catch the train east to Denver.

He arrived on March 3, checked into the Cosmopolitan Hotel and spent the rest of that day and evening double-checking and triple-checking his numbers. The next morning, he formally submitted Six Companies' bid. It totaled $48,890,000—$5 million below the next-lowest bid, $10 million below the highest and only $24,000 above the government's own estimates. Six Companies had won the right to build the world's largest dam. Within hours of the announcement of the awarding of the contract, its competitors were predicting it would go broke in the process.

On the face of it, there was much to suggest that they might be right. Emanating from the deep winter snows of the Rockies in Colorado and Wyoming, then cascading 1,700 miles to the Gulf of California, the

---

seriously ill. Representing them was Marriner Eccles, then 40 and a part owner of Utah Construction. The son of an Ogden, Utah, banker (it was he who supplied much of the Wattises' capital in building Boulder), Eccles later became Utah Construction's chairman. In 1934, he was appointed by Franklin Roosevelt to the board of the Federal Reserve System. Nominated two years later as Fed chairman, he served in that capacity until 1948. Both as a member of the Fed (from which he finally retired in 1958) and as chairman of Utah Construction, Eccles was to have a close personal and professional relationship with the Bechtel family. Utah Construction's ties with Bechtel continue to the present day in the person of Edmund Littlefield, who succeeded Eccles as Utah chairman and was named a senior Bechtel director in 1982.

Colorado is one of the world's mightiest rivers. Over the course of millions of years, it carved out the Grand Canyon. By the time it reaches Black Canyon, another of its creations, 270 miles downstream, it is roiling with red mud and moving at a rate of between 100,000 and 200,000 cubic feet a second. Dr. Elwood Mead, the Department of Reclamation's chief engineer, after whom the Boulder-created Lake Mead would later be named, likened its power at this juncture to "the force of a railway train." It was at the Black Canyon site, hard by the Arizona–Nevada border, 30 miles southeast of Las Vegas, that Six Companies proposed to put up its dam.

The Black Canyon site had been chosen for two reasons. One was the comparative shallowness of the river's bedrock. The other, even more important consideration was the relative narrowness—1,000 feet at the top, closing to 370 feet at the river's bottom—of the Canyon's gorge. Here, Six Companies planned to plug the Colorado with a mammoth concrete ledge, one that would extend 140 feet below the river bed and more than 700 feet above it—about the height of the Empire State Building, and nearly twice the height of any dam ever built.

It was a colossal and, in the opinion of many, insurmountable, undertaking, not merely because of the vast amount of materials that would be required, or the harshness of the desertlike conditions, but because of the power of the river itself. Even in the later summer and fall, when its water was low and sluggish, the Colorado could be capricious and deadly. During the preliminary work on Boulder, drill barges were frequently wrecked by a sudden rush of water down the canyon, and on more than one occasion, it seemed the entire project would be swept away. "The Colorado is a wild river," Frank Crowe said. "One day, it rose 40 feet in 40 minutes. It became a wall of yellow mud that kept rising and rising until I thought it was going to wash all of us right out of the canyon."[6]

Making working conditions even more harrowing were the extremes of weather. Sudden storms washed out roads and blew down workers' tents. Always fierce, the heat during the summer of 1931 averaged 12 degrees above normal, with temperatures at river level often hitting 120 to 130 degrees. With the heat refracting off the canyon walls, workers felt as if they were roasting in a huge oven. Such were the temperatures that gasoline tanks exploded by spontaneous combustion. The man who unthinkingly picked up a crowbar with his bare hands usually came away with a second-degree burn. During the first few months of building, heat prostration alone caused several deaths per week.

Yet thanks to the Depression, there was no shortage of workers eager to sign on. By the time Six Companies set up operations at Black Canyon in June 1931, upwards of 10,000 men from all over the country had converged on the Las Vegas area, lured by the newspaper stories about Boulder and by Six Companies' announcements of job openings. As a result, Crowe was quickly able to assemble a work force, picking and choosing from an enormous labor pool that had gathered almost overnight. Eventually, a thousand of the men would be housed in Boulder City, a company town with paved streets and shade trees that Six Companies was building seven miles from the damsite. Boulder City, however, would not be completed until 1932, and until then, the men lived in tents.

Getting a fast start on the project was critical for Six Companies, since in negotiating the Boulder contract, Crowe and his bosses—led now by Bechtel, who had been elected president after W. H. Wattis succumbed to cancer in September 1931—had built in performance incentives. The more quickly the work went, the fatter would be Six Companies' financial rewards in the form of paybacks and bonuses.

By July, when Crowe announced that Six Companies had begun "highballing" the project—going all out—the first of the building materials had started to arrive. Altogether, in building the dam Six Companies used 45 million pounds of reinforced steel, 8 million tons of sand, 840 miles of pipe and more concrete than had been needed for all fifty of the previous Department of Reclamation dams *combined*. On some days, Six Companies would take delivery of 60 railroad cars of cement and other building materials. Forty-two railroad cars were required simply to bring in parts for each of the 2-million-pound bulkhead gates used to open and close the tunnels Crowe's workers were digging through both sides of the gorge.

As materials kept arriving, conveyed by Six Companies' own truck fleet and twenty-nine-engine railroad, some of Crowe's crews began bringing in power lines from California to provide the electricity needed to drive much of the heavy equipment. Other workers, meanwhile, started laying hundreds of miles of railroad track and roads, while still others began spanning sections of the gorge with steel bridges and a network of cableways.

Once all these preparations were in place, workers began blasting and drilling thousands of feet of earth and silt from the canyon walls to find the bedrock that would ultimately anchor the dam. The so-called "high-scalers" hung like mountain climbers from ropes extending down the rim of the gorge and chopped away at loose rocks, the staccato clatter of their drills interrupted from time to time by the rumble of dynamite blasts. The army of workers below had to be on constant watch for falling rocks or, on occasion, the plummeting body of a comrade who had slipped or misstepped.

After the canyon walls had been cleared of silt, Crowe and his men began what was the most difficult phase of construction: the laying dry of the entire riverbed, which, in turn, required diverting the Colorado's course. Crowe's plan was to drill two mile-long tunnels, one on the Nevada side of the river, the other on the Arizona side. Each would have the approximate diameter of the Lincoln Tunnel and would start several thousand feet above the damsite, emerging nearly half a mile below it. The tunnels were the key to the project, and by midsummer, work on them had progressed to the point where Crowe could report to Bechtel and the other Six Companies partners that Boulder was well ahead of schedule.

The partners were pleased, and so was Crowe, who was rapidly living up to his reputation as the best dam-builder in the business. But though the work was going smoothly, there was trouble on the horizon: not from the Canyon or the River, but from the partners themselves.

They were, in their personalities and ways of doing things, a highly disparate bunch, and though they were united in wanting to build Boulder, each had distinct notions of how it ought to be done.* The result, during the first few months of construction, was a welter of

---

* Years after Boulder was built, Frank Crowe described to *Fortune* magazine what working for the Six Companies partners was like. "They were just about as different as men could be," he said. "Charlie Shea hated to write letters. If he wrote one a week, he thought that was too much. But Morrison . . . thought nothing of dictating a hundred letters in a morning. Morrison never drank, never smoked, never gambled; he was a Puritan. Charlie Shea didn't drink either, but he was crazy about gambling. I used to meet him and Felix [Kahn] at the [Southern Pacific] station when they came up from San Francisco and drive them across the desert to the dam. All the way—five hours—they'd shoot craps on the floor of the Lincoln.

"One day," Crowe continued, "I was driving down Montgomery Street in San Francisco. Kahn spotted Dad Bechtel headed for the bank. 'Drive over,' he said. 'This is going to cost Dad some money!' I pulled alongside the curb and Felix shouted, 'Dad, I'm matching you a double-eagle.' Dad didn't even say good morning. He just gave Felix a quick, disapproving look, dug into his vest pocket for a coin and slapped it on the car window. He took his hand off and said to Felix, 'You lose' and walked off without another word.

"They were a great bunch to work for," Crowe concluded, "because they stuck together. Charlie and Felix used to say to each other, to settle an argument, 'Right or wrong, you're right you son of a bitch.' They really felt that way toward one another."

---

conflicting orders to Crowe, who became sufficiently exasperated to begin seriously considering whether to quit. The problem was finally resolved when the partners agreed to leave the running of Boulder to an executive committee of four: Bechtel, Kaiser, Shea and Kahn. As Six Companies' president, Bechtel headed the committee, and ensconced in the fine Spanish-style mansion the partners built for themselves high above the damsite, he received regular progress reports from Crowe during a weekly pinochle game. It was Shea, however, who provided the day-to-day liaison with Crowe, straightening out difficulties before they reached the field superintendent. Kahn, meanwhile, added legal affairs and oversight of the workers' feeding and housing to his financial responsibilities. The fourth executive-committee member, Henry J. Kaiser, was designated chief lobbyist and dispatched to Washington. The posting was fine with Kaiser, who had suffered heat prostration during one tour of the damsite and was never to visit it again thereafter.

Soon after its formation, the four-man executive committee was confronted with a crisis that threatened to shut Boulder down. Under intense pressure from his profit-conscious bosses, Crowe had been driving his men mercilessly. "Some of the carpenters were working so fast, they'd put handfuls of nails in the cuffs of their pants, [so] they wouldn't have to keep going back to the keg for more," one Boulder veteran recalled. "One foreman was so tough, we used to say he had three crews: the one working with him today, the one he had coming on tomorrow, and the one he had just fired."[7] By August, the daytime temperatures at Boulder hadn't dropped below 98 degrees for a solid month, and the workers were ready to walk off the job. Led by a group of "muckers"—tunnel shovelers, whose salaries had been cut when they were displaced by mechanical shovels—the workers compiled a number of grievances. Among their complaints were the primitive sanitary conditions and the fact that they were being charged half of their $4-a-day salary for meals and the privilege of living in a Six Companies tent. They demanded that their pay be raised to match the $5.50 to $6 per day workers were making elsewhere in the Southwest, and that a number of safety improvements be made, including the provision of ice water on the canyon floor, where 13 men had already died of heat prostration. Unless Six Companies complied, the workers said they would strike.

Crowe was not intimidated. Rejecting the workers' demands, he reported to his superiors, "We are six months ahead of schedule . . . and we can afford to refuse concessions which would cost us $2,000 daily or $3 million in the seven years we are allowed to finish the work."[8]

In the face of Crowe's intransigence, the ranks of the dissidents, who had originally numbered no more than a few hundred, began to swell, and by August, totaled 1,400, two-thirds of the Boulder work force. Still unmoved, Crowe announced on August 10 that Six Companies was firing the entire group. They were to be given three days' pay and were to pack up and leave the damsite immediately.

To ensure that they did, and to quell possible rioting, the government sent in troops from Fort Douglas, Utah. Meanwhile, state and federal officials were brought in to search the workers' cars for firearms and liquor. In what would be the first of a series of bitter strikes at Boulder, the laborers, many of them members of the American Federation of Labor or the Industrial Workers of the World, refused their severance checks, took up pickets and set up their own camp in the desert.

The unions rallied quickly to their cause. "We feel it's a crime against humanity to ask men to work in that hell-hole of heat at Boulder Dam for a mere pittance,"[9] the AFL wired the U.S. secretary of Labor, William Doak. The Hoover administration, which tended to view any labor disturbance as "Red-inspired," was unsympathetic, and aside from halfheartedly pressing Six Companies to better the sanitary conditions, it did nothing. Crowe, meanwhile, stood fast. Cut off from support, with no prospect of victory, the strike finally collapsed. Six Companies agreed to rehire the dissidents, though at only their original salaries, and with no guarantees whatever of improving their plight.

With the crew back on the job, work at Boulder resumed in earnest, helped along by a drought that sent river levels to record lows, thus making it easier to control the Colorado and prepare the gorge for the laying of the dam. To accelerate the pace of construction even more, Six Companies brought in the most modern equipment on the market. Giant aluminum-bodied trucks roared back and forth across the construction site, transporting as much as 50 tons of material in a single load, while jumbo drilling rigs, fitted with as many as thirty different drills, attacked the canyon walls like crazed mechanical monsters, eating through 15 and 20 feet of solid rock in a matter of minutes.

By the beginning of 1932, Crowe was so far ahead of schedule that Six Companies had recouped its initial $5 million surety bond, and pocketed an additional $1 million in contract incentives. And more was yet to come, from savings on building materials—whose cost had fallen through the floor, thanks to the Depression—as well as from peculiarities in the contract, which allowed, for instance, an $8 charge for every cubic yard of earth excavated, when, thanks again to the Depression, it was costing Six Companies a third less.

In April, though, the project hit an unexpected snag when, unaccountably, Herbert Hoover, himself an engineer and a product of the West, failed to ask Congress for sufficient funds to carry on the work. In a panic, Kaiser mounted a whirlwind lobbying effort to get a deficit appropriation passed by Congress. As Kaiser buttonholed lawmakers, pressing on them the importance Boulder would have in relieving unemployment, Bechtel told reporters in San Francisco that unless funds were soon forthcoming, work on Boulder would be delayed as much as a year, forcing Six Companies to lay off nearly half of its 3,400-man payroll.

Dad's dire predictions, coupled with Kaiser's smooth salesmanship, eventually secured Boulder its congressional appropriation. Within months, however, Six Companies was under assault again, and this time from a far more dangerous quarter. In Washington, Senator William Oddie, Democrat of Nevada, charged that Boulder workers were being paid in scrip, spendable only at Six Companies stores, and that Crowe and his bosses were employing two sets of books to conceal pay irregularities and abuses of workers. Oddie's charges made headlines. What stung more, they were true.

At first, Six Companies attempted to brazen the situation out, ignoring Oddie. But despite denials from Hoover's Labor Department, and a marked improvement in worker living conditions brought on by the completion of Boulder City, the charges wouldn't go away. Moreover, the workers were once again restive. Indeed, another strike seemed imminent. Like the Veterans' Bonus March on Washington the same summer, Boulder was emerging as a national *cause célèbre*, polarizing left and right, labor and big business. Even novelist Theodore Dreiser managed to get into the fray. In an angry letter to *The New York Times*, he denounced Six Companies' management for failing, as he put it, "to catch any gleam of enlightment from beyond what they consider their closed and complete economic circle."[10]

Seemingly oblivious to the mounting controversy, Crowe pushed on, and by the spring of 1935, a full eighteen months ahead of schedule, was ready to begin pouring concrete. Oddie, however, was not ready to let the Boulder matter drop, and with Franklin Roosevelt now in the White House, the Nevada Democrat got a full hearing. He also got the support of FDR's Interior secretary, Harold L. Ickes, who ordered payment in scrip stopped and the launching of a federal investigation into Six Companies' labor practices. As a result of that investigation, Ickes charged the builders with 70,000 separate violations and fined them a total of $350,000.*

In response, Kaiser hired a public relations man to turn out a "quickie" book chronicling Six Companies' achievements at Boulder in breathless tabloid prose. Hundreds of copies went out to congressmen and federal officials. Leaving nothing to chance, Kaiser also took to the airwaves, and over a radio hookup, told Six Companies' side of the story to the nation. Kaiser's media blitz had its desired result. Inundated by angry letters and telegrams, the government commenced negotiations with Six Companies and eventually reduced the fine to $100,000.

At Boulder, meanwhile, the breakneck pace was continuing unabated. On April 10, 1935, the final phase of construction got under way, with the pouring of the first concrete. Crowe presided over the operation like a symphony conductor, orchestrating the movement and synchronization of each piece of equipment and the dozens of work crews. Blended at Six Companies' own mixing plants after it was brought to Boulder by train, the concrete was loaded into an unending succession of huge dump buckets, each of which was immediately placed on a waiting Six Companies train and transported to the damsite. There the individual buckets were unloaded and hung from hooks on one of four cable systems. The systems, in turn, functioned like marvelously efficient ski lifts, bearing bucket after bucket to the appropriate vertical column of the dam where the cement was finally poured. As the columns filled, the cement was cooled in summer and heated in winter by steel tubing inserted into it and carrying, depending on the season, cold or hot water—this to prevent the contraction that would have occurred had the concrete been allowed to harden on its own.

* One of the uglier facets of Six Companies' labor practices that Ickes' investigation uncovered was the company's treatment of blacks.[12] Until the government brought pressure to bear in 1933, no black workers were employed at the damsite. Thereafter, a token number were hired, invariably to labor at the most demeaning jobs. Six Companies, moreover, refused to provide them housing in Boulder City, and as a result, the blacks were forced to make a 30-mile drive twice each day between the damsite and Las Vegas. The bar against blacks' living in company-provided housing was finally dropped, but only after fierce complaints by Ickes.

Every few months, Six Companies poured half a million more yards of concrete, until, by the summer of 1935, all 3.25 million yards had been poured and the wedge that would contain the Colorado was in place. "A remarkable record," one of Crowe's engineers wrote, in describing the dam pouring for the Smithsonian Institution. "Twelve hundred men with modern equipment had in 21 months built a structure whose volume is greater than the largest pyramid of Egypt, which, according to Herodotus, required 100,000 men 20 years to complete."[11]

There remained a big mopping-up job, the construction of a power plant and the eventual building of a $100 million aqueduct; but Six Companies' work on Boulder was essentially complete. On September 30, 1935, President Roosevelt, accompanied by Ickes and a retinue of federal officials, reporters and governors and congressmen from the Colorado River Basin states, arrived at Boulder City. At precisely 11:00 A.M. Pacific Time, the president dedicated the dam in a ceremony broadcast live over both major national radio networks. Even Harold Ickes could not but be impressed. "It is a marvel of engineering skill," he recorded in his diary. "We were all struck with the wonder and marvel of the thing."[13]

CHAPTER 4

STEVE

T he building of Boulder Dam—later to be renamed for Herbert Hoover—changed the face of the American West forever. Power from its mighty turbines electrified cities as far away as Phoenix and Los Angeles, while its water, carried by aqueduct, filled Palm Springs swimming pools and transformed the Imperial Valley from parched desert into one of the richest agricultural areas on the world. Lake Mead, the 115-mile body of water that backed up behind its massive concrete walls, became one of the prime recreational areas of the Southwest. Without Boulder, and the rough-hewn men who built it, none of what was to become the Western sun belt would have been possible.

For the partners of Six Companies there were rewards as well. By building Boulder, they had, just as Henry Kaiser had predicted in Cuba, established themselves as world-class builders—and they had made a fortune doing it. After the deduction of taxes and a well-deserved $300,000 bonus for Frank Crowe, they could each count profits, depending on their share, of between $1 million and $2 million.

Flushed with their success, the partners of Six Companies would, in years to come, go on and build many New Deal–sponsored projects. Working together and sometimes independently, they were responsible for construction of the Moffat Tunnel in Colorado, Gray's Harbor in Washington and the Grand Coulee, Parker and Bonneville Dams.* Indeed, even before Boulder was completed, they had begun a project in some ways yet more daunting than the dam: the more-than-8-mile-long Bay Bridge linking Oakland and San Francisco. Built at a cost of $11.5 million and more than 50 lives—47 perished on one day alone, when, *en bloc*, they plunged through the safety nets and into San Francisco Bay—the Bay Bridge was counted as one of the engineering marvels of its time. Its foundations were the deepest ever laid, its building conditions—including treacherous currents, ever-shifting tides and gale-force winds—among the worst ever encountered. Yet against the odds, against the elements, the Six Companies partners had built it in under five years.** "This is the finest construction outfit on the face of

---

* Although the Six Companies partners would occasionally again build together, as they had at Boulder, in the future their partnership was often largely financial. One partner would find a project, then phone up the others, explaining how much capital was required and asking how much they were willing to invest. No lawyers were involved, and no contracts, and in the end, profits were simply divided in proportion to the capital each partner had put in. "This has always been a strict investment proposition," Felix Kahn said of the arrangement. "The sponsor's one advantage of doing the work was being allowed to make a little more money by taking on a larger share of the project."

An example of Six Companies' new way of doing things occurred shortly after Boulder's completion, when Henry J. Kaiser, who seemed determined to assume the mantle of Six Companies' *paterfamilias*, proposed that the partners build Bonneville Dam in the state of Washington. To his surprise, the others were reluctant to follow his lead, but offered, nonetheless, to provide financial backing. With his son, Edgar, as project manager, Kaiser built the dam on his own, improvising as he went along. The job was finished ahead of schedule, and Kaiser and his partners divided profits of $3 million.

Kaiser's independence did not sit well, however, with all the men at the Six Companies—particularly Steve Bechtel, who came to regard him as a self-promoting egotist. Eventually, the two parted ways and became rivals. Working alone, Henry J. Kaiser was to become one of the great industrialists and philanthropists in American history. He once said of himself, "Our real job is not the building of dams, ships, factories and hospitals; our job is to build and develop people, to bring out their courage, their talents, their zeal and their will to work." By the time of his death in 1967, at the age of 85, Henry J. Kaiser had done all of that, and more.

** On the Bay Bridge project, the Six Companies partners divided into two competing camps. The Kaisers and Bechtels formed Bridge Builders, Inc., while Morrison, Kahn, Shea and the others created the Transbay Construction Company. Though rivals, at

the earth today," Frank Crowe boasted. "You get the work lined up—we'll build it."[1]

And so they would, altering the Western landscape with their handiwork. One of their number, however, would be missing.

In 1933, with work on Boulder well under way, Dad Bechtel had received a most unusual invitation. Still not recognized by the United States, the fledgling Soviet government was then in the midst of a crash industrialization program, a key facet of which was building giant hydroelectric dams on all the country's major rivers. The largest of them all was on the Dnieper, near Kiev. Proud of Soviet handiwork, and in need of some outside engineering advice, the Stalin government asked Bechtel if he would come to inspect it. The invitation was one that Warren Bechtel, a leading *bête noire* of American labor, couldn't refuse. Informing his partners that "this is a good time to see what the rest of the world is doing,"[2] Dad, accompanied by Clara and Alice, set sail from New York in early August.

On arrival in Cherbourg, they went on by train to Vienna, where Clara and Alice had planned to attend the opera and do some shopping. Dad journeyed on to Russia alone—one of the few times in thirty-five years of marriage he had been separated from Clara.

He was 61 now, overweight and a diabetic, and his doctors in California had warned him against making the trip. At first, however, all went well. Arriving in the Russian capital, Bechtel took an instant liking to his hosts and they to him, and the next three days and nights were spent touring Moscow and conferring with leading technocrats and engineers. But on the night before he was to depart for Kiev, Bechtel suffered a severe diabetic attack. Fumbling with his syringe, he injected himself with insulin, something Clara had always done. Whether through unfamiliarity or grogginess, Warren overdosed and slipped into insulin shock.[3]

Russian doctors and nurses crowded round his bed at the National Hotel, worried looks on their faces. Then, briefly, Bechtel seemed to rally. Relieved, the medical personnel departed, leaving him in his hotel suite, sick, old and alone. That night, August 28, 1933, Warren A. Bechtel died in his sleep.

---

least on this job, the two organizations worked on the bridge together, with Bridge Builders, Inc., concentrating on the East Bay work and Transbay focusing on building the western portion of the crossing.

The death of the family patriarch staggered the Bechtels. Clara and Alice* had to arrange to get Dad's body out of Russia and back to America, where they were met by Warren, Steve and Ken. Though by now each of Dad's sons was involved in the family business, their father had left no plans for succession. Moreover during the last months of Dad's life there had been a dispute in the family over ownership of stock.[4] At the time of the company's incorporation, in 1925, Dad had given each of his sons 5 percent of his holdings. Initially, it had seemed a generous gift, but as the years went on and the boys began taking on more and more responsibility, Steve and Ken had begun demanding a larger share. Dad had resisted, and by the time of his death, a legal battle was in the works.**

It was against this backdrop that Dad was buried and the boys began sorting out the tricky question of which of them would lead.

Of the three, Warren junior seemed to have the clearest claim. Not only was he the oldest and most experienced, but he had also been his father's favorite. In personality, Warren was aggressive, boisterous, charming—the archetypal hail-fellow-well-met. Though not a college graduate (like his brothers, he dropped out of Berkeley before graduation), Warren was well read and intuitively bright. What he lacked, however, was seriousness of purpose. Work for Warren was work, and he preferred to have fun. By the time of his father's death, he'd already begun to lose interest in the family business.***

* While in Vienna, Alice had a brief romance with a well-connected but penniless Austrian count named Zucatur, who was on the verge of proposing marriage when Dad died in Moscow. The count was helpful in getting Dad's body out of Russia, but the romance cooled, and shortly after returning to the United States, Alice married Brantley M. Eubanks. Eubanks had worked for W. A. Bechtel on the Boulder Dam project in the finance department, but Steve viewed him as weak and eased him out of the company. Later Eubanks set up his own investment firm and Steve let him manage some of the Bechtel family fortune.

** In battling his father for a larger share of the company, Steve relied on the legal advice of Robert L. Bridges, a then-young attorney working in the San Francisco law firm of Thelen, Marrin (later to become Thelen, Marrin, Johnson and Bridges). The alliance with Steve put Bridges in a difficult position, as the firm's lead partner, Paul Marrin, had long represented Dad Bechtel's legal interests. Steve, however, was to reward him for his troubles. After Dad's will cleared probate, Bridges became Steve Bechtel's personal attorney, and later, chief counsel for the Bechtel Corporation.

*** Warren was active during World War II in managing copper projects for Bechtel-McCone, but had nothing to do with the family-owned business thereafter. He lived on his inheritance from Dad and later got by on funds provided him by Steve and Ken. A heavy drinker and womanizer much of his life, Warren was finally warned by his

Ken, the youngest son, was the quietest, most bookish and most reserved of the brothers, and also the most attached to his mother. In demeanor, he was cool, almost cold—hardly a quality suited to the rough-and-tumble of the jobsite. Ken, in fact, seemed always vaguely uncomfortable around his father's workers, and stuck to the office most of the time. Often on the occasions when he did appear at a construction project, he came dressed in a three-piece suit. For Bechtel's men, it was a uniform of his aloofness.

Which left the middle son, Steve.

Of medium height and slender build, with a soft-spoken manner that contrasted markedly with his father's boisterousness, Stephen Davison Bechtel was outgoing, intuitive and highly intelligent. He was also intensely ambitious. "Steve Bechtel," one of his father's friends put it, "must have climbed out of his crib determined to do something active and important."[5]

After graduation from Oakland's Technical High School, Steve had enlisted in the Army and gone to France with the 20th Engineers, American Expeditionary Force. Following his wartime service, he enrolled at the University of California at Berkeley in 1918. He seemed set on picking up a degree in engineering. But three months into his sophomore year, tragedy struck. While driving a carful of his classmates to a country-club dance, Steve ran down three pedestrians, killing two of them and seriously injuring the third.

The incident, which the Bechtel organization would go to great pains in later years to cover up—including, for a time, concealing the fact that Steve had even attended Berkeley*—was, according to friends, a deeply scarring one for Bechtel, and accounted for much of his subsequent obsession with secrecy. At the time, it also placed him in serious legal jeopardy, since the police arrested him and charged him with manslaughter. Then, something odd happened: the charges were dropped.

There was no explanation, either then or later, why Bechtel was not

---

brothers not to touch another drop of liquor or they would cut him off without a nickel. This threat was significant motivation for Warren to remain sober until he died at his Napa home in January 1976.

* The company's vagueness about Steve's academic background is evident in the Bechtel-McCone-Parsons performance record BMP published in 1942. It describes Steve simply as a graduate engineer—not saying that he attended UC (and failed to graduate). His partner, John McCone, on the other hand, is described as "a graduate mechanical engineer from the University of California."

prosecuted, and all that remains to account for it is a brief, suggestive story in the November 17, 1919, edition of the Oakland *Tribune:*

> Failure of the police or anyone else interested to file a complaint against Stephen D. Bechtel, University of California student, booked by the Oakland police on a manslaughter charge, caused the charge to be stricken from the docket in Police Judge Smith's court.
>
> Bechtel's car crashed into Dr. H. G. Chappel, Oakland dentist, Mrs. Jessie Chappel and Elizabeth Chappel, their daughter, causing the death of the mother and daughter and serious injury to Dr. Chappel, who is now under the care of a physician.
>
> The accident happened at Moss and Broadway, after the Chappels had stepped off a streetcar and were crossing Broadway to the sidewalk.
>
> Young Bechtel's car skidded 136 feet after the collision. The machine was filled with University students going to a dance at the Claremont Country Club.
>
> According to the evidence in the hands of the police, young Bechtel was driving over the 20-mile speed limit at Moss and Broadway. He admitted to going from 30 to 35 miles per hour.

Whatever spared Bechtel from prosecution—lack of evidence, the grief of Dr. Chappel or Dad Bechtel's influential intercession—Steve was shortly to drop out of Berkeley and join his father in business. Soon after, in September 1923, he married his college sweetheart, a handsome young woman from an old and well-respected California family named Laura Adaline Peart. On May 10, 1925, they had a son, Stephen Davison, Jr., and not long after, their second child, a daughter, Barbara, was born.

Initially, Steve was saddled with administrative chores, the nuts-and-bolts-fitting-together of the various elements that make a project work. His real love, though, was for developing new areas of business, and he was especially enthusiastic about pipelining and increasing Bechtel's involvement in the still fledgling but rapidly growing oil industry. With the approval of his father, a believer in giving his boys all the responsibility they could handle, Steve played increasingly larger roles in Bechtel's pipelining projects, and by the time he was into his mid-20s, was managing them on his own—so effectively so that by 1930 he became the functional corporate head of Bechtel-Kaiser Enterprises.

It was Boulder, however, that served as Steve's graduate school. What he hadn't picked up from working at Dad's side for twenty years he learned at Black Canyon, whether from watching Frank Crowe move men and materials, or listening as Felix Kahn explained the nuances of structuring a contract, or observing as Charlie Shea commanded armies of workers, or hearing Harry Morrison expound on the use and abuse of heavy equipment. More than anything else, though, Boulder opened Steve's eyes to the potential for large-scale, multidisciplinary construction projects—projects that in later years would dwarf even Boulder.

His job at Boulder was chief of administration—a title that put him in charge of, among other things, purchasing, assembling and transporting Boulder's vast store of materials. In terms of responsibility, the job was second only to Crowe's, and he went at it with zeal. Though he could be affable when he chose, Steve could also be tough—too tough for some tastes, including Crowe's. The two men had a fractious relationship, and more than once Crowe could be heard muttering that young Bechtel was "terribly ambitious."

Dad Bechtel had been ambitious as well in his youth, but Steve harbored even greater plans. Because of his wartime service, he was more sophisticated and worldly than his father, who, for all his success, was, at bottom, a knockabout earth-mover who threw up dams and gouged out mountains to make way for the roads and railways, never thinking much further ahead than the next job. Steve Bechtel did think ahead: beyond Boulder; beyond earth moving, railroads and road building. His vision set him apart from his father, and made him even more effective at selling than his father had been. "Dad did it [sold] simply and sincerely—with a lot of persuasion, but he didn't seem to be selling at all." Steve's brother Warren explained. "Steve had the same knack and the advantage of more kinds of work behind him and more contacts."[6]

Inevitably, the differences produced friction and, on Steve's part, a certain resentment. It had been Steve, for instance, who took the lead in pressing his father for a greater share of the company's stock, and when Dad refused, it had been Steve who called in the lawyers. Such enterprise did not always make him beloved. It did, though, make him a force to reckon with.

No one seemed to know that better than his brothers, who shortly after Dad's death named him president of Bechtel's operations. Later, Steve commented, "They wanted me to lead, and naturally, I was glad to do it."[7]

Despite the amicability of the settlement, Steve and Warren were to become increasingly estranged, largely over what Steve viewed as the dissoluteness of his older brother's ways. "Warren was a helluva nice guy," said a senior Bechtel executive who was friendly with both brothers, "but he had a penchant for liquor and he liked girls and the girls liked him. By 1936, when Dad's will cleared probate, Steve had become goddam angry with him."[8] So much so that in 1936, Steve, along with Ken, formed a new company, the S. D. Bechtel Company, leaving Warren to go off on his own. Concentrating on his father's railroad work, Warren would not be reunited with his brothers until World War II, and then only indirectly, through his management of Arizona copper projects in which both Steve and Ken had an interest. After the war, Warren retired from business and spent the rest of his life living off his inheritance, a move which succeeded only in alienating Steve all the more.[9]

Steve himself, meanwhile, had his hands full running the business. Like his father, he was eager to demonstrate what he could do on his own, and in 1936 he got his chance when the Department of Reclamation put up for bid a contract to build the Broadway Tunnel, a highway pass through the hills between Berkeley and Oakland. With financial backing from his Six Companies partners, Steve won the contract and became the project's prime contractor. It seemed a simple and straightforward job. Almost as soon as Bechtel's crews began to dig, however, they hit a quagmire of rock, water and mud. Work quickly ground to a near standstill. As the days wore on and costs mounted, Steve's frustration turned to anger and alarm. For under the terms of the $3.9 million contract, the S. D. Bechtel Company was required to pay all construction costs, and no money at all would be forthcoming until the job was done. Hiring a battery of lawyers to go over the contract's fine print, he charged that the Department of Reclamation's district engineers had grossly misrepresented underground conditions, and he threatened a lawsuit. Unfazed, the Department of Reclamation's engineers countered that the Bechtel organization was merely dragging its heels. In fact, the fault was largely Bechtel's. Ground conditions at the tunnel were horrendous, but Steve Bechtel, in his haste to secure the contract, had failed to properly "scope" the work. The result, he admitted years later, was a bid that was "too damn low . . . half of what it should have been. After Boulder," he added, "we were overly confident of our ability to do anything. . . . We should have protected ourselves against something like this. But we learned a lot from that tunnel. We learned we didn't have all the answers."[10]

At that moment, however, Bechtel was on the hook. Worse, Steve was, thanks to his carelessness, about to lose $2.4 million of his own and his partners' money. Hoping to salvage the situation, even at the cost of embarrassing Bechtel, Six Companies persuaded a reluctant Henry J. Kaiser to finish the job. Kaiser, however, fared no better than Bechtel, and in an attempt to recoup his losses wound up taking the Department of Reclamation to court. After an abortive attempt at negotiations—Kaiser offered to finish the tunnel if the Works Progress Administration guaranteed to give Six Companies an addition $3 million in work, a proposal the government flatly turned down—the U.S. District Court fined Kaiser $239,000 for defaulting on the contract and ordered him to complete the project. *

The Broadway Tunnel fiasco, though bitter and embarrassing, was an important learning experience for Bechtel. He would be far more cautious from here on, especially in his dealings with the U.S. government, whose great Depression-era spurt of building was, in any case, winding down. "We [Ken and I] had come to realize that competitive work for the government was unpredictable," he said in an interview half a century later. "More often than not it led to trouble, and many contractors went broke pursuing it."[11]

Neither Bechtel nor any of the Six Companies partners would ever go broke—on the contrary, all were to make millions more building government dams and roads—but they would increasingly seek work from the private sector, particularly the oil companies Steve Bechtel knew so well from his work in pipelining. In this effort, Steve Bechtel would join with an old college chum and business associate destined to become one of the pivotal figures in American foreign policy. His name was John A. McCone.

As presidents of both parties would come to realize, and Steve Bechtel knew already, John A. McCone was a man of considerable talents. The child of Scotch-Irish parents, he had been born in Los Angeles and raised a devout—many would say dogmatic—Roman Catholic. For a time there was some thought that he would be a priest, and no doubt McCone would have been a good one. With his dour demeanor and shrewd calculation, it was easy to imagine him as a hustling mon-

---

* Frank Crowe, who had been boss at Boulder Dam and worked on many later mammoth construction projects both for Six Companies and for Bechtel, was involved in the Broadway Tunnel not as a builder, but as the source of some timely advice. Seeing that there would be no end of lawsuits if Kaiser continued on his litigious path, Crowe, who could be as pithy as he was industrious, advised Six Companies to "Stop lawin' and start diggin'." They did, and the project was finally completed.

signor, whispering in the bishop's ear, even as he dispensed penance to those less straight and narrow. But somewhere in adolescence, priestly thoughts were put aside, and instead, McCone went on to the University of California at Berkeley, working his way through school as a part-time laborer in a steel factory. The exposure to the blast furnaces seemed to fire McCone's soul. He was graduated with honors from the college of engineering, ranked 10th in his class.

At Berkeley, McCone developed a reputation as a grind, a humorless sort more at ease with slide rules than he was with people. But exacting as McCone was—and there were few on the Cal campus who seemed as sober—he occasionally allowed himself the company of a few like-minded friends. One of them, an engineering student a year ahead of him, was Steve Bechtel. The two socialized together, and by the time Steve dropped out of school to join his father, they had become if not warm, then at least good friends.

Following graduation, McCone, who was determined to learn the steel business from the ground up, found work as a 40-cents-an-hour riveter for the Llewellyn Iron Works, a Los Angeles–based fabricator of steel frameworks for office buildings and storage tanks for the booming California petroleum industry. Before long he was promoted to foreman, and at the age of 26 he became construction manager. While Steve Bechtel was laying pipelines, his future partner was overseeing the production of the tanks they would fill.

It was not until 1931, however, that the two former schoolmates connected again. That year, McCone quit Llewellyn to become sales manager of Consolidated Steel. Headquartered in Los Angeles, Consolidated liked to boast that it was the "biggest steel fabricator west of the Mississippi," and until the Depression it had been prospering nicely, if unspectacularly. The Depression, however, changed everything. All at once, builders weren't buying enough steel to keep even a mid-sized concern such as Consolidated solvent. The company, which had lately built a big new fabricating plant, was in desperate straits, and McCone had been summoned in a last-gasp effort to turn corporate fortunes around. "It [1931] was a memorable year for sales managers," McCone later remembered. "I was in search of my first customer when the other sales managers were sure they had seen their last."

There was, however, one project that was using steel—tons and tons of it. That project was Boulder Dam, where, as it happened, John McCone's old friend from Berkeley was in charge of purchasing.

At Boulder, Bechtel was deferentially called "Mr. Customer" by the armies of peddlers and salesmen who called on him. Most he found a nuisance, and he hired an old Berkeley fraternity brother, William E. Waste—later to become executive vice-president and director of Bechtel—for the express purpose of keeping them at bay. McCone, however, was an old friend, and Bechtel welcomed him cordially. The terms McCone offered were favorable ones, and Consolidated eventually supplied Boulder with a total of 55 million tons of steel. The sale saved Consolidated from bankruptcy and young John McCone from unemployment.

In the years since, Bechtel and McCone had kept in close touch, hoping one day to go into business together. Both sensed that the core of America's industrial might, so long centered in the big smokestack cities of the East, was shifting westward, and that what was moving it was oil. "Steve and I shared a sense of imminent change," McCone recalled, "of great projects about to break at last upon the West. We were sure we could have a place in them."[12]

Securing that place was made easier by McCone's contacts in the oil industry—in particular with another Berkeley classmate, Reese Taylor, then chairman of Consolidated, and on his way to becoming chairman of Union Oil. From his pipelining projects, Bechtel had friends of his own in oil, especially at Standard Oil of California (Socal), where he had managed his first pipeline job at the age of 28. Both men, then, had entrée. The trick was coming up with something to sell after they got through the door. And here Steve Bechtel had an idea. Why not, he proposed to McCone, offer the oil companies an entire construction package? Not just pipelines, but storage tanks, refineries—the works. It would appeal to the oil companies, which would be spared the chore of dealing with dozens of subcontractors, and handling the complete job would enrich them both. John McCone peered through his wire-rimmed glasses and smiled. Why not, indeed?

The grand plan settled, Bechtel and McCone drew up a contract— one that named McCone president and gave Bechtel, as chairman, controlling interest in the Bechtel-McCone Corporation—rented a suite of offices in downtown Los Angeles and in May 1937, proclaimed themselves in business. It was not a two-man operation. With him, McCone had brought some of the technical talent Bechtel-McCone was going to need to survive—most notably, John C. Byrne, an MIT-educated Consolidated veteran, who was charged with handling the new company's cost and production estimates. Other key players came from Bechtel, including J. Perry Yates, a former Six Companies and

W. A. Bechtel field engineer. At Bechtel-McCone, Yates was initially put in charge of coordinating the work of the engineering, construction and purchasing departments; eventually, he became a senior vice-president and director of the company. Later, his son Alden went to work for Bechtel as well, and in 1982 he succeeded George Shultz as the Bechtel Group's president. Two other crucial hires were V. G. "Heine" Hindmarsh, a longtime engineering and construction manager (he specialized in building refineries), who brought with him a number of superintendents, foremen and mechanics; and Ralph M. Parsons, a former aeronautical engineer and naval officer, boss of his own Chicago-based engineering firm and holder of a number of patents covering various refinery processes and equipment. *

As the corporate team was being put together, Bechtel and McCone began calling on their friends in the oil industry, sounding them out on their "full-service" concept. The response was overwhelmingly positive; but for all the good wishes, no contracts were offered. Steve, however, had a card to play. In the spring of 1937, while McCone was winding up his affairs as Consolidated's executive vice-president, he and his brother Ken had approached Standard Oil of California about building part or all of a new refinery the company was planning at Richmond, California. It was complicated work, and given Bechtel's limited experience, Socal had been reluctant. Steve, however, had finally persuaded Socal to part with a portion of the contract. "Give us that work on any kind of basis and we'll show you we know what the hell we're doing," he had told him. "Let us prove ourselves."[13]

Prove himself Bechtel had, and by late summer 1937, work on the project was nearing completion, under budget and ahead of schedule. Impressed, Socal gave Bechtel-McCone a contract to build even more of the refinery. Steve was ecstatic. "We'll go to Richmond and build the refinery for nothing!"[14] he facetiously promised Socal. Of course, it was not for nothing. It was, for Bechtel-McCone, a multimillion-dollar contract, and the beginning of a long string of refinery construction for Socal and its competitors, in the country and out of it.

---

* Ralph Parsons was to play a vital role in the early years of Bechtel-McCone, and in recognition of his contributions, he was made a principal in the company—retitled the Bechtel-McCone-Parsons Corporation—in 1938. In 1944, however, after a series of personality clashes between Parsons and McCone, Bechtel and McCone effectively dumped him. After selling his shares back to the firm, he went on to form the Pasadena, California–based Parsons Corporation, which in later years, became one of Bechtel's chief competitors.

By 1939, Bechtel-McCone had mushroomed into an organization with more than 10,000 employees and was building refineries, chemical plants and pipelines from Montana to Venezuela. "We will build anything, any place, any time," Bechtel crowed. "The bigger, the tougher the job, the better we like it."[15]

He would soon be called on to make good his pledge. War had come to Europe, and the world was about to turn upside down.

CHAPTER 5

THE WAR YEARS

I n the crowded Washington restaurant, industrialists in wide-lapelled, double-breasted suits lunched on 75-cent sirloins, sipped sour mash and talked defense contracts with politicians and military brass. It was the summer of 1940, and much of Europe had already fallen to the Germans. In England, the British were mourning their dead and nursing their wounded from Dunkirk, even as they prepared for the soon-to-come Nazi blitz. At Number 10 Downing Street, the new prime minister, Winston Churchill, was hurling defiance at Adolf Hitler and begging his friend Franklin Roosevelt for help. "Give us the tools," he implored, "and we will finish the fight." America, they agreed, would be in the war soon: it was merely a matter of time.

At a corner table, five men lingered over their coffee long after the rest of the restaurant was deserted. Their host was the redheaded president of Consolidated Steel, Alden G. Roach. He had come to Washington to make a sales call on one of his lunch guests, Admiral Howard L. Vickery, number two man at the U.S. Maritime Commission and the person responsible for all naval ship construction and design.

Vickery, however, had more important matters on his mind. Recently, his office had received a telegram from the British Purchasing Commission (BPC) urgently requesting that the Maritime Commission arrange the building of 60 tankers to replace the ships the British had lost to German torpedoes. But as Vickery was well aware, U.S. shipyards on the Atlantic coast were already producing beyond capacity. If the British were to have their ships—and England needed them, if the war was to continue—a Pacific shipbuilder had to be found. Dropping his voice even lower, the admiral asked Roach if he knew anyone on the West Coast who could fill the bill.

"Give me a little time," Roach replied, "I might be able to help."[1]

Though he did not say so to Vickery, Roach already had his candidates in mind; and as luck would have it, they were staying at the same hotel. They knew next to nothing about building ships; but when an opportunity presented itself, Steve Bechtel and John McCone were always ready to learn.

Within twenty-four hours Roach had set up a meeting between the admiral and his two friends. He warned them in advance that Vickery was not going to be an easy person to deal with. An Annapolis graduate who had shown such promise as a naval architect that the Navy had sent him on to MIT, Vickery had a reputation for driving contractors hard. Let one of them fall behind schedule, and he would soon be on the receiving end of a bluntly worded telegram—one of "Vickery's needles"—warning him to get with it, or else.

But Vickery was also a good judge of talent. In selecting contractors, he looked for what he termed "management brains" as much as experience. He had never heard of Bechtel-McCone or Six Companies, but as he listened over lunch while Steve and McCone described their background, he couldn't help being impressed. With the Hoover Dam, and the numerous other projects Bechtel and McCone had undertaken since, they were clearly in the front ranks of American builders. Moreover, Vickery discovered, one of Bechtel's Six Companies associates, Felix Kahn, had run one of the nation's biggest shipyards during World War I. Lately, Bechtel and McCone themselves had become interested in shipbuilding, sensing, as Steve put it, that it "seemed about ripe to become a big-volume business." Indeed, so much interested had they become that they had already approached Six Companies with a joint-venture proposal, and bought a part interest in an existing Seattle yard.

Vickery was cautious, though. The scale of operation he envisioned would require quick turnaround, standardized design, production-line techniques—all the innovation necessary to turn out not just a few but dozens, even hundreds of ships. Did Bechtel and McCone think they could handle this kind of assembly-line work? "Admiral," Steve said evenly, "that's precisely the approach we had in mind."[2]

Roach couldn't believe how quickly everything had progressed. "The next thing I knew," he said, "they were in the middle of the ship-building business."[3]

When Bechtel and McCone returned to California, however, a rude surprise awaited them. The shipyards on the Pacific, including their own operation in Seattle, were as jammed with work as those on the Atlantic. To build new ships would require constructing an entire new yard. Looking around, Bechtel soon found two: the port of Richmond, and a former Northwestern Railroad terminal outside Sausalito on the shore of Richardson Bay. Here, near his original home base, he could draw on resources from the ongoing Socal work, and bring the talents of W. A. Bechtel into play.* Others were not so sanguine. Visiting Richmond in the fall of 1940, a BPC representative was shocked to discover that the Bechtel-McCone "shipyard" was, as he put it, in a nervous cable to London, "nothing but a vast sea of mud."

Bechtel and McCone had just begun clearing it when they were summoned to Washington for an emergency meeting with Vickery and his boss, Maritime Commission chairman Admiral Emory S. Land. There had been, Land and Vickery informed them, a slight change in the agenda. Besides building ships for the British, they would have to build them for the Americans as well. Not merely tankers, but Liberty and Victory cargo ships, troop transports, the whole makings of a merchant navy. Hundreds, perhaps thousands of vessels would be needed, and they would have to build them just as quickly as possible. America was heading into war.

It was apparent now that the Richmond and Sausalito yards alone would not suffice; a third yard would be necessary as well. The War Department found them a site on Terminal Island in Los Angeles harbor, not far from their corporate headquarters. Bechtel and McCone dubbed the operation "Calship" and called on Steve's old partners at Six Companies for help. On January 11, 1942, slightly more than a month after the Japanese attack on Pearl Harbor, the Maritime Commission awarded Calship its first shipbuilding contract; three days later, ground was broken at Terminal Island.

They were moving quickly—but as far as Land was concerned, not

---

* Though he'd formed several new companies since his father's death, Steve still operated the W. A. Bechtel Company and used it for earth moving and heavy construction projects.

quickly enough. In March, he telegraphed Bechtel and McCone with instructions to complete both shipyards as soon as possible. He added that he expected the first completed ships by the end of the year. "WE ARE NOW RELYING ON YOU INDIVIDUALLY," wired Land. "THE EMERGENCY DEMANDS ALL IN YOUR POWER TO GIVE YOUR COUNTRY SHIPS."[4]

Bechtel and McCone met the deadline with time to spare. Within little more than a year Calship was employing 42,000 workers and building as many as three dozen Liberty ships simultaneously on its prefabrication and subassembly lines. At the Sausalito yard—named "Marinship," for its proximity to Marin County—the pace was nearly as frantic. Under the direction of Steve's brother Ken, who, with brother Warren, was helping to run war-critical copper mines in Arizona and Mexico as well, Marinship was working around the clock and adding new workers every day.

The demands were backbreaking, and for some Bechtel-McCone executives, like George S. Cooley, Jr., hazardous as well. Called to the Philippines in the spring of 1941 to modernize an existing naval base in Manila and build an emergency airfield outside the capital, Cooley was in the midst of work when the Japanese attacked Pearl Harbor and, the next day, began massive bombing attacks on Clark Field, the main Philippine air base. These attacks were followed in quick succession by raids on Manila and the not-yet-completed bases at Cavite and Sangley Point. As the Japanese pressure increased, Cooley; his wife, Marjorie, and a small party of Americans retreated to the Mariveles Mountains to build emergency airfields and ammunition tunnels. Just as quickly, the Japanese landed in force. Aware that the enemy was tapping his phone, Cooley managed to get a last call through to Steve Bechtel in San Francisco. "You won't be hearing from me for about a month,"[5] he told his boss. He, Marjorie and the others were trapped.

Cooley had two choices, neither of them at all appealing: he could wait to be captured and imprisoned by the Japanese, or he could attempt an escape by boat to Australia through 1,500 miles of normally dangerous waters made more so by Japanese patrols. In early 1942, with the Japanese closing in and a number of other Bechtel executives already taken prisoner, he opted for the latter. Accompanied by his wife, another Bechtel couple and a British doctor from Shanghai, Cooley put to sea at night aboard a small pleasure boat and headed south. After a brief stop at Corregidor, where they were fired on before they could identify themselves, they crossed the Sulu Sea and landed on a small island just north of Borneo. There they transferred to a *kumpit*, a native sailboat, and set out once again, this time for the British-controlled port of Sandakan. They arrived to find the British gone and the Japanese in control. Increasingly desperate, Cooley continued on, slipping the *kumpit* into a tidal river and gradually making his way past the Japanese to the shelter of a rain forest, where the group made camp for the night.

At daylight, it was apparent that the fragile *kumpit* had been so battered by storms they had passed through that it was no longer seaworthy. Cooley set off in hopes of finding a nearby native village where he could buy another boat. Unable to pass through the dense jungle, he waded into the river and began swimming upstream. He had not gone a thousand yards when he encountered a *kumpit*-sized crocodile which sent him scampering up a mangrove tree. He was still perched in its branches, waiting for the crocodile to depart, Cooley recounted in a privately published account of his wartime experiences, *Manila, Kuching and Return*, when a Japanese patrol boat spotted him. The crew found his situation quite amusing. Cooley, his wife and the rest of the group would spend the remainder of the war in a disease-ridden Japanese prison camp.

In the United States, meanwhile, Bechtel-McCone's shipbuilding efforts were continuing. By September 1942, less than six months after work on the Richmond yard had begun, Marinship had christened its first Liberty ship. Hardly was the christening ceremony over when Ken received one of Vickery's needles. "NOW THAT THE SHOUTING IS OVER REGARDING YOUR FIRST LAUNCHING," the admiral wired, "WHEN IS THE NEXT LAUNCHING AND WHEN WILL SHIPS BE DELIVERED, OR WAS THAT [the christening ceremony] MERELY A PUBLICITY STUNT?"[6] Two months later, Ken wired back apprising the admiral that Marinship had completed its first, fully outfitted tanker, the *Mission Purisima*. "IT'S A GIRL (PURISIMA) DELIVERED AT SIX PM NOVEMBER 23. CHILD IS VERY HEALTHY. ALL PARENTS WEAK BUT WILL RECOVER. REGARDS." Vickery's retort came back the same day. "DELIVERY WAS STIMULATING NEWS. I HOPE THE NEXT PERIOD OF GESTATION WILL NOT BE THAT OF AN ELEPHANT."[7] From the acerbic Vickery, that was high praise.

John McCone also received his share of Vickery's needles, but he had his own special incentive for keeping production at Calship in high gear. Henry Kaiser had followed Bechtel-McCone's lead into shipbuilding, and during the first few years of the war the two companies had emerged as the country's leading shipbuilders, running nearly neck and neck in the speed and volume with which they turned out vessels.

But Kaiser had the decided edge for self-promotion, and as a result, the media began characterizing him as the captain of America's war effort, a gutsy, down-to-earth patriot-capitalist who managed to keep defense plants humming twenty-four hours a day and never forgot to bid "Good morning" to Rosie the Riveter. "The Atlas Industrialist," *Fortune* called him. "The most portentous industrial phenomenon in the U.S. today."

A proud man, McCone was irked that Kaiser was getting so much publicity and claiming so much credit. Bechtel was annoyed as well, but neither he nor McCone was ready to tangle with Kaiser publicly. Lacking Kaiser's self-promotional skills, they beat him where it mattered—on the production line. Each time one of Kaiser's shipyards announced an increase in production, McCone and Bechtel would push Calship's up another notch, always maintaining a slight lead. At his peak, during the summer of 1944, Kaiser was turning out 18 ships a month. By October, Calship was producing 20, winning for Bechtel and McCone the satisfaction of running the most productive single shipyard in the world.

By then, Bechtel and McCone had become involved in other wartime enterprises, some of which would later come back to haunt them. There was, for one notorious example, the Alaska pipeline.

Until Pearl Harbor, the Army had not thought much about Alaska; but then, not many people had, including Bechtel and McCone. Alaska was far away, barren, cold; it seemed an altogether useless piece of real estate. In the jittery months after the Japanese attack, though, that estimation rapidly changed. All at once, Alaska was important—indeed, vital, for it was here, Army intelligence concluded, that the Japanese would likely mount an invasion and from here, after securing their position, sweep southward through Canada and into the United States itself.

Defending Alaska, where military installations were few and exceedingly far apart, would be difficult—impossible without supplies, most critically oil, from the "lower forty-eight." Without oil, the fighter planes based in Alaska couldn't take off, and the bombers that landed there on their way to the Pacific couldn't refuel—nor, for that matter, could any of the cargo ships and ferries bound for Russia with Lend-Lease war matériel.

Work on one oil route, the Alaskan Highway, was already under way, but even when completed, the highway would be closed two-thirds of the year by fierce subarctic storms. Alaska needed another means of supply, and Lieutenant General Brehon Somervell, head of the Army

Sources of Supply Command, had already decided to build a major refinery at the Norman Wells oilfields in Canada's Northwest Territories, and run a pipeline from there 1,200 miles southwest through the Yukon Territory into Alaska.

It was, to put it mildly, an ambitious proposal. The territory the pipeline would traverse was among the most remote wilderness areas in the world. Much of it had never been explored and was unrecorded on any map. In winter, temperatures dropped to 70 degrees below zero. But it could be done. Somervell, who had been an Army engineer for thirty years, was sure of it. So confident was he of the project's success that he had already committed several thousand Army Corps of Engineers troops—many of them blacks from the South—to do it. But the bulk of the work—the building of refineries, tank farms and the pipeline itself—would fall to a civilian contractor recommended to him by Standard Oil of California. That contractor was Steve Bechtel.

Initially, Bechtel was reluctant. With Calship and Marinship, he and McCone already had more work than they could handle. Somervell, though, was not an easy man to deny. A West Point graduate who had served under "Black Jack" Pershing in the punitive raids against Pancho Villa's forces in northern Mexico, he had the swagger of a soldier and the mind of an engineer. There was an appealing forcefulness about him that even Bechtel found hard to resist. Also, the deal Somervell was offering was a sweet one: Bechtel was to be guaranteed a 10 percent profit on the project, and would have the right to select his own subcontractors, including, if he chose, the W. A. Bechtel Company and Bechtel-McCone. Any remaining doubts Bechtel may have had were banished when Secretary of War Henry L. Stimson called him into his office and in no uncertain terms, ordered him to take the job. Said Stimson: "This is what your country has decided you are going to do during the war. Now get out of here and get to work, goddammit."[8]

So Bechtel would build Somervell's pipeline. But Somervell had one more condition: the work on "Canol," as it was called, after "Canadian oil," had to be done in secret, with no contract and no one outside the War Department and Bechtel's own organization knowing about it. It wasn't so much the Japanese Somervell was worried about as the old curmudgeon Harold Ickes.

Just as the Interior secretary had been a thorn in Bechtel's side at Boulder, Ickes was a longtime enemy of Somervell's as well, repeatedly attacking the general since the days when Somervell was building La-

Guardia Airport and a host of other New York projects for the WPA. Now, in addition to his Interior post, Ickes was named head of the Petroleum Administration for War, a job that put him in charge of ensuring that the oil industry met the military's needs, and which, in Somervell's eyes, made him all the more dangerous. If Ickes got wind of the pipeline project, Somervell told Bechtel,[9] he would no doubt try to assume control of it or even attempt to cancel it. But Bechtel needn't worry about the project's funding. With the consent of Stimson—no friend of Ickes' either—Somervell had already buried an initial $25 million[10] for it in a massive war appropriations bill. All Bechtel had to do was keep his mouth shut.

The final approval for Canol came through in April 1942, and shortly thereafter, notices began appearing in employment offices in the United States and Canada. They neither named the project nor described its location, but they made the challenge of building it clear enough. "THIS IS NO PICNIC," the posters warned. "WORKING AND LIVING CONDITIONS ON THIS JOB ARE AS DIFFICULT AS ANY CONSTRUCTION JOB EVER DONE IN THE UNITED STATES OR FOREIGN TERRITORY... IF YOU ARE NOT PREPARED TO WORK UNDER THESE CONDITIONS... DO NOT APPLY."[11] Eager to avoid the draft, hundreds of welders and iron-workers, truck drivers and mechanics, cat skinners and carpenters ignored the warning, and within a month, Bechtel had put together and shipped north a work force of several thousand men. They were soon joined by 2,500 troops from the Army's Corps of Engineers and hundreds of Bechtel engineers and technicians. They had their work cut out for them.

There were no roads where they had gone, deep in the Canadian wilderness, a thousand miles from the nearest city of Edmonton; no airports, no railway tracks, no electricity, no creature comforts of any kind. Everything had to be brought in from outside, shipped by barge across Great Slave Lake and up the Mackenzie River—both frozen solid most of the year.

To facilitate the shipment of materials, Bechtel's crews began hacking out roads and laying down railroad tracks. An airport was built, and soon Bechtel was operating its own airline. By autumn, work had progressed sufficiently that Steve Bechtel, who was flying in on personal inspection tours once a month, had decided to commission a private film on what his men were calling "the greatest project since the Panama Canal."

His optimism proved premature. With the onset of winter, work once merely nightmarish quickly became impossible; blizzards halted construction. Then in the spring and early summer as the frozen sub-soil began to thaw, it swallowed up men and machinery like quicksand. As the work fell further and further behind, the project's cost, initially budgeted at $35 million, began to skyrocket. Then, the worst happened: Ickes found out.

Given the Interior secretary's network of contacts, and his passion for uncovering secrets, it was probably inevitable that Ickes would uncover Canol sooner or later. To Bechtel and Somervell's chagrin, it turned out to be sooner. During a business trip to London, in May 1943, an Ickes associate named Ralph K. Davies had a chance encounter in the Mayflower bar with a builder acquaintance, who told him of an incredible project in Canada that sounded as if it had been inspired by a Jack London novel. Davies passed along the information to Ickes, who initially didn't think much of it. "Our first impulse," he recorded in his papers, "was to discount the report, because we assumed that if a project of this kind was being considered, we would have been officially informed."[12]

But as the days went on, additional rumors about Canol kept drifting in. Finally, Ickes pressed Stimson's office for information. Yes, there was something in the works in Canada, the War Department admitted, but Stimson couldn't supply many details. Furious, Ickes demanded to at least see the contract for the project. Sorry, Stimson responded: there were no contracts.

In high dudgeon now, Ickes started digging, and bombarded the War Department with letters detailing what he was finding. He also briefed his friends in Congress, including an obscure senator from Missouri named Harry S. Truman. Chairman of a Senate subcommittee investigating the national defense program, Truman convened hearings on Canol in November 1943. His star witness was Harold Ickes.

Voice dripping with sarcasm, Ickes told the committee: "The whole Canol project grew entirely out of a one-page memorandum from General Somervell, who was anxious to conserve paper. . . . The congressional authorization was for $25 million, which was buried in one of the huge authorization bills.

"General Somervell," Ickes continued, "in 1942 defended his visionary scheme on the allegation that it was strategically vital to the defense of the United States. He defended it again in 1943 as still being strategically necessary, although by that time our Navy had turned back the Japanese at Midway. Guadalcanal had been captured and North

Africa was being invaded."[13] Moreover, Ickes went on, the pipeline itself was useless. Four inches in diameter—slightly larger than a man's wrist—it would pump in one year as much oil as "one average-size tanker could supply . . . making four trips between the mainland and Alaska." And the cost? Not including the expense of transporting, feeding and housing 4,000 Army troops working on the project, So-mervell, said Ickes, had spent more than $100 million on Canol—and the project was at least a year from completion.

Somervell himself seemed unperturbed. "A check is just the same size, no matter what you write on it," he blithely told one senator, and with that, excused himself from the hearings,* leaving the task of further defense to his chief advisor, James G. Graham. A dollar-a-year man ("And worth every penny of it," cracked Ickes), Graham did not turn in a stellar performance.[14]

"How many miles did you think the pipeline was going to be?" Hugh Fulton, the committee's chief counsel, asked him.

"About five or six hundred," Graham responded.

FULTON: "How many did it turn out to be?"
GRAHAM: "I do not know."
FULTON: "Are you aware that it was longer than contemplated?"
GRAHAM: "No. I do not know."
FULTON: "How much did you estimate it would cost in terms of materials and manpower?"
GRAHAM: "On war projects, I never make an estimate."
FULTON: "Who . . . made an estimate of any kind?"
GRAHAM: "None was made that I know of."

Bechtel himself never appeared before Truman's subcommittee. Privately, however, he made no apology for his Canol work. It was the Army that had specified the use of 4-inch and 6-inch pipe, he insisted,[15] not he, just as it was the Army, in the person of Somervell, that had insisted on no contracts and keeping the pipeline secret from Ickes. The delays, the cost overruns, the tens of millions wasted, they were to be expected from a project as difficult and complex as Canol.

---

* A good part of the reason for Somervell's passivity in front of the committee was the fact that he was desperately trying to conceal the existence of another Army Corps of Engineers undertaking far more expensive—and even more critical—than Canol. That undertaking was the Manhattan Project, which resulted in the creation of the first atomic bomb.

He, Steve Bechtel, had only been a good soldier, following his country's orders.

As for the pipeline and the refinery, they were finally finished in May 1945—three months before the Japanese surrender, and two years behind schedule. They managed, for a time, to pump some oil—at a cost of $150 per barrel, rather than the $5 to $10 Somervell had promised Stimson—but after less than a year the entire operation was abandoned, left to rust in the Canadian wilderness. The cost to the taxpayers had been more than $134 million.

Bechtel, however, had profited handsomely. Not only did he get a percentage of the costs, but, all told, three Bechtel-owned companies, W. A. Bechtel, the Bechtel Company and Bechtel-McCone, received contracts fom the War Department for Canol.

Thanks to projects like Canol, Bechtel-McCone was booming. By 1943 it had grown tenfold since the beginning of the war, with revenues exceeding $50 million—a figure that did not include moneys from shipbuilding or Canol. At the direction of the War Department, it was building pipelines and refineries in Mexico, Venezuela and Bahrain, off the coast of Saudi Arabia, and Bechtel had already set up a planning department for more such work when the fighting was over. In what was to be a pivotal move, he had also acquired a company called Industrial Engineering, which had invented, and held the exclusive patent rights on, a process that could keep pipelines from corroding for fifty years—five times their normal lifetime. When the war was over, the process would provide Bechtel with a competitive edge no other pipelining company could match. Until then, there were still other opportunities for Bechtel-McCone to exploit. The biggest—and most controversial—was the Army's Willow Run Aircraft Modification Plant in Alabama.

Bechtel and McCone had wanted to get into the aircraft-building business largely because Henry J. Kaiser was in it and by all reports, doing quite well at it. In July 1942, they mentioned their interest to Somervell,[16] who promised to check with his friends in the Air Corps to see what projects were available. Somervell came back to report that while the Army had enough new planes in the works, the service was planning to erect the Willow Run modification facility, not far from Birmingham, Alabama, to modify newly built aircraft for specific climatic missions. A bomber destined for missions in North Africa, say, would be modified with one sort of equipment, while one destined for Lend-Lease shipment to the Soviet Union would be fitted with another sort. Studies for the factory had already been requested, and a total of fifteen companies, including Kaiser's, had submitted proposals. But if they moved quickly, Somervell said, he could ensure that a Bechtel-McCone proposal would get a good hearing. Soon thereafter, McCone sent the Army an engineering study, attaching to it a bill for $25,000.[17]

Stunned—all the other companies had done studies at no cost—the Army at first refused to pay. McCone, however, had been counting on that, just as he had been counting on the fact that by entailing a bill, Bechtel-McCone's study would stand out from the rest. Both assumptions were correct. The Army paid, and—partly because it had paid—awarded Bechtel-McCone the contract.

The document was a builder's dream. In it, the Army committed itself to pay all the company's costs plus 5 percent on work estimates submitted every six months. Those estimates were to be made not by the Army, but by Bechtel-McCone. The company was thus in the enviable position of deciding how much it wanted to profit. Moreover, the Army paid Bechtel-McCone *whether or not* its estimated work was completed.[18] It was, as events would later demonstrate, an invitation to abuse.

Nonetheless, the Army went forward. In time, a 300-acre factory was duly built, and 8,000 employees hired to staff it. All that was missing was the airplanes, which, according to the Army's original calculations, should have been pouring out at the rate of hundreds a month. By the summer of 1943, not one had shown itself in the skies. "The planes are not even flying over the city, much less away from the city as finished products," a *Birmingham News* reporter named Marguerite Johnston wrote a friend in August that year. "Employees of the company [Bechtel-McCone] both at the plant and at the downtown office will talk glibly of men being paid large . . . salaries for 'waiting orders' week after week; of stenographers hired by the score who cannot type or take shorthand." Johnston added that she had also heard stories of "some sort of investigation about to be launched."[19]

Some sort of investigation was indeed about to be launched, triggered by a conversation a Birmingham lawyer named Talbott Ellis had with a woman for whom he was handling a divorce. During the talk, the client told Ellis that she was working at Willow Run, and that the only thing being modified at the plant was the employees' bank accounts, which were getting fatter and fatter. She herself went in every day at 9:00, punched the time clock, then went home, not to be seen again until 5:00, when she returned to punch out. She added that all her colleagues did the same.

Subsequently, Ellis repeated what he had heard to a local stockbroker named George P. Alexander. Outraged at the tale, and helped along, perhaps, by a bounty that was being paid for turning in war profiteers, Alexander and Ellis began collecting affidavits from Willow Run workers. One was a truck driver who said he drove the same load of gravel into and out of the plant as many as eight times a day without unloading it. Another worker, who, with a number of other laborers, was laying a concrete apron in front of one of the modification buildings, said he was told by a superintendent to throw all his tools into the concrete "to reinforce the base." From this Alexander drew the obvious conclusion: Willow Run's management, namely Bechtel-McCone, wanted to buy new tools, which would increase the estimate for the job—and thereby Bechtel-McCone's profits.

On the basis of these affidavits, Alexander filed suit against Bechtel-McCone in federal district court on July 31, 1943. Charging that the company had made "many and various claims against the government of the United States, or a department or officer thereof, knowing such claims to be false, fictitious or fraudulent," Alexander sought to recover $2 million under the provisions of Title 31, Sections 231–235 of the United States Code. *

Alexander's suit soon produced a visit to Birmingham from John D. Sparkman, then congressman, later U.S. senator from Alabama and later still, Adlai Stevenson's vice-presidential running mate. Dispatched by a congressional investigating committee, Sparkman met with McCone and several other Bechtel-McCone officials and apparently satisfied that there was no wrongdoing, returned to Washington without seeing either Alexander or Ellis, or for that matter, any worker from Willow Run. [20]

In the courts, meanwhile, a Bechtel-hired lawyer had succeeded in having Alexander's suit thrown out, on the ground that it lacked specificity. Not easily put off—"We were highly patriotic" Alexander said of himself and Ellis—Alexander secured affidavits from more Willow Run employees and on September 13 filed an amended complaint,

---

* Under these provisions, since recodified as Section 3730, a private citizen can bring a civil suit on behalf of the U.S. government against another individual for knowingly making a false or fraudulent claim to the U.S. government. If the government proceeds with the action, the person bringing the action may receive an amount the court decides is reasonable for disclosing evidence or information the government did not have when the action was brought. The amount may not be more than 10 percent of the proceeds of the action or settlement of a claim and shall be paid out of those proceeds.

detailing a laundry list of alleged instances of fraud and abuse. *

On the face of it, Alexander seemed to have a compelling case. It hinged, though, on the provision in the contract calling for Bechtel-McCone to receive a guaranteed 5 percent profit above what it estimated as its future costs. Without that provision, there could be no motive for committing fraud; without the motive, there could be no case. In a never-published May 17, 1943, interview with *Fortune* magazine, however, John McCone, who was famed for the exactitude of his memory, stated that the contract was indeed written the way Alexander claimed it was. As McCone put it: "Every six months, we estimate how much work we expect to do in the next six months and then we get a fee of five percent of the estimated amount of work *regardless* [author's emphasis] of how much work we actually do turn out."[21] The contract Bechtel-McCone's lawyers presented in court, however, said no such thing. After reading it over, the judge had no choice but to dismiss the case. "In its original complaint," said his judgment, "the plaintiff averred that the defendant under its contracts was to be reimbursed on the basis of a percentage of the amount expended by the government. The contracts in evidence conclusively show that defendant's compensation was on a fixed fee basis."[22]

If McCone's memory was, in fact, accurate, the contract wording, it seemed, had been changed. However it was accomplished—if, indeed, it was accomplished—Steve Bechtel and John McCone had been legally saved. They had also made a great deal of money: a total, when the final figures for Willow Run were added up, of $3,375,000.

All in all, World War II was a most lucrative enterprise for Bechtel-

* The extent of the abuses at Willow Run was reflected in Alexander's lengthy court papers. The affidavits taken from a number of Willow Run workers related one fiscal horror story after another. Employees were paid for doing no work; others were trained —at great government expense—for doing auto mechanics rather than airplane modification; chauffeurs racked up overtime pay driving Bechtel-McCone officials (along with McCone's wife) on personal errands. Some of the allegations—like the charge that a training class of 50 people passed their time making aluminum ashtrays and fishing-tackle boxes—were petty, while others—such as the claim that Bechtel-McCone diverted government funds for its own corporate use and discharged employees who threatened to complain—were serious indeed. Taken together, the tales of featherbedding, cost overruns and outright theft made for a disturbing document, one reflecting many of the practices of what would later be called "the military-industrial complex."

McCone. According to the General Accounting Office of Congress, Calship alone had brought in revenues of $44,423,014, while Marinship had added $11.8 million more. Another $23.55 million in estimated revenues flowed in from an equity interest Bechtel-McCone owned in Henry Kaiser's shipbuilding operations, and there were additional millions from Canol, Willow Run, the Bechtel-owned copper mines that Warren had run and the refineries the company had built for the war effort, both at home and abroad. When everything was totaled, Steve Bechtel and John McCone had grossed well over $100 million. Their net investment: considerably less than $400,000.

There were those in Congress who thought it all obscene, and with the conclusion of hostilities, hearings were held on war profiteering. [23] The result was embarrassment, a few bad headlines, but nothing that substantively damaged the reputations of Steve Bechtel and John McCone. They were heroes in the eyes of the War Department, and in October 1945, shortly after the shutdown of the shipyards, Admiral Vickery, who had done so much to make their careers possible, hosted a small congratulatory ceremony. Recently released from a Japanese prison camp, a gaunt George Cooley stood by his friend Steve Bechtel and listened as Vickery lauded their accomplishments. * They had, said Vickery, built the ships that carried the guns that had won the war. America had triumphed, and as much as to anyone, the victory belonged to Steve Bechtel and John McCone.

---

* Cooley was fortunate to have survived the war. Other Bechtel executives, including one who attempted to escape with Cooley, were not so lucky, and perished during their internment. After recovering his strength, Cooley himself went on to become one of Bechtel's most valued and colorful executives. In the mid-1950s, while on assignment in the Amazon, he acquired the nickname "Shoot-from-the-Hip" for downing an attacking ocelot with a revolver. In 1958, however, during a bloody revolution in Iraq, Cooley's luck ran out. Attempting to escape from Baghdad with a small party of Europeans and Americans, Cooley was dragged from his car by a mob, beaten, bludgeoned and dismembered. Despite the personal efforts of then Secretary of State John Foster Dulles and his brother, CIA director Allen Dulles, Cooley's body was never recovered. The loss was particularly devastating to Steve Bechtel, Sr. Cooley had been his closest friend, and even years later, Bechtel could not talk about his death without becoming emotional.

CHAPTER SIX

▲

IN HIS
OWN IMAGE

The same war that had enriched Steve Bechtel and John McCone had also drained them. After five-plus years of eighteen-hour days, seven days a week, they were burned-out and exhausted, each looking forward to nothing so much as a long rest. It would mean dissolving the Bechtel-McCone Corporation and divvying their profits, and this they accomplished quite amicably not long after the war. By now, both men could well afford it. In addition to the money they had earned together, each had made millions through a series of shrewd wartime investments—the bulk of them in Bechtel's case with the oil and steel companies with which he would later do business.

He was one of the wealthiest men in San Francisco now, with a fortune that put him in the same league as the Huntingtons, Crockers and Stanfords and the rest of the city's moneyed elite. Dad Bechtel had never been able to get through the door of clubs like the Pacific Union and Bohemian; by 1946, his son was a leading member of both. He had become a power in California, and before long, his quiet reach would stretch across the country and the globe as well. For the moment, though, he was content to play golf, dabble in real estate and acquaint himself with the family he'd nearly forgotten.

Laura, his wife of twenty-five years, knew their peaceful life couldn't last. It was fine having Steve lounging around the house, or puttering around "Villa Bechtel," the oceanfront estate he'd bought not far from Monterey, and it was better still seeing him develop a relationship with his children, particularly his pride, Steve junior. But within months, she knew, Steve would be getting restless. And within months, so he was. His weekly golf games with friends like Cooley and McCone or his luncheons with brother Ken, who now was running the fast-growing family-owned insurance company, no longer seemed to engage him. He was getting bored collecting dividends* and watching over real estate. For all his protestations of enjoying retirement, Steve Bechtel missed the action.

His company missed him as well. Largely for tax reasons, Bechtel and McCone had liquidated their corporation and sold off its assets. Its place had been taken by a new entity titled "Bechtel Brothers–McCone," which put under one corporate roof all the Bechtel and McCone interests that had existed before and during the war. While Bechtel controlled the lion's share of the stock, he—along with McCone and the rest of Bechtel-McCone's senior executives—was deterred by tax considerations from playing an active management role.[1] Instead, the company was being run by a coterie of former Bechtel middle-managers, led by Steve's Berkeley classmate and Boulder colleague Bill Waste. Though Waste and his confreres had landed several major contracts, none had produced any major profits, and by the end of 1946, Bechtel Brothers–McCone was foundering.[2] To continue, it needed a fresh infusion of cash. But more than anything, it needed Steve Bechtel.

He returned without much persuasion, and after buying out the interests of McCone and brother Ken** and pumping in several million dollars of his own funds, set out to turn the company around.

---

* Steve made it a practice to buy large blocks of stock in companies like Socal that were Bechtel clients and over the years amassed a portfolio worth hundreds of millions of dollars.

** Following the war, Kenneth Bechtel took over management of the family's insurance concern, Industrial Indemnity, and built it into one of the largest such firms in the country. As time went on, however, relations between Ken and his brother Steve became increasingly strained, in part because of Ken's marriage to Elizabeth Hay, a wealthy San Francisco socialite. Among Steve's objections to Betty was the fact that she collected Impressionist paintings. Steve viewed this as a frivolous and expensive practice and strongly disapproved. After growing irritation, Ken and Betty finally moved out of the Bechtel-owned Lakeside apartment building, and thereafter refused to attend Bech-

Rechristened Bechtel Corporation, the company soon snapped up several major contracts, including one to build a 200-mile portion of the Texas–California gas line, another to erect a $7 million oil refinery for Socal in Salt Lake City and still another to build several factories in California for Owens-Corning Fiberglas. "With Steve back as salesman," said his friend and lawyer Bob Bridges, "the company took off like a rocket."[3]

The men Bechtel gathered around him to build and guide that rocket were very much like himself. Virtually all had been born in California and educated at Berkeley, Stanford or USC. With few exceptions, they were hardworking WASP Republicans with equally hardworking WASP Republican wives. They sent their children to good public schools, attended church, played active roles in the Boy Scouts and PTA. In their personal habits, they were carefully temperate: they didn't go to nightclubs or stay up late, and if they drank or smoked, it was never to excess. A rollicking good time for them was having over a few friends (invariably other Bechtel employees and their wives) and throwing some steaks on the grill, followed by a hand or two of canasta or bridge. A few, like Bridges, who could dictate complex contracts off the top of his head, and Jerry Komes, were extraordinarily bright; an even lesser few, like George Cooley, who was fond of regaling the office with demonstrations of how he fended off poison arrows with his bare hands, and who enjoyed taking in cases of whiskey and fresh-cut flowers as gifts to Bechtel managers and their wives in Saudi Arabia, were highly colorful in their own right. Most of the "Bechtelians," though, were determineded middlebrow sorts: earnest, drab, decent, distinguished primarily in their work. In an era of *Leave It to Beaver* and *Father Knows Best*, they were archetypal Middle Americans.

Now and again, however, there was an exception, a figure not from the mold. One was Laura's uncle and Steve's chief confidant, John L. Simpson.

A native San Franciscan and nine years Steve's senior, Simpson pos-

---

tel family functions. A rapprochement of sorts occurred in 1961, when Ken announced he was divorcing Betty (who collected a $4 million settlement) to marry Nancy Slusser, until then the wife of Bechtel's popular chief counsel, Willis Slusser. Almost as quickly as family peace was restored, though, it began to unravel, in large measure over Ken's growing involvement in the environmental movement, one of whose principal targets was the Bechtel Corporation. After a number of conflicts, Ken resigned from the Bechtel board in 1971, and shortly thereafter retired from Industrial Indemnity to devote himself full time to the cause of conservation. He died in February 1978.

sessed a worldliness and sophistication no one else in the Bechtel organization, including its president, could match. After graduating from Berkeley, he had gone to work for the Commission for Relief in Belgium, a joint U.S.-British project that provided food and clothing for Belgian refugees during World War I. He spent five years in Europe schooling himself in Continental finance, making the social rounds (most notably in Vienna, where he married a well-connected socialite, Margarete Mandel), and developing a close friendship with CRB's head and his fellow San Franciscan, Herbert Hoover.

On his return to the United States, Simpson joined the J. Henry Schroder Banking Corporation, a leading New York investment house with branches throughout Europe. *

One evening during the mid-1930s, as Simpson was thrashing through an especially difficult contract, his friend and boss, Prent Gray, dropped by his office and suggested that the two of them seek advice from Sullivan & Cromwell, a law firm headquartered in the same building. During the Paris Peace Conference, Gray had met one of the firm's partners, who had impressed him as a "very smart fellow."[4] His name was John Foster Dulles. Perhaps, Gray suggested, he could help.

"Foster" did help, not only that night, but on many days and nights in the years ahead. Dulles, in fact, proved so helpful that he and his brother, a rather owlish fellow named Allen, were subsequently awarded all of Schroder's legal work. Schroder, in turn, began arranging financing for a growing number of Sullivan & Cromwell clients. It was a mutually beneficial relationship, and during the course of it the brothers Dulles became fast friends with the bank's rising young executive vice-president, John L. Simpson.

Simpson himself, meanwhile, was continuing to prosper. Named a

---

* J. Henry Schroder was something more than an ordinary Wall Street investment bank. It was owned by the wealthy, titled Schröder family of Germany who, following World War I, moved to renew commercial ties with Great Britain and the United States. Baron Helmut von Schröder moved the bank's headquarters to London in 1914, and later opened major operations in New York, Switzerland, Central and South America, Canada and Lebanon. While Helmut von Schröder was building his banking empire, a cousin, Baron Bruno von Schröder, was gaining notoriety as a close associate of Adolf Hitler. In 1932, Bruno brought Hitler and Germany Army chief of staff Franz von Papen to his home for a meeting that helped clear the way for Hitler's becoming German chancellor the following year. Bruno's activities and the bank's German origins produced accusations during World War II that the bank was tied to the Nazis. Fact was that the J. Henry Schroder bank gave valuable assistance to the Allies, including affording cover for a number of agents of the Office of Strategic Services.

Schroder director, he became the firm's international contact man, and as war clouds gathered over Europe, he began shuttling between Washington, New York and Central and South America. Officially his missions were undertaken for the bank, but at the suggestion of his friends the Dulleses, he began doing the government favors as well, including "smoking out," as he later put it, whether Schroder's South American clients would remain loyal to the Allies. Simpson passed along the results of his private intelligence-gathering to two men who were regular lunch partners in Washington: Dean Acheson, later to become Harry Truman's secretary of State, and William "Wild Bill" Donovan, founder of the OSS.

During World War II, when Allen Dulles was organizing OSS networks from Switzerland, Simpson took time off from the bank to become chief financial advisor for the U.S. Army in Europe. After the Allied landings in Italy in 1943 and subsequent Italian surrender, Simpson, working with another Schroder executive attached to the OSS, in effect controlled the country's treasury. After completing that task in 1944, he returned to San Francisco for what he imagined would be a brief rest at the home of his niece and her husband, Steve Bechtel. Bechtel, however, had an offer for him: a consultancy position with Bechtel-McCone.

"I'm not an engineer," Simpson protested.

"We have plenty of engineers," Steve replied. "But you've had broad experience, and the very fact that you're different makes it interesting."[5]

Simpson accepted and brought to Bechtel's various enterprises a financial expertise they had been sorely lacking. But his real worth was as a door-opener, a skill he demonstrated at the inaugural meeting of the United Nations in San Francisco in April 1945.

Assembled at the conference were many of Simpson's friends from Washington and New York, and he made a point of introducing most of them to Steve Bechtel, who showed them around his shipyards. One who got the tour was Thomas Finletter, later to succeed James Forrestal as Harry Truman's secretary of Defense. Another was a State Department aide named Adlai Stevenson, who evidently was impressed. "Dear John," he wrote afterward:

> I have been meaning ever since I got back from San Francisco to report to you how much I enjoyed meeting Steve Bechtel. . . . He is a most stimulating and interesting citizen and I was awed by all that he has done with which I was unfamiliar during the war period.[6]

In 1946 Simpson decided, at Steve's urging, to go to work for the Bechtel Corporation as its chief financial officer and *éminence grise*. He and Steve had adjoining offices in the headquarters Steve set up at 153 Sansome Street, and they were close personally as well as professionally. Seldom, if ever, did Steve undertake a major move without checking it first with "Uncle John."

Despite Simpson's influence, there was never any doubt who was in charge at 153 Sansome. At the monthly meeting of the board of directors, recalled Jerome W. Komes, a key Bechtel executive who had joined Steve after working for John McCone at Calship, "Steve would say, 'This is what I think' and the rest of us would nod: 'That's a hell of an idea, Steve.'[7] He was the dominant, vital force in the outfit, with great imagination and salesmanship."

He also had very definite ideas how he wanted that outfit to function. After the war, Bechtel had seen a number of his fellow contractors go broke, and others, like Henry Kaiser, who went barreling into the manufacturing of aluminum and automobiles (Kaiser-Frazer), lose tens of millions. Steve was not about to repeat their mistakes. His would be a service company, one that would travel light and keep overhead to a minimum. There would be no factories, no assembly lines, no big capital outlays, and despite his excellent lines of credit at Bank of America and other major West Coast financial institutions, no major debt. His father had borrowed and lived to regret it. Steve wouldn't. Instead, he would deal with customers who financed their own projects with big advance payments and had a record of paying their bills on time. He wanted the biggest clients with the biggest projects—projects Bechtel would not only build, but conceive and design; and with his own contacts and those provided by Simpson, he could afford to be selective. "We'd rather be known to a hundred key people than to a hundred million," he told his executives, "because those hundred are the ones from whom we could obtain business."[8]

The hundred key people came to be known at the Bechtel Corporation as "the sweetheart clients"; and one of the sweetest and most helpful was James B. Black, chairman of Pacific Gas & Electric.

A native San Franciscan, Black had excellent ties in the East, where he had spent fifteen years in high-level government and corporate positions before returning to California to take over PG&E, the fastest-growing utility in the country. As PG&E's chairman, Black soon became close to Bechtel, who had been a prime construction contractor for the utility since the days of Bechtel-McCone. In the company of

Jack Horton, chairman of Southern California Edison, another Bechtel customer, the two men socialized and, eventually, became members of the same Bohemian Grove lodge. As the friendship deepened, Black began doing important favors for Bechtel, like arranging for him to become a director of New York's J. P. Morgan & Company, a position that provided Bechtel with entrée to the world of East Coast finance. Black was also responsible for Bechtel's becoming one of the few California members of the Business Council, a Washington-based organization composed of the leading businessmen in the country.

Soon Bechtel was flying frequently to the East, returning, often as not, with a contract in his pocket. "Steve . . . would come back and say, 'I agreed we'd do this, and now it's up to you guys to do it," Komes recalled. "Usually, the project was something that at the outset, we would regard as impossible. But then Steve would start talking and we'd realize that as long as he said it, we could do anything."[9]

In pursuing the clients who gave these contracts, Bechtel was the master of the soft sell. He shunned advertising, and rarely, if ever, made an overt sales call. Instead, over a long lunch or a round of golf, he'd ask about a CEO's business, what his problems were, what he thought the future held. Seemingly casual, he would then listen as the man unburdened himself of whatever difficulty was bothering him. It usually didn't require much before Bechtel devised a way his company could help. "Steve had incredible intuition," his attorney Bob Bridges noted. "If there are ten relevant facts that relate to a decision, most men need to have at least six or seven of them in their grasp before they can make up their minds. Not Steve. He'd make a decision based on two or three facts—and most of the time he would be right."[10]

How the Bechtel method worked was demonstrated in 1949 when Steve found himself sitting next to Robert L. Minckler, president of General Petroleum, the West Coast subsidiary of Socony Mobil, at a lunch at the California Club in Los Angeles. During the course of the meal, Minckler began describing a major oil discovery that had been made near Edmonton, Canada, an area Bechtel knew well from building the ill-fated Canol project. "If I could ever run a pipeline from that field to the West Coast," Minckler said offhandedly, "I'd build a refinery up north, and I think some of the other companies would do the same."[11]

Bechtel sympathized with Minckler's perplexity: there was all that oil, seemingly there for the taking, and no way to transport it to where it was really needed—not with tanker companies charging their extortionate rates. A pipeline was indeed the solution. As the waiters cleared away the dishes, Bechtel pulled a pen from his pocket and began sketching lines on the tablecloth. Minckler pulled out his own pen and started jotting figures. By the end of the meal, it was decided: perhaps Steve Bechtel could help.

On his return to San Francisco, Bechtel dispatched a team of engineers to reconnoiter the Canadian Rockies by jeep and plane. At the company headquarters, meanwhile, draftsmen began preparing "scope books"—hundreds of pages of data and drawings of the projected pipeline. As that work continued, Bechtel commissioned a study of the potential for oil usage in the Pacific Northwest from the Stanford Research Institute of Palo Alto. That the study would produce a favorable conclusion Bechtel was more than reasonably certain: he had been one of SRI's principal founders and had bankrolled its operations heavily. *

Sure enough, SRI turned in a study fairly glowing with promising predictions for northwestern oil, and armed with it, Bechtel began calling on banks and lining up underwriting. He then summoned to a meeting at the Links Club in New York Mickler and representatives from six other oil companies to finalize the deal. The last detail—assuaging the sensitivities of the Canadian government, across whose

* Founded in 1946 by a group of West Coast businessmen, including Steve Bechtel and Henry J. Kaiser, and originally affiliated with Stanford University, the Stanford Research Institute eventually grew to become the second-largest corporate–government "think tank" in the country. Its business was supplying government and industry with the latest in applied research, economic analysis and management techniques. Among its many programs, SRI evaluated the U.S. strategic force; conducted laser radar studies in the upper atmosphere; analyzed ballistic missile defenses; drew up studies for improving Air Force reconaissance and surveillance systems and played a leading role in developing the U.S. response to the launching of the Soviet *Sputnik* satellite. Its multimillion-dollar involvement in defense work, combined with its work for the Defense Department during the Vietnam War, provoked violent student demonstrations on the Stanford University campus, and led the university to sever its connections with the institute in 1969.

Since SRI's founding, Bechtel has been one of the institute's major clients and supporters. SRI has conducted numerous studies for the company, including evaluating the development potential of Jubail, Saudi Arabia, and drawing up a blueprint for Bechtel's industrialization of Indonesia during the Sukarno regime. Over the years, the Bechtel family has donated millions to SRI and was principally responsible for the funds used to build SRI's 42,000-square-foot headquarters which opened in 1969.

At the time, SRI listed 68 individuals and companies—among them, such corporate heavyweights as IBM, the Wells Fargo Bank and Standard Oil of California—as permanently affiliated with it. Included in this list of "associate members" are no fewer than six Bechtel entities. No other company or family matches this total.

national territory the pipeline would be built—Bechtel handled personally.

His first move was to camouflage American interests by creating a Canadian company to oversee the pipeline. Dubbed "Transmountain Pipeline Company of Canada," it was supported by the companies that had attended the Links Club meeting and featured none other than Stephen Davison Bechtel as its chairman and major stockholder. To dilute the American flavor of the venture still further, he also farmed out most of the actual construction work to Canadian firms, restricting Bechtel participation to the role of project manager. Finally, Bechtel representatives paid a call on acting Canadian prime minister C. D. Howe to outline the benefits building the pipeline would bring Canada. To no one's astonishment, least of all Bechtel's, Howe conferred his government's blessings. [12]

Stretching across the Canadian Rockies from Edmonton, Alberta, to Vancouver, British Columbia, and from there south across the border into the United States, the 718-mile, 24-inch-diameter pipeline was finished in 1954. It had been built at a cost of $93 million and would bring oil into the United States at a rate of some 150,000 barrels a day. For Bechtel, the job—the first time his companies had been involved in a pipelining project from inception to completion—was especially satisfying. "There was never," he told the press, "a tougher . . . pipeline job." [13] Nor had one produced such financial rewards. By the end of the pipeline's first year of operation, Bechtel had received a total of $200 million in revenues, both from the pipeline and from the number of refineries he had built along its route. The contracts were coming thick and fast now, including one from the Canadian government, which, delighted with Bechtel's work, wanted him to build another pipeline, this one east from Alberta to Montreal. *

* Not every Bechtel pipeline project moved so smoothly, and there were several that were cancelled because of government or political pressure. One was a 2,500-mile line that was to have run from Kirkuk, Iraqi, to Paris. With 300 additional miles of branch lines, it would have supplied Iraqi gas to most of Eastern and Western Europe. The project was killed for a number of reasons, not least of which was the 1958 Iraqi revolution that resulted in the death of George Cooley. Another petroleum project that died aborning was a refinery Bechtel was to have built for British Petroleum in Haifa, Palestine, in 1948. Thirty days after the contract for the job was signed, Israel declared itself a state and war commenced with the Arabs. As a result, the refinery was never built. The loss was a bitter one for Bechtel, which had to forgo millions in potential profits, and according to several company executives it was a major factor in the company's growing anti-Semitism.

Proud as he was, though, Bechtel never lost sight of the larger goal. "Remember," he told his senior executives, "we are not in the construction and engineering business. We are in the business of making money." Nowhere would the truth of that statement be more fully realized than in a vast stretch of sand called Saudi Arabia.

CHAPTER 7

▲

SAUDI ARABIA

T he deal that would forever alter the fortunes of Steve Bechtel and
the company that bore his name had its beginnings in a phone
call one otherwise uneventful morning in the spring of 1943. On the
other end of the line was R. G. Follis, a senior executive with the
Standard Oil Company of California, Bechtel's largest nongovernmen-
tal customer. Politely but urgently, Follis asked Bechtel if he could
drop by Socal's offices that afternoon. Something had come up that
required Bechtel's assistance.

Follis, who would soon be named president of Socal, hadn't specified what that something was, but as he rode the elevator that afternoon to the eighteenth floor of the oil giant's headquarters at 225 Bush
Street, Bechtel knew two things: it had to involve oil, and it would
mean more business for his company. The elevator doors opened and
Bechtel walked past the ranks of black male receptionists in two-tone
brown livery to Follis' office. Follis greeted him cordially, pumped his
hand and motioned him to a seat. He came right to the point. Socal
needed Bechtel—not in California, but halfway across the world in the
Kingdom of Saudi Arabia.

At that moment, Steve Bechtel, like most Americans, had only the dimmest knowledge of Saudi Arabia: only that it was hot, long dominated by the British, far off—and brimming with oil.

Though Britain initially had no idea there was an abundance of oil in Arabia, it had taken the precaution in 1922 of having Arab leaders sign an agreement stipulating that they would grant oil concessions only to agents appointed by Britain. A decade later—in July 1932, as this agreement was about to expire, two Americans and an Englishman met for lunch in London at the fashionable Simpson's in the Strand.[1] Present were Harry St. John Philby, a Cambridge-educated Arabist and close advisor of the Saudi king, Abdul Aziz ibn Saud, and Francis B. Loomis, former U.S. under-secretary of State and a senior executive for Socal. Socal, as Philby knew, had already struck oil on the independently ruled island of Bahrain in the Red Sea just off the Saudi coast, and was eager to extend its drilling to the mainland. Socal's problem was the British, who owned the kingdom's exclusive petroleum rights. Those rights, however, were soon to expire, and for a secret retainer of the equivalent in sterling of $1,000 per month, Philby offered to intercede in Socal's behalf with ibn Saud. By the time dessert arrived, the deal was set.

From London, Philby repaired to Saudi Arabia, where, unbeknownst to Socal, he began playing the British against the Americans. Faced with the loss of their concession, the British offered ibn Saud £10,000 in exchange for retaining their rights. It was, they were confident, a sum far greater than Socal would pay for what was, in the main, a worthless stretch of sand. They were wrong on both counts. Socal offered £35,000 down, £20,000 more after eighteen months and £5,000 more plus a royals of 4 riyals—equal to 8 shillings—per barrel for the duration of the concession. Prompted by Philby, ibn Saud accepted, and in a ceremony on July 3, 1933, in the Saudi capital of Jeddah, the Americans were awarded the concession. The Standard Oil Company of California had won the exclusive fifty-year right to search for oil across 395,000 square miles of the most oil-rich country on earth.*

* St. John Philby was a man of ever-shifting loyalties, both corporate and national. During World War II, he was imprisoned by the British for pro-Nazi sympathies. Following his release, he became a Communist and returned to Saudi Arabia, where, working on yet another secret retainer, he attempted to undermine Bechtel's interests in favor of British companies. Meanwhile, Harry's son, known as Kim, found employ-

Being granted the right to search for oil, however, was one thing: actually finding it was quite another. Dry hole followed dry hole, and it was not until late 1937, five years after signing the agreement with ibn Saud, that the Americans found oil in commercial quantities. Socal's lack of European distribution capability and the onset of World War II delayed full development of the Saudi fields another five years. By then, Socal had concluded that it couldn't penetrate the European market on its own and had agreed to sell half its interest in the Saudi concession to the Texas Oil Company (Texaco), which was both well heeled—it paid Socal $50 million for its interest—and well connected in Europe. The new partners called their joint venture Caltex; but in 1948, after Standard Oil of New Jersey and the Mobil Oil Corporation bought into the company, it was rechristened the Arabian American Oil Company—Aramco, for short.

While the oil giants were working out their deal, the U.S. government was not paying Saudi Arabia much heed. The country was regarded as a diplomatic backwater, and U.S. interests, such as they were, were represented by a lowly minister, who routinely deferred to the oil companies for guidance. The result, according to J. B. Kelly, a British historian and diplomat who spent much of his career in the Middle East, was that "conduct of American relations with Saudi Arabia [fell] into the company's keeping. Naturally," Kelly added, "Aramco saw this as only logical and fitting, since its management firmly believed there was a broad coincidence of interests between Aramco and Saudi Arabia, between Saudi Arabia and the United States and between the U.S. government and American oil companies operating in the Middle East." Aramco, Kelly noted, "was far from being alone in holding that view."[2]

World War II, however, changed everything. Worried that U.S. oil supplies were dwindling, Ickes ordered Aramco to develop its Saudi fields posthaste. Shortly thereafter, the call went out to Steve Bechtel.

The meeting at the Socal headquarters did not last long. The company's needs were as succinct as they were urgent: the immediate construction of additional refinery facilities and storage tanks at Bahrain,

ment with MI-6, the British equivalent of the CIA. Eventually, he rose to become chief of MI-6 counterintelligence—one of the most sensitive positions in the whole of Western intelligence. Unbeknownst to his superiors, Kim Philby was also an agent for the Soviet KGB. His treachery was discovered in 1963, but before he could be arrested, he fled to Moscow, where he was decorated as a hero of the Soviet Union and still lives.

then the laying of an underwater pipeline 23 miles across the strait of Bahrain to the Saudi port of Ras Tanura. Though Bechtel's resources already were being strained by its other wartime commitments, Steve was not about to say no to his friends at Socal.

He immediately dispatched crews to begin the refinery and underwater pipeline work and would soon begin building a big refinery at Ras Tanura as well.

In undertaking the work in Saudi Arabia, Steve sensed the makings of an opportunity. That sense grew in 1944 with the visit to San Francisco of Prince Amir Faisal, Saudi Arabia's foreign minister and ibn Saud's second son. Upon Faisal's arrival, Steve conducted the prince, who would one day become the Saudi monarch, on a tour of Marinship, the showcase of Bechtel's wartime efforts. Faisal proved no less susceptible to Steve's amiable, low-key salesmanship than Bechtel's other clients and returned home with glowing reports of the American builder and his accomplishments.

Three years later, having emerged from self-imposed "retirement," Bechtel created a new division, International Bechtel, Inc., that was to focus exclusively on the Middle East. Van Rosendahl, a Bechtel veteran and one of its top pipeliners, was put in charge of the operation, while George Cooley was named second in command. The IBI executives had barely ordered their new business cards when Steve informed them he was off to Saudi Arabia.

The chief purpose of Bechtel's visit was to meet with the Aramco people, who were then keen on building a pipeline from the Persian Gulf fields to the Mediterranean. Shortly after his arrival, though, Bechtel was told by Earl English, his principal Middle East troubleshooter, that the Arabs were eager for the company's services as well. Suddenly flush with oil revenues—in 1946 alone Aramco had paid $10 million in royalties—ibn Saud was in a spending mood, and with his finance minister, Abdul Suleiman, had drawn up a plan for building a railway from the capital of Riyadh to the port of Damman, 375 miles away. English had already tried to dissuade the Arabs, pointing out the difficulties of laying track across nearly 400 miles of desert. Suleiman, however, had brushed aside his concerns. There had not been a working railroad in Saudi Arabia since T. E. Lawrence's guerrillas had knocked out the Hejoz line during World War I, Suleiman told him, and ibn Saud was determined to see one built.

The king's insistence put Bechtel in the awkward position of having to choose between two masters, the king and Aramco. Aramco, however, would have to come first. Without oil, ibn Saud would have no money, and to get the oil to the European market, the company had to rely on tankers which made a twenty-day, 7,000-mile round trip down the Persian Gulf, across the Indian Ocean to the Red Sea and through the Suez Canal, where the British were charging a toll of 13 to 17 cents a barrel. Though it would be a vast and enormously expensive undertaking, costing no less than $100 million and requiring that 550,000 tons of pipe and other material be shipped in from the outside, an 850-mile pipeline from Saudi Arabia through Syria and on to the Mediterranean would eliminate that journey. Better yet, it would quickly pay for itself in saved Suez tolls.

Aramco had wanted to build the pipeline for the Saudis since 1944, but had been stymied both by the war and by Arab anger over U.S. support for the creation of a Jewish state in Palestine. Indeed, at one point ibn Saud had become so furious about Palestine that he threatened to cancel the American oil concessions altogether. Whether or not the king was bluffing, the Americans had been sufficiently concerned that they had mollified him with $6 million a year in Lend-Lease aid during the war. Since the halt of those payments, the king's temper had again begun to fray, and he was once more charging the United States with "betrayal." Aramco had tried to soothe him by lining up financing for the pipeline in the form of a $100 million U.S. loan to Saudi Arabia. Nonetheless, it was far from certain whether the king would give the pipeline his approval. The question hung, Aramco said, on how he got on with Bechtel.

There turned out to be no cause for alarm. Predisposed to like Bechtel by the reports of his son, the king took to the American businessman quickly, and the American to him. For all their obvious differences, the warrior king and the builder shared a pragmatic, unsentimental understanding of how the world worked, and how, given vision on both sides, it might work in the future. Suleiman and the other court ministers might question the king's enthusiasm for the railroad, as had Bechtel's Earl English, but Steve could readily grasp the project's significance. As for the pipeline, ibn Saud didn't seem overly concerned about it, and after Bechtel pledged not to hire "Jewish elements"[3] and to switch the pipeline's terminus from Egypt to Lebanon, readily gave the project his assent.

Indeed, Bechtel and ibn Saud got along so splendidly that by the end of the audience, the king, helped along by an offer of a $10 million loan Bechtel had promised to secure through the U.S. Export-Import

Bank, had commissioned IBI to build not only the railroad, but a port facility at Damman, a modern pier at Jeddah and the electrification of the entire city of Riyadh as well. Afterward, U.S. minister J. Rives Childs cabled Washington: "STEPHEN BECHTEL INFORMED ME TODAY HIS FIRM HAS ASSOCIATED ITSELF FOR EXTENSIVE OPERATIONS NOW PLANNED IN THIS COUNTRY.... BECHTEL STATES WORK CONTRACTED FOR WILL REQUIRE AT LEAST 2000 AMERICANS AND 10 TO 20 THOUSAND SAUDIS AND PLANS ARE BEING MADE TO GO AHEAD FORTHWITH."[4]

On his return to San Francisco, Bechtel himself called the pipeline project "the biggest news since Boulder Dam" and claimed that the 30-inch, 400,000-barrel-per-day line "will be the mightiest ever laid. In the Middle East program," he continued, "I cannot help but foresee tremendous possibilities pointing towards the biggest development of natural resources ever undertaken by American interests."[5]

In Saudi Arabia, meanwhile, work on the pipeline and the king's railroad had commenced simultaneously. Like different divisions of the same army, the Bechtel crews—"Camel Legionnaires," they called themselves—and thousands of Arab laborers pushed across the desert, laying down pipeline and railroad tracks along the routes ancient caravans had traversed for thousands of years. It was an expensive undertaking—the transportation and housing costs for each American alone amounted to $5,000, and in addition, Bechtel paid workers who completed their eighteen-month tour the bonus equivalent of a year's salary—and for the workers, who labored ten hours a day in 100-degree-plus heat, a backbreakingly dangerous one as well. Traffic accidents in which Arabs, unaccustomed to the presence of motor vehicles, were struck by speeding, often inexperienced American drivers were frequent—so frequent that Bechtel developed an unofficial compensation policy. As a memo from the American Consulate in Dhahran explained it: "Such cases are usually settled with company cooperation by a payment or bribe to the Arab, the amount varying with the degree of his mental or physical health."[6]

Within the work camps, which were fitted out like self-contained "Little Americas," drunkenness and brawling were a constant problem, despite the presence of Bechtel's own armed force of security men. One IBI worker, Robert W. Agnew, became so unsettled by the conditions that he demanded to be sent home, with full pay, fifteen months before his contract was up. His charges that the company condoned violence, gambling and drunkenness were largely ignored until he threatened to sue and put together a rambling brief detailing what he claimed were regular beatings, forced labor and general abuse of Arabs, including depriving them of water. Before the document could be made public it fell into the hands of the American consulate, which reported to the State Department that Agnew was "either mentally unbalanced or attempting to extort money from his employer." As for Agnew's charges, the consulate conceded that many of them were true. It then went on to warn: "This interesting document... if publicized, would tend to bring into disrepute not only International Bechtel, Inc., but all American citizens living in Saudi Arabia." The "interesting document" was not publicized and Agnew was sent home, accompied by a recommendation from the consulate to the State Department's Passport Division that "his future activities abroad may well be regarded with suspicion."[7]*

Despite the problems and privations, the Bechtel projects moved ahead, either on or close to schedule. George Cooley had taken charge of the pipeline—"Tapline," as it was designated by Aramco—and by February 1948, construction had begun on the Abqaiq-to-Qatif section.** After being unloaded at the port of Ras el Mesha and by use of giant cranes, tons of 30- and 31-inch pipe—large enough to transport 450,000 barrels of oil per day—were welded into 93-foot-long sections and then packed aboard specially outfitted trailers and trucks for transport across the desert. Upon reaching the building site, they were set into place on ring girders mounted on cement supports. Though practical and economical, placing the pipeline aboveground would later cause problems, when Bedouin pitched their tents over the line to warm themselves by the flow of the heated oil. Horrified that the Be-

* Agnew was not the only disgruntled Bechtel employee, nor the only one to leave. Despite the Western-style amenities, life in the Bechtel work camps was hard, and working for Cooley even harder, so much so that the workers at one jobsite dubbed it "CCC"—"Cooley's Concentration Camp." The result was constant turnover—according to one company estimate as much as 77 percent annually. Bechtel executives referred to terminated employees as "Termites" and often sent them home via the slowest and least agreeable means of transport available.
** Cooley's duties included screening prospective employees to ensure that none were Jewish. The exclusion of Jews from Bechtel projects was quietly sanctioned by the State Department, which at the time did not employ Jews in Saudi Arabia either. Nor were any Jews employed by Aramco. Cooley also refused to hire homosexuals. According to his associates during that period, his means for discovering a prospective employee's sexual proclivities was to ask, "Are you a cocksucker?" If the candidate reacted by cursing Cooley or hitting him, he was hired. Those who hesitated or stammered were abruptly dismissed.

douin campfires might ignite the oil, the Americans as well as Saudi soldiers guarding the line continually had to drive them off. When that effort proved unsuccessful, each section of the pipe was marked with a royal emblem. Fearful of ibn Saud's wrath, the Bedouin kept at bay.

The railroad presented a different set of difficulties. Many of the builders had laid rail across forbidding country before, but they had never experienced anything quite like Saudi Arabia. Miles of rocky, desolate flatlands; sand dunes the size of small mountains; jagged lava fields that stretched for miles all had to be crossed or circumvented. Exclaimed one newly arrived engineer: "This is a helluva place to build a railroad!"

Finally, though, after four years and the expenditure of $50 million, built it was. The trick was teaching the king's subjects to use it. Not understanding that stated prices were nonnegotiable, long lines of Arab customers haggled incessantly over ticket prices, and as a result, American-planned train schedules quickly became meaningless. Such trains as did run were accompanied by Saudi soldiers, there to keep a watchful eye on the cars crammed full of gun-toting Bedouin. Other problems were not so easily dealt with. According to one Arab custom, if an Arab engineer ran over someone—a not infrequent occurrence on the Saudi line—the victim's relatives were entitled to kill the engineer on the spot. This occupational hazard made it difficult to recruit and train qualified engineers.

Bit by painstaking bit, however, the country was being modernized, and IBI was flourishing. By 1947, the company's Saudi business amounted to $3.6 million, exclusive of its Tapline work, and by the end of the next year, it would double. Pleased, ibn Saud contracted with Bechtel to do even more: build sewer systems, roads, power plants, airports; even tear down the centuries-old walls of Jeddah and reconstruct much of the city. There was trouble, though, in the offing.

It came first from members of the royal family, who, seeing the wonders Bechtel could work in the desert, sought to put the company's talents to their own use. The king's brother Abdullah, for instance, insisted that IBI build him a castle in Riyadh, on which he wanted to spend no more than $1 million.[8] When Earl English looked over the plans and informed Abdullah that his castle would cost at least $3 million, the prince threatened to complain to his notoriously indulgent brother. Another prince, Amir Saud, became inordinately fond of American food and ordered IBI to provide him with ten full meals a day at his palace in Riyadh.[9] To do so, Bechtel was required to import a cook from the United States and then fit out the palace with electric lights, water heaters, refrigerators, air conditioners and a huge, ultra-modern $50,000 kitchen.

The demands—and there were numerous others—put Bechtel in an impossible position. If the company refused, the princes would complain to ibn Saud, jeopardizing IBI's position. If it complied, precious resources were lost and work was delayed, infuriating Suleiman. Precisely that had happened when Steve Bechtel's friend Crown Prince Faisal "borrowed" a Bechtel bulldozer to level sand for his new palace, holding up construction of a badly needed road for a month. Suleiman, enraged, had threatened to complain to ibn Saud himself.

Suleiman, in fact, was turning out to be a major headache. He too had pet projects he wanted Bechtel to undertake, including running power lines to his summer house, at a cost of $20,000. In addition, senior Bechtel officials learned that the finance minister was using funds owed to IBI to buy and sell currency on the black market.[10] As time went on and the practice continued, IBI began losing patience. Finally, Thomas Borman, International Bechtel's vice-president and project manager for all the Saudi work, warned Suleiman that if he didn't soon pay his debts, Bechtel was pulling out of Saudi Arabia.

The problem seemed to be smoothed over after a visit to the kingdom in May 1948 by Steve Bechtel and his son, Steve junior, then just 23 and fresh out of the Marine Corps and Purdue. Saud received them warmly and assured the elder Bechtel that the moneys due IBI would be paid at once. In token of his goodwill, he sent Steve back to California with a number of valuable gifts, including one of his prized Arabian stallions for Steve's horse-loving daughter, Barbara.

Despite the king's promises, Suleiman failed to pay up, and by the end of the year, the Saudis owed IBI more than $1 million, of which nearly $600,000 had been spent by the finance minister's wife on a recent shopping expedition to Paris.[11] When Borman questioned him about the missing funds, Suleiman smilingly explained that they had been withheld as Saudi "income taxes."

Eventually, Borman came to the conclusion that Suleiman not only was profligate and a cheat and an alcoholic to boot—the last apparent from the nips of gin he kept taking during meetings—but, given the punishments he meted out to those who defied his word, also was losing his grip.[12]

Suleiman, however, was cagier than the Americans imagined. Not only did he have a hold on ibn Saud—who tolerated his minister's excesses even as he indulged in grander ones himself—but Suleiman had also set out to undermine Bechtel's position by entering into discussions with several British firms about taking on some of Bechtel's work. The British were eager for a piece of the Saudi action, and by paying their largely Irish work force a third of what Bechtel's American engineers were making, could underbid to get it.

To complicate matters further, Borman was facing a rival in his own ranks. John Rogers, a Berkeley-educated Bechtel veteran who had accompanied Steve Bechtel on his latest visit, was taking an increasingly active interest in IBI's Saudi Arabian operations, and an increasingly jaundiced view of Borman's performance. Borman had better take care, his friends warned him: Rogers was after his scalp.

Borman managed to get Bechtel's contract renewed for 1949; but the situation in Saudi Arabia, his own and IBI's, was deteriorating rapidly. Suleiman still owed Bechtel hundreds of thousands, and rather than bringing him to heel, ibn Saud had begun complaining about IBI's delays and high costs. Growing more worried, Borman sought the counsel of J. Rives Childs, the American minister and a good friend. Childs was sympathetic. He admired Borman and valued his straightforward honesty, a quality rare in Saudi Arabia not only among the Saudis, but among a number of Aramco executives as well. In their dealings with the Arabs and the American government alike, the Aramco chiefs were haughty and imperious and routinely disregarded Childs's advice. By contrast, Borman was low-key, deferential and on a number of occasions, greatly helpful to U.S. interests. Still, Childs knew his friend was in trouble, and when Steve Bechtel reappeared in Saudi Arabia in early March, he invited him to the Mission residence to talk out the problem. After several brandies, Steve hit on a possible solution. Why not beat Suleiman at his own game, he suggested, and invite in George Wimpey & Company, Ltd., one British firm with which Bechtel had established a good working relationship, to handle the housekeeping that was consuming so much of IBI's time? That way, he went on, IBI could give its undivided attention to projects of prime importance.[13]

There was merit in Bechtel's suggestion. Childs agreed—but before calling in Wimpey, perhaps IBI should set up a program to train Arab workers to perform less technically demanding chores, like plumbing, or radio and appliance repair. It would free up IBI's resources, undercut Suleiman and best of all, provide a vivid demonstration of how "a great American company" was working to help underdeveloped countries, rather than merely profiting by them.

Bechtel leaped at the suggestion and soon reported back to Childs that the king, Suleiman and the rest of the Saudi government were enthusiastic as well. Moreover, Steve had been assured that the government was "fully satisfied" with IBI's work. As for the outside contractors, that would be fine, but only if Bechtel wanted them, and only on the condition that IBI itself approved of them. In the interim, the government wanted to start the training program immediately.

Borman was relieved it appeared that the crisis had passed. Now that his beloved railroad was complete, even ibn Saud was in good spirits—delighting in the electrification of Riyadh, finished in 1949, and even more so in an X-ray machine the Americans had given him as a gift. The X-ray pictures so amused him that he had them taken of his harem and the entire royal family.

But despite ibn Saud's mood, Borman was not completely in the clear. A Palestinian Arab, Badr Fahuum, who had been assigned by the king to act as a liaison between Suleiman and IBI, was proving uncooperative; like Suleiman, he was also dipping into the Bechtel till. Childs and others who knew the man concluded that he was trying to ingratiate himself with the Saudis at IBI's expense. A different view was taken by Borman's rival John Rogers, who had the full beaucratic backing of IBI's president, Van Rosendahl, and who was now spending most of his time in Saudi Arabia. The problem, said Rogers, wasn't the Palestinian: it was Borman.

Rogers himself was making new friends in the kingdom. He publicly quarreled with U.S. officials, most notably General Richard O'Keefe, the commander of the Dhahran airfield—and was openly critical of Borman, [14] who did his best to ignore the attacks. It particularly seemed to gall Rogers that Suleiman kept him waiting for a week for an appointment, while the nonconfrontational Borman could walk into the finance minister's office at any time.

The hostilities finally came to a head just before Christmas 1949 when, with the backing of Rosendahl, Rogers announced that Borman was being removed from his post. The change, Rogers asserted, represented nothing more than a routine transfer of Bechtel managers; but there was no doubt that Borman was being fired. Rogers had ordered him out of Jeddah in three days.

Childs had seen the dismissal coming, but was nonetheless shocked and extremely upset. "WHEN NEWS OF BORMAN'S REMOVAL BECAME KNOWN... HIS MANY FRIENDS WERE OUTRAGED," he cabled Secretary of State Dean Acheson. "BORMAN'S REPUTATION FOR ABSOLUTE INTEGRITY AND FAIR DEALING HAS EARNED HIM THE HIGHEST RESPECT OF THE

SAUDI OFFICIALDOM AND THE FOREIGN BUSINESS COMMUNITY IN JED-DAH."[15]

When they learned of Borman's dismissal, the Bechtel crew working on the huge Jeddah pier threatened to resign *en masse* in protest. They were dissuaded only when Borman told them to stick it out. He reflected, Childs noted, "A REMARKABLE LACK OF BITTERNESS... CONSIDERING WHAT HE HAD TO CONTEND WITH."[16]

Suleiman was also unhappy with Borman's dismissal and wired Steve Bechtel asking that he be allowed to stay on. Childs followed with a letter making the same entreaty and stating that "Tom holds an almost unique position of confidence with the Saudi Arabian Government, with the American and foreign community in Jeddah and with the United States Air Force in Dhahran." But there was no reprieve.

In the end, Childs attributed Borman's demise to Rogers' extreme jealousy. Rogers, he said, was a ruthlessly unprincipled executive. According to Childs, Rogers' charges, notably that Borman was more concerned with Arab needs than with those of IBI, were grossly unjust, and merely a smoke screen for his own overweening ambition. Before leaving Saudi Arabia himself a few years later, Childs noted that under Rogers, Bechtel's policies had come to mirror those of Aramco, which saw itself as an extension of the U.S. government and was viewed as arrogant and overbearing by many of the State Department officials stationed in Saudi Arabia. Only Bechtel had taken what it had learned from the oilmen one step further. At just about the time Borman was being ordered to leave Jeddah, for instance, Bechtel hired a high-powered Washington lobbyist named A. J. Shaw. Though he was nominally in the employ of Bechtel, Shaw's actual job was representing the Arabs in their dealings with the U.S. government. While Socal and Aramco had served as the surrogate representatives of the United States in Saudi Arabia, it was Steve Bechtel's company that took the lead in representing the Arabs in the United States. *

---

* Bechtel's lobbying activities on behalf of the Arabs were summarized in an April 1949 report provided to the State Department by A. J. Shaw. Shaw's report stated that Bechtel "personally aids and assists the Saudi Arab Embassy and Government in many ways." According to Shaw, these services included:

> Personally representing the Saudi Arab Government before the various divisions of the International Emergency Food Committee of the Food and Agricultural Organization of the United Nations as both representative and technical advisor;
>
> Personally representing the Saudi Arab Government in contacts with all the United States Government departments...

Personally representing the Saudi Arab Government as alternative delegate to the International Wheat Conference;

Completely handling many matters which the Commercial Department of an embassy would normally handle;

Executing the purchasing and shipment of many and diverse personal items for members of the royal family in Saudi Arabia, as well as for the Washington Ambassador and his staff.

In an addendum to the report, a senior State Department official added that Shaw's office had "acted as a commercial attaché of the Saudi Arab Embassy. The Saudi Arab Ambassador, Sheik Asad Al Faqih, depends on Mr. Shaw for his commercial contacts, dealings and negotiations."

CHAPTER 8

LUCKY MAN

It was the fifth of November 1950, and in the Bechtel Corporation mess hall in Dhahran, Saudi Arabia, Steve Bechtel; his wife, Laura, and Steve's oldest friend, George Cooley, had just finished dinner. Suddenly, the lights went out. Steve grimaced: the Bechtel-built power plant appeared to be on the blink. Seconds later, his features softened into smiling surprise: there, being borne into the room on a silver tray, was a birthday cake, ablaze with fifty-one candles—one for each year of Steve Bechtel's life and one more to wish on.

Laura, who had conspired all day with the kitchen help to make the cake in secret, beamed at her husband's response. They had been married twenty-seven-years now, and however remote the jobsite, she was almost always at his side. Her husband squeezed her hand and kissed her on the cheek. Then, after blowing out the candles and hearing the staff sing a raucous chorus of "Happy Birthday," Steve got up to speak. "My friends," he said, "I am unquestionably the luckiest man in the world."

Certainly, he was one of the most successful. In the coming year alone, some thirty new projects would be brought into the Bechtel fold. Among them: 1,200 miles of pipeline; three refinery jobs; four chemical plants; four steam-powered electric plants and ten industrial plants. The company's interests now stretched from California, where it was in the process of building the largest electric plant in the state, to Indonesia, where, on the island of Sumatra, it was beginning construction of an oil-processing complex that when finished would be the largest such facility in Southeast Asia. The San Francisco–based construction and engineering firm was now a corporate power around the world; and despite its proprietor's speech in Dhahran, very little of its success had to do with luck.

Instead, Bechtel's $200 million a year in revenues was the result of shrewd calculation and careful balancing. To protect his company from the boom-and-bust cycles that regularly ravaged the rest of the U.S. construction industry, Steve Bechtel had set a goal of dividing the company's workload 50/50 between international and domestic projects. When one area or the other went soft—and rarely did both do so at once—he leaned on the other. He buffered himself further by diversifying, adding to Bechtel's established petroleum, mining and construction work new areas like shipping and building of chemical and industrial plants. What luck there was in all this planning was largely a matter of being in the right place at the right time.

Such a time was 1952, when a subsidiary of U.S. Steel decided to extract half a billion tons of high-grade iron ore from the Orinoco region in Venezuela. The one American construction company that had extensive Venezuelan experience, as well as expertise in mining, was Bechtel, which was awarded the contract to coordinate construction and administration of the job, one of the largest the steel company ever sponsored outside the United States.

Bechtel's good fortune, however, was more than simple happenstance. Twenty years earlier, when Steve was purchasing steel at Boulder, he had given considerable business to a John McCone salesman named Alden Roach. Later, the same Alden Roach had become chairman of Consolidated Steel and had set up the meeting with Admiral Vickery that led to the Bechtel-McCone shipbuilding work. Later still, Roach headed a subsidiary of U.S. Steel which at Roach's suggestion contracted with Bechtel to do the mining work in Venezuela. In the world of Steve Bechtel, an effect invariably had a cause.

This was especially true in the Middle East, where Bechtel's operations were rapidly expanding beyond Saudi Arabia. During the late 1940s and early 1950s, Bechtel crews moved into Yemen, Kuwait,

Lebanon, Iraq and Iran, with the Kuwait Oil Company the first to seek out Bechtel's services. "Their people came down to take a look at what we were doing in Saudi Arabia and we went up there to check out their operations," Bechtel recalled in an interview. "Pretty soon, they had us building refineries in Kuwait. Then their parent company, British Petroleum, which also owned Iraq Petroleum, asked us to build the pipeline from Kirkuk to the Mediterranean for Iraq Petroleum.

"In this business," he went on, "you get to know people, sit on their boards, and one day when something comes up, they ask you to take on a project. One thing leads to another."[1]

It was not, in fact, that simple. The dominoes first had to be lined up before they could topple over in quick succession. By eventually letting George Wimpey & Company, Ltd., share in the Saudi work, and later providing the British firm with access to desperately needed steel, Steve established an important liaison with Wimpey's head, Sir Godfrey W. Mitchell, one of the most powerful businessmen in Britain. The two began socializing, and eventually Mitchell put Bechtel in touch with Basil Jackson, the head of British Petroleum. The work in Kuwait and Iraq followed.

In 1951 an even bigger project came along, when BP, having been temporarily ousted from Iran by the Mossadeq revolution, asked Bechtel to build a 120,000-barrel-a-day refinery in nearby Aden. Such a project normally required four years to complete; Bechtel said he could built it in less than two. To underline his seriousness, he agreed to a provision in the contract compelling him to pay $10,000 for every day the project ran over schedule. In turn, BP committed itself to paying a $1 million bonus if Bechtel finished under the deadline. Steve, who was so confident Bechtel was going to get the job that he'd ordered the preliminary work to commence even before the contract was let, collected the bonus with three months to spare.

In the United States, Steve Bechtel had friends as well. And few were better—or more valuable—than his old partner, John McCone.

After the breakup of Bechtel-McCone, McCone had used part of his wartime windfall to buy the San Francisco–based Joshua Hendry Iron Works. The company, in which Bechtel had a minority interest, had built ship engines during the war, and like many such enterprises, had gone into a slump with the coming of peace. To turn it around, McCone added generators and earth-moving machinery to its product line. At the same time, he became increasingly involved in shipping, an area he and Bechtel had gotten into after the war, when, along with

Socal in 1947, they assumed ownership of a shipping company, Pacific Tankers, Inc. Transporting oil for the Navy from the Middle East to the United States, Pacific Tankers' fleet eventually grew to 90 ships, and by the end of the war had become the largest oil mover in the world.

With McCone as majority stockholder and Bechtel and several West Coast associates as silent investors, the company had since been rechristened Pacific Far East Lines and had extended its operations to Japan, China and the Philippines. In addition, McCone, along with Bechtel, had entered into a partnership with Henry Mercer, the New York owner of States Marine Lines and U.S. Lines, companies with vast fleets that operated in the Atlantic. When all McCone's interests were totaled together, he ranked as one of the dominant shipping figures in the world.

In between business chores, McCone had also found time to serve as a director of the Stanford Research Institute and as a trustee and chief fund-raiser for the California Institute of Technology, whose scientists had played a critical role in the development of the atomic bomb and were now on the leading edge of nuclear research. McCone's first love, however, was government.

Admitting himself "a little restless"[2] with the business world, McCone found the challenge of government work stimulating, particularly when it was for the Department of Defense, where he was able to give full vent to his hard-line anti-Communist views. Even the Bechtelians, who were hardly Reds, were sometimes startled by the fervor of their former colleague's pronouncements. To hear McCone tell it, the Soviets were bent on nothing less than world domination. The free forces would survive, he said, only if they were strong, and they would be strong only if they understood that the atomic bomb was not so much a weapon of destruction as a God-given means of defending the American way of life. "He was a rightest Catholic," said political pundit I. F. Stone. "A man with holy war views."[3]

McCone's chance to translate those views into action came in 1947, when he was invited to Washington to become a member of the President's Air Policy Commission. Charged with examining the then-moribund aircraft industry and devising methods to revive it, the commission turned out a dramatically titled report, "Survival in the Air Age," which recommended that the United States convert its military planes from piston-engined to jet and that the country build up nuclear-weapon stockpiles as quickly as possible. The report, whose military conclusions were written by McCone, became a major rationale for increasing the Defense budget.

Impressed with McCone's handiwork, Secretary of Defense James Forrestal, the most hard-line member of the Truman cabinet, asked him to draw up the budget for the newly formed Department of the Air Force. McCone threw himself into the task with the same relentless dedication he had shown at Calship. "I've never worked for anyone who demanded as much as this guy or wanted as much," one Air Force colonel who labored under McCone told Bechtel executive Jerry Komes. "He wakes us up at six in the morning, and at midnight we're still working for the son of a bitch."[4] And woe be to those who didn't produce. When that happened, McCone would take out his gold pocket watch and begin twirling it, the rotations becoming more and more rapid as his displeasure grew, until the motion became a blur. "That's when the explosion came," a former colleague said. "You wanted to run for cover."[5]

Nonetheless, the McCone method got results. As his stature in the Defense Department grew, he became close to California Senator William Knowland, a leading proponent of beefing up the Air Force, as well as to the former supreme commander in Europe, Dwight D. Eisenhower, whom McCone first met when Eisenhower returned to Washington to take up duties as Army chief of staff. Another important friendship made during this period was with Allen Dulles, later to be McCone's predecessor as director of Central Intelligence.

The occasion that initially brought them together was a dinner party at the Dulles town house in New York, called to celebrate the expected victory of Thomas E. Dewey as president. Taking a brief respite from his Washington duties, McCone had been staying as the houseguest of Grete and John Simpson, Steve Bechtel's chief confidant. When the Dulleses asked the Simpsons to dinner, Uncle John brought McCone along. During the party, McCone and Dulles chatted amiably, interrupting their conversation now and again to listen to the latest election bulletins. With each announcement, it became clearer that the biggest upset in American political history was in the making. On a deflated note, the party broke up, but not before John McCone had made an important friend.[6]

With Truman's reelection, McCone returned to California to resume his business career. He saw Bechtel frequently, and the two men often golfed together, sometimes in the company of McCone's friends from Washington, including Eisenhower. "We Republicans are fond of golf," McCone explained to *Life* magazine,[7] "because by and large, we're a sociable lot."

McCone's socializing was interrupted in June 1950 by another summons to Washington. With war in Korea looming, his Air Policy Commission colleague Thomas Finletter, now secretary of the Air Force, wanted him by his side.

Though McCone's title was deputy secretary, it quickly became apparent that he was the department's real boss. McCone's first order of business: Get aircraft production moving on a crash basis; get the Sabre jets needed to combat the Russian-built MiGs out of the plants and into the skies over Korea.

In his new role, McCone also revamped the entire Air Force, approving the development of a new generation of jet fighters and bombers and providing the principal inspiration for the creation of the Stategic Air Command, whose nuclear-laden bombers remained constantly ready to strike the Russian homeland.

McCone could draw satisfaction from the fact that one of his key recommendations in "Survival in the Air Age"—the buildup of U.S. nuclear-weapons stockpiles—had been put into effect by Truman. As part of the effort, the president authorized the tripling of capacity at the principal weapons plant at Oak Ridge, Tennessee, and the building of ancillary gaseous-diffusion plants at Portsmouth, Ohio, and Paducah, Kentucky. McCone was heartened by Truman's move. So was Steve Bechtel, whose company was chief contractor on the work.

McCone, meanwhile, kept drawing closer to Eisenhower, now NATO commander and being touted by both parties as a presidential candidate. Eisenhower himself, however, was being coy about his candidacy, and indeed, had yet to declare his party affiliation. Then, in early January 1951, Henry Cabot Lodge, Republican senator from Massachusetts, told the press that he had learned that Eisenhower would soon announce his candidacy as a Republican. McCone, who was in Paris, vacationing with his wife, hurried to Eisenhower's headquarters outside the French capital.[8]

Escorted in through a back door and away from a mob of reporters waiting out front, he found Eisenhower and three senior U.S. generals convened around a large conference table littered with coffee cups. They looked as if they had been up all night.

"Cabot Lodge made this statement and we've got to answer it," Eisenhower told McCone. "We're drafting an answer and I'd like you to help with it."[9]

Ike said he was ready to declare his candidacy; the trouble, McCone quickly discovered, was that he had still not made up his mind whether he was a Republican or a Democrat. McCone pressed and argued with him until Ike finally gave in: all right, he was a Republican. The next step was formulating a statement for the press, broadly hinting at Eisenhower's candidacy, without formally declaring it. The hours dragged out as the five men in the room haggled over phrasing. Finally, at 3:00 that afternoon, the statement was ready and released to a throng of reporters waiting outside. The bridge had been crossed; Eisenhower was in.

As president, Dwight Eisenhower would remember his friends, including John McCone, whom he would name chairman of the Atomic Energy Commission. Under McCone's aegis, the nation would begin gearing up for the age of expectedly cheap and trouble-free nuclear power. Dozens of new plants, costing billions of dollars, would be necessary. Required too would be a construction company to build them. As "lucky" Steve Bechtel had put it, one step was following another.

1

1. *Each summer the Bechtels and their friends from government and business visit the Bohemian Grove for their annual encampment. Here under the redwoods members and guests gather around a bonfire. (Woodfin & Camp Assoc.)*

2

3

2. In 1906, the W. A. Bechtel Company was awarded one of its earliest contracts, a grading job for Western Pacific. This was the first time the company utilized a steam shovel. (Bechtel Corporation)

3. With their fortunes improving by 1915, the Bechtels posed for a family portrait. From left to right standing are Clara, Warren and Steve. Seated are Ken, Alice and "Dad." (Bechtel Corporation)

4

4. By 1924, W. A. Bechtel was one of the biggest contractors in the West. Here during a break on a railroad job he posed with his three sons. (Bechtel Corp.)

5. In June 1927, en route to the Bowman Dam construction site high in the Sierra Nevada, "Dad" and Clara Bechtel chatted with operators of one of the big "Cat 60" tractors used by the company. (Bechtel Corp.)

5

6. "Dad" Bechtel died in Russia before his crowning achievement, Hoover Dam, was completed. Here his middle son, Steve (far right), joined other officials of the Six Companies on an inspection tour of the project in 1937. (Bechtel Corp.)

6

7

8

9

7. *Steve Bechtel (right) and John A. McCone went into business together in 1937 and later during World War II ran many of the major shipyards and construction projects in support of the war effort. (Bechtel Corp.)*

8. *When Prince Amir Faisal, Saudi Arabia's Foreign Minister and King Ibn Saud's second son, visited San Francisco in 1944, Steve Bechtel took him on a tour of Marinship, the showcase of Bechtel's wartime efforts. Years later when Faisal became the Saudi monarch, he would award Bechtel some of the biggest contracts in Saudi Arabia. (Bechtel Corp.)*

9. *Bechtel built many pipelines, including Tapline, which brought Saudi oil to market. Some extended thousands of miles across the desert. (Bechtel Corp.)*

11

12

10. *After Bechtel had established it-self as a major presence in Saudi Arabia, Steve Bechtel moved the company into nuclear power. In 1949 the Atomic Energy Commission asked Bechtel to build an experimen-tal breeder reactor at the agency's Nuclear Reactor Test Station west of Idaho Falls, Idaho. Called ERB-1, the facility was designed to test whether nuclear power could be con-verted to electrical power. (Depart-ment of Energy)*

11. *Working with General Electric, Bechtel also built the Dresden Nuclear Power Station for Commonwealth Edison. Located outside Chicago, Dresden was America's first major power plant.*

12. *One of the chief architects of Bechtel's nuclear program was W. Kenneth Davis, who left the company in 1981 to serve as Deputy Secretary of Energy in the Reagan Administration. (Department of Energy)*

13

13. Bechtel counted on President Nixon and Eximbank chairman Henry Kearns to help further its interests during the early 1970s. With Nixon's blessing, Kearns approved hundreds of millions of dollars in low-interest loans to underwrite foreign nuclear power projects Bechtel was pursuing. (Export-Import Bank)

14

14. *In January 1971, President Nixon called Steve Bechtel, Jr. (second from right), and other construction-industry leaders to the White House to ask their advice in halting the wage–price spiral. Soon after, the Bechtel chairman helped resolve a long-standing feud between the President and the AFL-CIO's George Meany. (UPI/Bettmann)*

15

15. *After Nixon resigned, Bechtel turned to President Ford for support in furthering its nuclear development plans. Here Steve Bechtel, Jr., who was serving as chairman of the World Energy Conference Organizing Committee, welcomes Ford to the committee's opening session in Detroit on September 23, 1974. (UPI/Bettmann)*

From the mid-1970s through 1982, Bechtel's business boomed as never before. 16. The company built most of Indonesia's major liquefied-natural-gas facilities, such as the one shown here, in Sumatra. These helped transform Indonesia into a major oil power and strengthened the Suharto government. (Bechtel Corp.) 17. In New Guinea, Bechtel used helicopters to transport men and equipment to a huge copper project located in some of the world's most rugged and remote terrain. (Bechtel Corp.) 18. In the mid-1970s, Steve Bechtel, Sr., posed in front of a prototype car for the Bechtel-built Bay Area Rapid Transit (BART) system. (Bechtel Corp.)

19

19. *Bechtel's most ambitious project, perhaps the biggest construction job ever undertaken, was the $30 billion-plus Jubail Industrial Complex the company began building for the Saudi government in the late 1970s. (Bechtel Corp.)*

20. *Suliman Olayan, one of the wealthiest men in the world and Bechtel's partner in Saudi Arabia, helped the company obtain the Jubail contract. He later became furious when Bechtel executives enlisted the help of a Saudi prince to land a multibillion-dollar airport contract. (Woodfin & Camp Assoc.)*

20

"HE'S IN WASHINGTON NOW, TOO — IS THERE ANYONE ELSE YOU'D LIKE TO SPEAK TO?"

21

22

23

21. *Bechtel's revolving door to Washington was the subject of a Herblock cartoon in* The Washington Post. *(Copyright 1982 by Herblock in* The Washington Post*)* 22. *It was occasioned by Ronald Reagan's nomination of Bechtel Group president George Shultz as Secretary of State in June 1982. (Bechtel Corp.)* 23. *At that time Bechtel's former general counsel Caspar Weinberger was serving as Secretary of Defense. (UPI/Bettmann)*

Passage through the revolving door between Bechtel and Washington moved in both directions. Among the former senior-level government officials who ended up working for Bechtel, both as consultants, were 24. ex–CIA chief Richard Helms (Black Star) and 25. onetime State department official Philip Habib. (Woodfin & Camp Assoc.) In July 1982, The Washington Post revealed that Habib was serving as President Reagan's Middle East envoy at the same time he was on Bechtel's payroll.

26. Bechtel's people played key roles in mapping out the campaign strategy of Ronald Reagan's 1980 campaign. Here Reagan confers with Bechtel lobbyist Charls Walker (far right) and Bechtel Group president George Shultz (second from right) during a September 1980 meeting in Middleburg, Virginia. (UPI/ Bettmann)

27

27. *Steve Bechtel, Jr., pictured here inspecting a jobsite, struggled desperately to get his company back on track. He initiated severe cutbacks, laid off thousands of employees and took on small, run-of-the-mill jobs Bechtel would have declined during its heyday. (Bechtel Corp.)*

28

28. *By the spring of 1987, Bechtel's belt-tightening measures had proved effective. The company had weathered the recession and regained its position as the world's leading construction and engineering company. To celebrate, the lights in the twenty-three-story Bechtel building in San Francisco were left on to spell out the number "1." (Bechtel Corp.)*

CHAPTER 9

▲

ATOMS FOR PEACE

Y ears before John McCone became chairman of the AEC, Steve
    Bechtel had realized the potential of atomic power and positioned
his company to capitalize on it.

The company's involvement had begun at the dawn of the Atomic
Age, when in the early 1940s, Bechtel, through its connections with
General Somervell, had built several "heavy water" storage plants at
Hanford, Washington, as part of the Manhattan Project—the program
that developed the atomic bomb. Later, after the bomb had proved its
destructive potential at Hiroshima, Bechtel had been one of several
contractors and utilities that had built the "Doomsday Town" in the
middle of the Nevada desert. Complete with model homes, electric
lines and its own power plant, the town had been erected so that the
AEC and major utilities could assess what would happen if a small
nuclear device were detonated in the midst of a typical middle-sized
American city. Would, for instance, the power keep running in, say,
Memphis or Indianapolis? The companies got their answer at 5:10
A.M., on a mid-October morning in 1952, when, as one witness recounted, "the switch was tossed and the soft pearly dawn of the desert

went white and orange." Sad for Memphis and Indianapolis, the Doomsday Town was leveled.

For Bechtel, the Doomsday study was one of a series of early projects the company carried out for the AEC in conjunction with a number of its energy-minded customers like PG&E. It was work that in the coming years would do much to define the emerging nuclear industry. Not coincidentally, it would also establish the Bechtel Corporation as the world's largest purveyor of nuclear power.

Bechtel had already gained a foothold in the rapidly expanding power industry through his connections with California utilities, for which he had built—and would continue to build—a number of highly profitable steam and hydroelectric plants. He was eager to extend that business to other utilities across the country; "going nuclear," he calculated, was the way to do it. "Nuclear power was a mechanism for getting Bechtel into the power-plant business," said a senior Bechtel executive. For Steve, "it was a considered move."[1]

Other Californians were making similar calculations. James Black of PG&E was on the verge of committing his company to nuclear power, while Henry Kaiser had already gotten into the game in typically high-rolling fashion by securing a $110 million contract for Kaiser engineers to modernize and expand the Hanford facilities. Meanwhile, Cal Tech and Bechtel and McCone's alma mater, Berkeley, were in the process of supplanting Eastern universities as important centers of atomic research. Almost overnight, it appeared, the West Coast was becoming a hotbed of nuclear development.

At the center of much of this activity was Ernest O. Lawrence, a Berkeley scientist who had worked on the Manhattan Project and who, after the war, had been a principal supporter of Edward Teller's proposal to build what was then called "The Super" and later became more familiarly known as the hydrogen bomb. In October 1949 the AEC temporarily put off building the weapon, but awarded Lawrence and his colleagues at Berkeley a contract to build a top-secret project with the cover name "Materials Testing Accelerator."[2]

Lawrence had a lifelong obsession with building big machines, and this one more than fulfilled it. Nearly 4,000 feet in length and employing giant magnets and thousands of tons of steel, the MTA was designed to be a kind of massive nuclear oven, wherein uranium was bombarded with neutrons to create fissionable plutonium—the explosive "stuff" of H-bombs. Even with uranium from the Belgian Congo quickly being depleted and the AEC as yet unaware of the great store that lay in western Colorado and Utah, Lawrence believed he could create large quantities of this, the most dangerous substance on earth.

He headquartered the project on an abandoned World War II naval air station 40 miles southeast of the Berkeley campus in what would later become the site of the Lawrence-Livermore Laboratories, one of the largest developers of nuclear weaponry in the world. The contract for building the facility went to the California Research Group, the research-and-development arm of Socal. Socal promptly subcontracted the engineering and construction to Bechtel.[3]

Work on MTA had scarcely gotten under way when in December 1949, the AEC called on Bechtel to build what would become an even more significant project: an experimental breeder reactor and chemical-processing plant at the agency's Nuclear Reactor Test Station in the arid sage and lava plains 40 miles west of Idaho Falls, Idaho. EBR-1, as it was called, was to test whether nuclear energy could be converted to electric power. The effort, said Lawrence R. Hafstad, director of the AEC's Reactor Development Division, was "a daring adventure in nuclear science."[4]

The adventure proved successful, giving Bechtel an important head start in what would soon be a headlong, high-stakes race to convert America to nuclear energy. The timing was most propitious. For just as EBR-1 went on line, Dwight Eisenhower took over at the White House. "My chief concern and your first assignment," he instructed his AEC chairman, Lewis Strauss, "is to find some new approach to the disarming of atomic energy."[5] Eisenhower expanded on the theme in an "Atoms for Peace" address delivered to the United Nations General Assembly less than a year later. "The United States knows that peaceful power from atomic energy is one dream of the future," the President declared. "That capability, already proved, is here—now, today." "Nuclear materials, he urged, should be used "to provide abundant electrical energy in the power starved areas of the world . . . The greatest destructive forces can be developed into a great boon for the benefit of all mankind."[6]

The business of effecting that development fell to private industry. Ignoring the counsel of Harry Truman that nuclear energy was "too important a development to be made the subject of profit-seeking," Eisenhower wanted the AEC to be able to issue licenses to private companies to build and operate nuclear power stations. In drawing up the Atomic Energy Act in 1954, the Republican-controlled Congress granted him his wish.

Wasting no time extending Bechtel's lead, Steve flew to Washington, where McCone introduced him to AEC chairman Strauss, whom he had come to know when both men were working for the Department of Defense. Bechtel had his own friends at the AEC as well. One was W. Kenneth Davis, the agency's director of reactor development, who, as Socal's research director, had worked with Bechtel during the construction of the MTA. Three others, working out of the AEC's West Coast office, were Harry Brown, Steven V. White and Ashton O'Donnell. Eventually, all four men would leave the agency and ultimately work for Bechtel, later prompting Connecticut Senator Abraham Ribicoff to complain that the AEC had spawned an industry "so incestuous, it is impossible to tell where the public sector begins and the private one leaves off."

While Bechtel was ingratiating himself at the AEC, he was also moving to enhance his standing with the utilities. Part of that task had already been accomplished. In 1951, at the invitation of the AEC, Bechtel and PG&E chairman James Black had formed a joint Bechtel-PG&E team to prepare an in-depth study of the commercial uses of nuclear power. Soon other big utilities were clamoring for a share of the action. "Most of the heads of these utilities, men like Wesley McAfee [president of the Union Electric Company of St. Louis], were well known to us," Bechtel said in an interview. "And as they began to talk among themselves about the prospects of nuclear power, they became more and more excited by it."[7]

In 1954, seven of the most enthusiastic utilities, joined by Bechtel, formed an association called the National Power Group. Based in Chicago, the consortium carried out economic and design studies for the AEC, and evaluated different prototype reactors, determining which was best for commercial power generation.

It was an exclusive, well-connected club, but membership was costly: a minimum investment of $1 million to support research, with no guarantee of any return. Bechtel's attorney, Bob Bridges, who attended some of the early NPG meetings, said later that "the amount took our breath away. It was," he went on, "like a high-stakes poker game and you have one chip—and that's a million-dollar chip."[8] Despite the worries of several of his key advisors, Bechtel anted in.

He began getting his return on his investment almost immediately. The same year NPG was formed, PG&E contracted with Bechtel to build a 300,000-kilowatt power plant near San Luis Obispo, California, the first in the country to use evaporators to convert seawater to fresh water. At the same time, Bechtel was on the verge of closing a total of $300 million in other power-plant deals from California Edison, Utah Power & Light and utilities in Arizona and Hawaii. Quickly, Bechtel had gone from a regional, not terribly important builder of power plants to perhaps *the* leading contractor in the field. Steve Bechtel was also ready to extend his company's reach overseas.

His chance came during an around-the-world trip with Union Electric's Wesley McAfee in 1954. During a stopover in South Korea, Steve met with Tyler Wood, economic coordinator of the U.S. Foreign Operations Administration, who asked him to meet with South Korean President Syngman Rhee about problems Rhee was having with the United States, which had failed to follow through on its promise to build power plants in South Korea. "Rhee complained that the Koreans needed electricity," recalled Bechtel executive vice-president Jerry Komes, who would head up the Korean work and later succeed George Cooley as chief of Bechtel's international operations. "Rhee said the U.S. had agreed to help, but all that had happened so far was that studies had been done."[9] Steve thereupon gave Rhee an impromptu lesson on dealing with the U.S. government. As Komes described it: "Steve told him he ought to decide on one standard design, figure out how many plants he needed and then tell the U.S. government to get off its butt and get going. Rhee took him more or less literally at his word. Then he asked Steve, 'Will you take charge of the project?' and Steve said, 'Sure.'"[10]

The result was that before long, the Bechtel Corporation was building three coal-fired plants in Korea, the first of which was ready to come on line within two years of the company's arrival in the country. But when the project was nearing completion, Komes discovered that 17 miles of expensive copper cable had been stolen. Komes went right to the government. "I told them, 'Our plant is finished . . . but your people have stolen our cable. Unless we can get the cable back in a reasonable time, we're pulling out,'" he related. "In three days, we had the cable all back."[11]

Bechtel displayed the same hardball approach in 1954 in building the Joppa steam plant for the AEC's weapons-manufacturing installation at Paducah, Kentucky. The $830 million plant had been begun by one of Bechtel's rivals, Ebasco Services, Inc., but was only a third finished when a jurisdictional fight between local workers and the AFL brought the project to a standstill. Invited to take over by the AEC, Bechtel promptly shut down the operation and fired the entire work crew. The strikers responded by accusing the company of importing goon squads to intimidate them, and there followed a series of lawsuits, threats and violent confrontations. Bechtel, however, refused to budge. Unless labor peace was soon restored, the company warned the unions, the Joppa project would be abandoned.[12] The unions eventually buckled, and with help from the AFL, Bechtel began rehiring—refusing, however, to take back workers it deemed to be troublemakers. From there on, work proceeded smoothly.

With Joppa's completion, Bechtel's reputation soared even higher at the AEC and among the utilities. But there was one link in the nuclear chain still missing: an affiliation with either General Electric or Westinghouse, the nation's principal reactor manufacturers. In October 1953, Steve forged it during a relaxing weekend in the company of America's business elite.

The Homestead is the unlikely name of an elegant, antebellum hotel nestled high in the Blue Ridge Mountains of Virginia. Here, twice a year, the 160 or so members of the Business Council gather to discuss the concerns of corporate America, shucking their somber pin-striped suits for brightly hued sport jackets and golf trousers. Invariably, they are joined by top-ranking government officials, who are whisked into the nearby Hot Springs airport aboard Air Force jets, or as was the case with President Lyndon Johnson in 1964, ferried by helicopter to the manicured Homestead lawns.

The council was established in 1933 to serve as a meeting point between the private sector and government. Over the years, dozens of its members have served in presidential cabinets, while the council itself has advised a succession of presidents, both Republican and Democratic, on everything from taxes to inflation. "Its power to influence the nation's economy—and the decision-making of its elected officials—is little short of awesome," noted a business journal.[13]

Here, as in the Bohemian Grove, Steve Bechtel was in his element. Since being elected a council member in 1950, he had developed a cordial personal—and oftentimes financially beneficial—relationship with many of his comembers. Through the council, for instance, Bechtel met Pan American Airways founder and chairman Juan Trippe, for whom he later built the worldwide chain of Inter-Continental Hotels. It was also at the council that Bechtel came to be friendly with IBM founder Thomas J. Watson and his son, Tom junior;

later, Bechtel would build a number of major facilities for both men, and his son, Steve junior, would serve on the IBM board. United States Steel Chairman Roger Blough was still another friend made at the council; it was Blough's company that had given Bechtel the Orinoco ore project. In terms of furthering Bechtel's nuclear development, though, the key council member was Ralph H. Cordiner, chairman and chief executive officer of General Electric.

Cordiner and Bechtel had known each other slightly before serving together on the council. GE had managed the plutonium-processing reactors at Hanford, and Cordiner, like Steve, was a frequent participant in various energy conferences. But it was at the council meetings at Homestead that their friendship really firmed. During the long weekends, the two men would often slip off to a quiet corner and discuss their plans and ideas for nuclear energy until late into the night.

GE, Steve was well aware, had dropped to second position in the reactor industry, following Hyman Rickover's decision to award reactor development for his nuclear submarines to the company's archrival, Westinghouse. He also knew that Cordiner was eager to regain the lead—as eager as Bechtel was himself to gain GE's support. With its reactor-building capacity, its long history as one of the country's leading consumer electric companies and its considerable clout on Wall Street and in Washington, politically conservative General Electric could be to Bechtel's nuclear ambitions what Socal had been to its pipeline and refinery business.

During a break in the Homestead weekend, Steve drew Cordiner aside and told him that his company had decided to earmark 10 percent of its pretax earnings for nuclear development and training. Cordiner was impressed; he had had no idea Bechtel was so committed to nuclear power. Bechtel was in the nuclear game to stay, Steve added, going on to describe the work it had done already in developing EBR-1. Again, Cordiner was impressed; the liquid-metal fast breeder reactor, such as the one at EBR-1, was a design GE favored, rather than the water-cooled models Westinghouse was building for Rickover. Finally, Bechtel came to the point. Why not, he proposed, get beyond all the testing and endless discussion over which type of reactor was best for generating commercial power, and simply built a nuclear plant—not just another prototype, but an actual, full-scale, money-making plant that ran on atomic energy.[14] Cordiner's eyes lit up. The proposal was bold, but Bechtel was talking sense.

By the end of the weekend, Bechtel and Cordiner had concluded a handshake agreement to go to the National Power Group and ask which of its members was ready to stop talking and start building. When Commonwealth Edison of Chicago volunteered to build a plant at Dresden, Illinois, not far from its corporate headquarters, General Electric and Bechtel were in business.

As Cordiner and Bechtel were optimistically readying their plans, their friend AEC chairman Lewis Strauss was not having an easy time of it. Since taking office, he had been drawing increasing fire from the Democratic-majority Joint Committee on Atomic Energy. Members of the committee, most notably its chairman, New Mexico Senator Clinton P. Anderson, had repeatedly charged that the AEC's long-range nuclear power program was fuzzy and inadequate. So intense had the grilling been during committee sessions that Strauss was no longer on speaking terms with most of the members. During one hearing, he burst out: "This room is decorated with my blood!"[15]

By November 1957, Strauss had had enough and told Eisenhower he would not seek reappointment to another four-year term. The man he recommended to replace him was John McCone.

Since the fateful meeting in Paris, McCone had remained close to Eisenhower and had provided a steady stream of advice during the 1952 campaign. McCone had also struck up a warming friendship with Eisenhower's vice-president, Richard Nixon, whom he had known since Nixon emerged as an ardently anti-Communist California congressman, and John Foster Dulles, who had asked McCone to be his deputy secretary of State. Washington itself, however, had lost much of its charm for McCone, largely because of the flak he had taken as under-secretary of the Air Force for awarding a contract to build Flying Boxcar transports to his former business partner Henry J. Kaiser. The seeming impropriety of the arrangement nettled a number of congressmen, who were even more upset that McCone was paying Kaiser three times as much as it had formerly paid the Fairchild Corporation, another Air Force contractor, to build the identical plane.[16] Eyebrows had gone up also when it was revealed that the Kaiser-Fraser Corporation, the financially strapped Kaiser partnership that was building the planes, was partly owned by McCone's good friend and former business partner Steve Bechtel. McCone, Republican senator from Wisconsin Alvin O'Konski charged, was "merely on leave of absence from his position as Bechtel-McCone Corporation president."[17]

Partly as a result of the Flying Boxcar episode, and partly, too, be-

cause he wanted to attend to business affairs in California, McCone
had informed Eisenhower that he was not interested in serving during
the general's first term. In 1954, however, Eisenhower briefly lured
McCone back with an invitation to serve on a committee that was
devising ways of restructuring the U.S. Foreign Service, which had
been decimated by the McCarthyite purge. The following year, Eisenhower sent him to Rome as his personal representative for the observance of the birthday of Pope Pius XII. McCone, however, was
reluctant to do more. His growing shipping business was on its way to
making him the American Onassis. Indeed, when the call came in
from White House chief of staff Sherman Adams summoning him to a
meeting with the president in May 1958, McCone was about to launch
a new $75 million 14-ship fleet.

Nonetheless, McCone did not turn the president down. Offered the
AEC post over lunch at the White House, he asked for three days to
think it over, then accepted.*

The agency John McCone took over had a budget of $2 billion per
year, operated $7 billion worth of facilities, employed 105,000 persons
and was counted as one of the most complex and diffuse organizations
in the federal government. Despite all its resources, however, the AEC
had been slow in developing commercial nuclear power—a delay
McCone attributed largely to lack of leadership. In the words of one of
his aides: "He thinks the commission should lead where it has been
following."

McCone quickly took charge. One of his first—and for Bechtel,
most important—moves involved AEC funding for the private nuclear
industry. Under Strauss, the AEC had underwritten research and
development, but nothing more. McCone recommended that federal
subsidies be paid to utilities for the construction of prototype

---

* During McCone's confirmation hearings, several senators made much of the fact
that during the 1956 presidential campaign, McCone, then a trustee and principal
fund-raiser for Cal Tech, had attacked ten of its scientists who had written a letter
supporting Adlai Stevenson's proposal to suspend H-bomb tests. According to one well-
placed Cal Tech source, McCone had stormed into a trustees' meeting "bright purple"
and asserted that the scientists' letter was designed to "create fear in the minds of the
uninformed that radioactive fallout from the H-bomb endangers life." When the
trustees refused to muzzle the scientists, McCone had resigned as chairman of Cal
Tech's fund-raising effort. Questioned about the incident during the confirmation
hearings, McCone defended himself by saying that the scientists were "using their
position in the institute" to "inject themselves into what appeared to be a political
argument." Apparently satisfied, the Senate quickly confirmed McCone.

nuclear plants. Paying such subsidies, he argued, would make up all or more of the difference between the cost of nuclear plants and the lower price tags for conventional oil- or coal-fired plants, hastening the nuclear industry on its way. Another decision McCone made was to halt uranium-buying from foreign sources; henceforth radioactive ore was to be obtained exclusively through U.S. companies, principally Union Carbide (a major customer of the McCone-and-Bechtel-owned Joshua Hendry Corporation), Kaiser and Utah Construction. Next, he appointed three executives from Standard Oil of California and the president of PG&E—all of them major Bechtel customers —to study the question of federal subsidies for reactors, such as those being built by General Electric. Not surprisingly, the resultant study called for "a vigorous [government-supported] developmental program."

All these measures were taken without much critical comment. Then, in June 1958, McCone overstepped himself.

What proved his undoing—at least in terms of public embarrassment—was a contract let by the U.S. Maritime Commission for the operation of the $40 million S.S. *Savannah*, the world's first—and, on the basis of the *Savannah*'s costly experience, last—nuclear-powered commercial merchant ship. Operating the *Savannah*, which Hyman Rickover later branded "a huge boondoggle," was rightly counted as a financial plum, and lest there be any hint of impropriety, the Maritime Commission appointed a professional selection board to sort out the qualifications of six bidders, among them States Marine Line, a company in which McCone and Bechtel had a working partnership through Joshua Hendry shipping.

When the rankings were announced, States Marine placed next to last, trailed only by yet another McCone entity, U.S. Lines, and just below still another, Pacific Far East. Thereupon, Commerce Secretary Sinclair Weeks, a friend of both Bechtel's and McCone's, overrode his own board and directed its members to reconsider. They did, and bumped States Marine up three slots to second place. At that point, ferocious lobbying commenced, and when it was over, States Marine had won the contract.

Despite being pilloried by the likes of public-affairs columnist Drew Pearson, McCone shrugged off the incident, though, under pressure, he did agree to place his various shipping interests in an irrevocable trust. In any event, the *Savannah* affair did nothing to diminish

McCone's enthusiasm for nuclear power. With the approval of Congress and the administration, he began spreading U.S. nuclear technology overseas, providing foreign aid in the form of experimental reactors to a host of countries large and small. The idea, as McCone explained it in an interview in 1974, was to give these countries reactors "so they would become accustomed to the operation of a reactor and to the handling of radioactive material. We did that in a great many countries," McCone went on. "Some were not prepared to enter the field, such as Vietnam, Korea, other less advanced countries. I've forgotten how many of these reactors were set up around the world, but maybe a hundred of them. I think that, in retrospect, we went a little too fast on that."[18]

McCone was equally zealous in his support of U.S. nuclear-arms development, but here Eisenhower finally drew the line in late summer 1958, when he told his staff that the joint efforts by the AEC and DOD to build up America's nuclear arsenal had gotten out of hand. He was, said the president, firmly committed to imposing a ban on all nuclear-arms testing. The ban was bitterly opposed by McCone, who was keen on firing a nuclear missile in the general direction of Cuba, and the idea lay dormant until the Kennedy administration. Eisenhower, though, was able to have his way with one McCone-sponsored project: providing private companies like Bechtel with small nuclear explosives to help them extract oil from deep underground and to blast tunnels through mountains. McCone was positively rabid about the notion. Think, he asked, of the things a Bechtel or a Socal could do with a few atomic bombs in its toolbox! Eisenhower killed the plan with a one word response: "No."[19]

Nonetheless, thanks to McCone, Bechtel and General Electric were moving right along, and by the fall of 1959, the Dresden I nuclear plant was complete. At the dedication ceremonies, Cordiner threw the switch, while flashbulbs popped and McCone, Bechtel and the representatives of the nation's largest utilities beamed. McCone hailed the facility as "the largest, most efficient, most advanced nuclear plant in the world." Bechtel predicted it would do more to "establish nuclear power than any other project in the world."

It seemed to matter little that after only a month of operation, Dresden I suffered the first of numerous shutdowns and accidents, and that it proved far more expensive to operate than conventionally powered plants. Nor did it matter overly that the Bechtel Corporation had yet to make a profit on any of its nuclear operations. A toehold in the new age had been established, and in the years to come, billions upon billions would flow in.

John McCone had helped his friend Steve Bechtel in other ways as well. He had, for one thing, done much to make him a frequent and familiar face in Washington, including at the White House. Sensing a direct, low-key bluffness not unlike his own, Eisenhower seemed quite taken with Bechtel. They golfed together at Burning Tree, swapped stories, exchanged affectionate notes. "I know you did a lot of work in the recently concluded political campaign and that, in addition, you helped materially on the financial end," Eisenhower wrote Bechtel after his 1956 reelection. "This note is merely to express my lasting appreciation of the personal compliment implicit in your action."[20]

More substantively, Eisenhower also sought out Bechtel's counsel and appointed him to a number of prestigious government posts. In 1954, for example, he named him to the National Highway Committee. Chaired by Berlin blockade hero General Lucius Clay, a figure who would join with Bechtel in a number of business ventures in coming years, the committee presented to Congress a blueprint for the creation of the Interstate Highway system. In 1957, Eisenhower appointed Bechtel as one of a number of business executives (among them Bechtel's own John L. Simpson) to work with Under-Secretary of State Douglas Dillon in drafting a report that would determine policy for distribution of foreign aid and development loans—many to countries which would use them to employ Bechtel. "This is wonderful," exclaimed Eisenhower, when he reviewed the group's findings. "I can read it myself."[21] Later, the president wrote Bechtel: "I am grateful to you. Your concern and your action as a private citizen surely reflect the spirit of initiative and the sense of firm conviction that are essential to our democratic life itself." He added: "Steve Bechtel is the kind of American you want to have on your side," Ike advised Richard Nixon when the vice-president was preparing to make a White House run of his own. "He'd make an excellent cabinet member." Taking the counsel, Nixon penciled Bechtel in as a potential secretary of Commerce.

There were many chores Steve Bechtel and his company would perform for presidents, many favors they would do—and had done—for the organs of government, including, though few knew it, the Central Intelligence Agency.

CHAPTER 10

THE COMPANY
AND THE COMPANY

I t seemed a small thing at first, these assorted favors the Bechtel Corporation did for U.S. intelligence; and so, at least in the beginning, they were.

The process had started, as did so much else for Bechtel, in Saudi Arabia shortly after the conclusion of World War II. At the time, the United States had two principal concerns in the Middle East: the Soviets, who were already beginning to put pressure on the northern provinces of neighboring Iran, which itself would shortly be torn by civil war and a CIA-sponsored coup; and the Jews, thousands of whom were streaming into what was then British-controlled Palestine, in hopes of creating their own state. Both developments were potentially explosive, and beginning in 1947, Bechtel started lending the U.S. government a hand.

That year, the company approved the assignment by the Navy of several nonuniformed officers to the Bechtel-built Saudi Arabian refinery at Ras Tanura. The officers' nominal task was looking out for saboteurs; but it became apparent as time went on that their larger mission was gathering intelligence. This in turn was transmitted through a secret Bechtel-built naval communications center at Ras Tanura.[1]

As tensions in the region continued to worsen, Bechtel began doing more, including making its personnel available for intelligence debriefings. One such occasion was in mid-July 1948, when Buzz Clarke, the IBI personnel director, led Dan Catlin, an intelligence officer with the U.S. legation in Dhahran, out to meet an IBI truck convoy that had arrived after a six-week crossing of the desert. Israeli planes had been bombing oil-storage tanks, much needed by the Arabs, who were preparing to mount an offensive against the fledgling Jewish state. Catlin debriefed each of the drivers, obtaining extensive information on troop movements and the bombing damage they had witnessed. Subsequently, he passed along a report to Colonel Francis E. Meloy, the American vice-consul in Jeddah. Said Catlin: "The Jews bombed the large gas reserve on the Trans-Jordan frontier and completely destroyed one large storage tank and one small reserve tank. A conservative estimate would be 200,000 American gallons [destroyed]."[2] The Saudi king, Catlin added, apparently on the basis of what Bechtel executives had told him, "is trying to again build up a reserve on the frontier . . . so it would be hard for the Zionists to locate and destroy the Trans-Jordan mobile fuel units . . . The King has again asked IBI to lay 30" pipe filled with gas along a new route of transport for the Saudi Army. So far nothing has been done by IBI."[3]

Bechtel's Saudi boss, Tom Borman, himself passed along intelligence when he happened on something important. On October 14, 1947, for instance, he notified Francis Meloy of pending trouble on the Palestine border. Reported Borman: "Yesterday we were told by a very intelligent Arab here [Jeddah], who speaks English fluently, that the situation is very critical. He said, 'You may not know it, but the Arabian army has been moved north to the border, and the tribes are all gathered for immediate action in the event that Palestine is partitioned.'"[4]

State Department documents reveal that Borman was suspected of providing material help to the Saudis, notably by flying to Belgium to arrange the purchase of a shipment of arms. Borman denied the charge, but Belgian-made arms nonetheless came into the Saudi arsenal, including, according to a State Department report, "the new snub-nosed rifle made in Belgium . . . with grease packed around their working parts which would indicate a recent shipment."

The arms, which helped improve Bechtel's relations with King ibn Saud and his troublesome finance minister, Abdullah Suleiman, were of small concern to the State Department, which at the time had a heavily pro-Arab bias. Of genuine worry to State, though, was the prospect of the Soviets' entering the conflict and gaining control of U.S. oil supplies. To guard against such an eventuality, the State Department drew up plans for Bechtel and Aramco to place explosives at all refineries and oil wells in Saudi Arabia and Bahrain. According to top secret State Department documents,[5] the explosives were to be used to destroy the facilities in the event "of the Soviet Union entering the hostilities." The plan was scotched by the National Security Council, and when war finally came, in 1948, the Soviets did not intervene.

The war itself went badly for the Arabs, and afterward, the Syrian government, furious at U.S. support for Israel, cancelled an agreement to permit the Bechtel-built Tapline pipeline to cross its borders. Had the policy stood, Bechtel would have lost millions. But in 1949, the civilian Syrian government was overthrown in a CIA-sponsored coup and replaced by a military dictatorship, friendlier to U.S. interests. Shortly thereafter, Bechtel was granted permission to build Tapline across Syria.

Though the coup came at a most propitious moment for Bechtel, the company denied any involvement. However, State Department documents from the period state that an unidentified "multinational corporation" had indeed had a hand in overthrowing the Syrian government, notably by supplying arms and funding to the rebels. According to J. Rives Childs, U.S. minister to Saudi Arabia, the "multinational corporation" was most likely International Bechtel.

At the very least, Bechtel was heavily enmeshed with the CIA. Among those attesting to the company's relationship was a former Aramco executive, Michael Cheney, who after ten years in Saudi Arabia returned to the United States in the 1950s to write a book about his experiences in the Middle East.[6] Cheney was particularly withering in his assessment of the CIA, whose Saudi operatives, he asserted, were "naive young men just out of Princeton and Yale who didn't know the first thing about the Middle East." The only real, effective intelligence-gathering, Cheney claimed, was being conducted for the CIA through a "large private company." At the time, the only such company in Saudi Arabia was International Bechtel Incorporated.

In the United States, meanwhile, Bechtel's John L. Simpson was strengthening his ties with the brothers Dulles, particularly Allen, who had bought a brownstone on Simpson's New York block and had become a frequent dinner companion. In 1951, after British Petroleum was expelled from Iran and had asked Bechtel to build a refinery in Aden, Simpson met with his friend and briefed him on what Bechtel had learned about developments in Iran. A year later, after the appointment of Dulles as deputy director of the CIA, the two met again in San Francisco on November 30, 1952, when Dulles stopped off on his way to Korea, where his son had been seriously wounded. Despite his personal anxiety, Dulles was happy to see Simpson, and according to the Bechtel executive's papers, the two discussed the concern that the Mossadeq government was considering shipping Iran's vast store of oil to the Soviet Union. During their meeting, Dulles asked Simpson if Bechtel would undertake a study to determine whether the Iranians had the technical know-how to build a pipeline to Russia. Two weeks later, Simpson wrote back:

Regarding that particular matter which we discussed and as to which you think our organization might have some information and opinions of value: I have talked this over with Steve [Bechtel] and he entirely agrees with me that we should like to do anything we possibly can to be of service. We are going to ask one of our very able men, who has spent considerable time in that part of the world, to give special thought and attention to this. He will make contact with the other members of our organization who are most conversant with the territory and the problem and we shall endeavor to put together the best ideas we have on the subject.[7]

The "very able" man Simpson referred to was George Cooley, Jr., Bechtel's pipeline chief and senior vice-president. With the assistance of a number of Bechtel engineers, Cooley put together a study which concluded that the Iranians could indeed build a Russian pipeline. Fearing the worst, the CIA shortly thereafter undertook "Operation Ajax," the CIA-sponsored coup which in 1953 restored Shah Reza Pahlevi to the Peacock Throne.

Besides their plotting, Simpson and Dulles were also engaged in a chatty correspondence. Many of the letters from Dulles were gloomy. At one point, he wrote to Simpson:[8]

So far as I can see we are likely to lose our position throughout the entire Far East, India, Indonesia, etc. Also, as far as I can see, we are not doing anything effective about it.

Simpson tried to buck up Dulles' spirits with flattery. In June 1954, when Dulles, by then CIA director, was being pilloried by Senator Joseph McCarthy, Simpson wrote, beginning in a jocular vein:[9]

I want to give you my personal assurance that I do not believe you are or were a Communist. This unequivocal statement on my part will, I feel sure, bring great comfort to you, because in a time of trial it is well to have the confidence of one's friends.

Seriously speaking, I cannot tell you how disgusted and outraged I was at the suggestion that you would tolerate any looseness in an organization for which you are responsible. I do not know what we have all done to warrant this blight being inflicted upon us.

Here's to you, Allen, in the hope that you are having a great deal of satisfaction out of the fine contribution you are making to our country and to us all.

Dulles evidently appreciated the sentiments; in any event, he began sharing all manner of confidences with Simpson. Immediately after the downing of the U-2 plane over the Soviet Union, for instance, he met with Simpson in London and over breakfast,[10] revealed precise details of the plane's mission—at the time, the United States was claiming that the aircraft had strayed while collecting weather information—including the number of U-2s possessed by the United States, a highly classified military secret.

Dulles also tried to come to Bechtel's aid in July 1958 when George Cooley was abducted and killed in Iraq. "MY FRIENDS REPORT THAT COOLEY STILL MISSING BUT THAT SEARCH IS CONTINUING," Dulles cabled Simpson on July 20, 1958. "KILLIAN [Bechtel executive Lou Killian] AND WIFE DEPARTED FIRST EVACUEE PLANE."

Simpson had also developed a close relationship with Allen's brother, Secretary of State John Foster Dulles. In mid-September 1953, shortly after the Iranian coup, Simpson, Steve Bechtel and Dulles met for cocktails at the Waldorf-Astoria in New York and talked over world problems and the difficulty of securing reliable information in areas like the Middle East. Afterward, Simpson and Bechtel decided to make Dulles a proposal. Simpson described it in a letter to the secretary of State dated September 29, 1953:

In talking over our meeting afterward, both Steve and I had a thought which I would like to mention. Our organization has, as you know, rather far-flung activities in engineering and construction throughout the world. We have projects under way and under consideration at numerous points in both hemispheres, and our key executives have considerable familiarity with resources and transportation in many countries.

It might just happen that in this connection, or with regard to some particular matter, we could furnish information or be of assistance to your organization. Occasionally a private concern can perform a function or develop certain aspects of a problem with greater facility than a government agency.

Three days later, Dulles wrote back thanking Simpson for his offer and promising to "remember it if the occasion arises."

The occasion arose quickly, and by the early 1950s, according to an Aramco governmental-affairs executive named William Mulligan, the Saudi Arabian operations of both Aramco and Bechtel were "loaded with CIA. . . . The agency didn't have to ask them [Bechtel and Aramco] to place its agents," Mulligan said in a 1987 interview. "Bechtel was delighted to take them on and give them whatever assistance they needed." After a time, so many CIA men were working for Bechtel and Aramco that Frank Jungers, then an Aramco executive in Saudi Arabia, later to become the company's chairman, complained to the CIA that too much information was being generated, much of it contradictory or wrong. "We told them, 'We'll help you and open up whatever areas you need, but you must work through one central source,'" Jungers recalled in an interview.[11] Eager to oblige, the CIA appointed a chief liaison officer for both Bechtel and Aramco.

As Bechtel's business expanded through the area, the CIA moved with it. According to published reports, denied by Bechtel but independently confirmed with former Bechtel employees, the company was especially accommodating to the agency in Libya, where between 1963 and 1970, "cover" employment was provided to two CIA men in Bechtel's employee-relations department.

Usually, such cover arrangements were made quite discreetly. But not always. The Allen Dulles papers on file at Princeton University contain a letter from Dulles to Simpson in January 1962[12] casually asking if Simpson would provide covert employment for a CIA agent named Jens Jebsen whose cover position as an executive with the London office of Manufacturers Hanover bank was being eliminated in a corporate consolidation. Simpson cheerfully replied that he would try to arrange it with Lynn Coughham, an executive with Bechtel's London office.

The approval for CIA covers came directly from Steve Bechtel, who had his own ties to the agency. In March 1951, while his company's Middle East crews were pushing toward Tapline's Mediterranean terminus, Bechtel became a charter member of the National Committee for a Free Asia, an organization devoted to fighting Communism and promoting free enterprise. The brainchild of Allen Dulles, NCFA, which later changed its name to the Asia Foundation, included in its membership such Bechtel friends and associates as Henry Kaiser, Socal chairman Gwin Ferris and Pan Am chairman Juan Trippe. Together, the members of the Asia Foundation sponsored a number of propaganda activities, most notably "Radio Free Asia," a Far Eastern counterpart of Radio Free Europe. In 1967,[13] after press reports identified the Asia Foundation as a CIA front, the group's trustees admitted that funding for RFA and its other activities had come from the CIA. Subsequently, the Asia Foundation was banned in India, Thailand and most of the other countries in which it had operated.

According to Simpson's papers, the Asia Foundation membership was only one of a number of links Bechtel had with the CIA. At the invitation of Allen Dulles, Steve Bechtel also served as the agency's liaison with the Business Council, and in that capacity provided regular reports on tidbits council members had picked up overseas. In addition, Steve and many of his colleagues on the council like John T. Connor, chairman of the Allied Chemical Corporation, were debriefed by the agency after they'd made trips abroad.

In reciprocity for their cooperation, the government often provided Steve senior and his colleagues with privileged information that could prove vital to their operations overseas. As an example, Council records indicate that on several occasions in 1964 and 1965, CIA director John McCone and U.S. ambassador to Indonesia Howard Jones privately briefed Steve senior and other Business Council members on the rapidly deteriorating situation in Indonesia. Bechtel, Socal, Texaco and other companies headed by Council members had extensive dealings in that part of the world and were concerned because Indonesia's President Sukarno was nationalizing U.S. business interests there. On behalf of the Business Council, Steve expressed his immense gratitude to McCone and Jones for these briefings and monitored developments in Indonisea closely. In October 1965, in what a number of CIA alumni have since charged was an Agency-backed coup, Sukarno was ousted and replaced by President Suharto, who proved far more receptive to U.S. business interests than his predecessor.

Steve senior and John Simpson were Bechtel's liaisons with the intelligence community at the high levels, but in the field, Bechtel worked with Washington through one of its key executives, a dashing figure in Savile Row suits with the redoubtable name of C. Stribling Snodgrass.

A native of West Virginia, Snodgrass had attended Annapolis and seen combat action during World War I. In 1927 Snodgrass had resigned from the Navy and moved to London, where he found employment as a consultant to several major oil companies, among them Standard Oil of California, which subsequently introduced him to Bechtel. On trips home to the United States, Snodgrass met frequently with Bechtel, and a friendship took—one that was to be most useful to both men in the years ahead.

In 1939, with war in Europe imminent, Snodgrass had returned to the United States and duty with the Navy as a senior-level nonuniformed officer on the British desk of Naval Intelligence. He remained interested in oil, however, as did the Navy, which in 1942 detached him to work for Harold Ickes' Petroleum Administration for War. Snodgrass rose eventually to become head of the PAW's foreign-operations division, and Ickes appointed him in that capacity to a top-secret delegation dispatched in 1943 to survey the world's oil reserves and plan how they might be developed for the war effort.

Headed by Everette Degrolyer, assistant deputy administrator of the PAW, the Degrolyer Mission, as it came to be called, was stocked with men who would later play key roles in the U.S. oil industry. Besides Snodgrass, they included Ralph K. Davies, on leave from Socal, James Terry Duce, on leave from the Texas Oil Company and later to become Aramco's chief contact with the State Department and CIA, and Earle E. Garde, former director of Union Oil of California and since 1938, director of process engineering for Bechtel-McCone.

Garde, who was the PAW's head of economic warfare, proved his worth when the Degrolyer Mission reached Mexico in late August 1942. They were met at the airport by U.S. Ambassador George S. Messersmith, who arranged for them to meet with senior Mexican officials and survey Mexican oil fields and facilities.[14] Garde reported in detail on what they saw to Secretary of State Cordell Hull. Quietly, he also briefed Bechtel, who within days of the mission's return to the United States contacted Hull to volunteer Bechtel-McCone's services in upgrading the Mexican petroleum infrastructure. Six weeks later, in October 1942, Garde filed a report to Degrolyer spelling out what needed to be done to beef up the Mexican fields. One month after that, this time wearing his Bechtel hat, Garde submitted an engineering study based on his work on the Degrolyer mission to a Mexican Shell company—Compañía Petrolera La Nacional, SA—which consisted of one American lawyer working out of a room in Washington's Shoreham Hotel. On the basis of that engineering study, Compañía

Petrolera La Nacional secured $20.8 million in funding from the United States and hired Bechtel-McCone to build a new refinery and pipeline system.

Snodgrass, meanwhile, had not been idle. In December 1943, he and several of his fellow Degrolyer Mission colleagues (among them a smoothly polished State Department official named Alger Hiss) spent three weeks surveying oil potential in the Middle East. They found oil aplenty, and in their report asserted that "the national security of the U.S. may depend on availability of Middle East oil." The report, whose highlights Snodgrass passed to Bechtel, paid special attention to Saudi Arabia, recommending that the United States do everything possible to develop the kingdom's oil-producing capabilities forthwith. It was that report, drafted largely by Snodgrass, which had led to Bechtel's collaboration with Aramco.

Snodgrass himself spent the remainder of the war as head of the PAW's foreign-refinery division, working with the military and the State Department in devising plans to secure oil installations against sabotage and attack. According to PAW records, he also furnished "military agencies with maps and other data concerning refinery installations in enemy territory"—information that was critical in planning bombing attacks. What refineries were left standing were under Snodgrass' purview as well. In tandem with the Army and Navy, Snodgrass, according to PAW records, drew up "secret plans for the rehabilitation of facilities . . . occupied by enemy forces." Snodgrass was happiest, however, as a field agent. After Germany's surrender, he flew there and personally coordinated the transfer of German oil assets for use in the Pacific campaign.

The end of the war also meant the end of the PAW. Snodgrass, however, did not lack for employment. The administration had barely closed its doors when he was hired by Steve Bechtel, who appointed him, in the words of his letter of introduction to Abdullah Suleiman,[15] "Executive Representative in charge of all affairs and relations between the Saudi Arab Government and International Bechtel, Inc., pertaining to operations in the Kingdom of Saudi Arabia and elsewhere."

Such, at least, was Snodgrass' title. In fact, he functioned—both for the CIA and for Bechtel—as a Middle East intelligence agent.

His main contact in Washington was Richard Sanger, then head of the State Department's Saudi Arabian desk. Routinely, Snodgrass would brief Sanger on Bechtel's activities in Saudi Arabia and receive information useful to Bechtel from Sanger in turn. Soon Snodgrass started asking Sanger for favors as well. Initially, they involved small items, like arranging priority air travel for a party of Bechtel engineers soon to leave the United States to prepare a detailed study of Saudi Arabia's transportation needs.[16] As time went on, however, Snodgrass' needs became more complex and he began turning to more sensitive sources for help. One was General S. F. Chamberlain, director of intelligence at the War Department, who in June 1947 provided Bechtel with a secret aerial survey of eastern Saudi Arabia, which Bechtel subsequently turned over to the Saudi government, then feverishly laying out roads in preparation for war.

Snodgrass proved so valuable in Saudi Arabia that Bechtel began dispatching him on economic intelligence-gathering missions to Europe and the United States as well. After one especially busy mission to Europe in April 1946, Snodgrass wrote to Bechtel detailing no fewer than eight major projects being undertaken by Bechtel customers and rivals. Included were a French fuel-oil plant in Le Havre; a series of cement plants being planned by the Swiss; a British refinery in Southampton; a power plant in Belgium and assorted major petroleum projects scattered across the Continent—all of which Snodgrass had learned about in less than twenty-four hours.

He was equally adept at picking up political information from his friends in the CIA. After receiving a decoded agency cable from one of his sources in Saudi Arabia in July 1950, shortly after the outbreak of the Korean war, Snodgrass passed along the data to Bechtel. It read:

Judging by the statement Jeddah Arabs and local diplomats from other Arab countries Egypt refusal to support UN action in Korea has made unfortunate favorable impression. Hope still held that Saudi Arabia and Lebanon may support UN. Basis of neutrality propaganda is bitter Arab experience with UN and U.S. in Palestine and fear that action in Korea may also be contrary to wishes inhabitants South Korea. Voice of America and other U.S. propagandists would do well to cite evidence South Koreans want U.S. armed help instead of citing UN authority for U.S. actions. Policy of Iraq and Jordan will depend on British pressure. Unfortunately British in Jeddah have been referring cynically to "America's little war in Korea" instead of "our war."[17]

Inspired by Snodgrass' cloak-and-daggering, Steve Bechtel embarked on intelligence-gathering missions of his own. After one such foray to Teheran in October 1950, he shared with Snodgrass what he had learned at the U.S. Embassy, apparently from Kermit Roosevelt, son of

President Theodore, chief of the CIA's operations in the Middle East, and later architect of the coup that overthrew the Mossadeq government:

> Our friend in Teheran feels that there will be no actual movement southward by the northern neighbors [the Soviet Union] unless it is part of a world-wide activity. He says while they are there and ready, every indication is that they recognize that any movement whatsoever would be the spark that would set off a world-wide program [World War III].
>
> Our friend is more worried about the dilatoriness and slowness of the Export-Import Bank than anything else. He chafes under the delays and red tape. This amuses me because of the fact that he, more than most people, should know of the problems of getting anything done in Washington.
>
> All in all, we had a most pleasant trip to Teheran, the result of which is that I feel better about the situation in that area.[18]

Bechtel was at least partly correct. Bluntly warned by the United States that intervention in Iran would indeed trigger a "world-wide program," Soviet troops stayed behind their borders. The internal situation in Iran, however, continued to deteriorate, and in 1951, with the oil companies under increasing pressure from Mossadeq, Snodgrass took a year's leave of absence from Bechtel to return to government service as chief of foreign operations for the Petroleum Administration for Defense. One of his first assignments was to go to Teheran to confer secretly with Mossadeq. According to Snodgrass' diary notes of October 26, 1951, the socialist prime minister did not appear to bear the oil companies any particular grudge. The British, he said, could continue pumping and distributing Iranian oil, as long as Iran maintained control over the operation. As for the United States, Snodgrass quoted Mossadeq as calling it "the world leader in maintaining peace."

Mossadeq's good wishes were apparently not sufficient for Snodgrass' superiors, and shortly thereafter, the CIA's Operation Ajax got off the drawing board.

Snodgrass himself soon returned to Washington, where he helped undercut Mossadeq's position by developing alternative sources of oil and was a frequent participant in National Security Council meetings and CIA briefings. He also kept in continuing touch with Bechtel, to whom he relayed such helpful items as U.S. government projections on Middle East oil reserves, and tips on upcoming refinery projects, such as one in Puerto Rico that Bechtel later built. At the same time, Snodgrass continued to provide the company with an ongoing stream of classified political intelligence, including information—contained in a confidential letter to IBI vice-president Van Rosendahl, December 31, 1952—that a last-ditch attempt by Mossadeq to make peace with the United States was expected to fail.

In 1952, Snodgrass wound up his work as Bechtel's unofficial man in Washington, and went back to work for the company as a consultant. From this vantage point, he was able to feed intelligence about Saudi Arabia and other oil-producing countries in which Bechtel did business back to the intelligence community, even while lobbying for the Saudis in Washington. In 1954, Secretary of the Interior McKay appointed Snodgrass to a twenty-one-member military petroleum board that was to advise the United States on oil and gas matters which related to national security and defense. Subsequently, Snodgrass formed several Washington-based international consulting firms which counted Bechtel among their clients.

Snodgrass' new career took him all over the globe. He popped up in Pakistan in the early 1960s, advising the government on the development of its natural-gas reserves; emerged in Iran as a paid "energy consultant" to the Shah; spent time in Syria, New Zealand and Australia reviewing oil and copper production there and in 1972 was named petroleum advisor to the Sultan of Oman, while simultaneously serving as natural-resources advisor to Jordan's King Hussein—all the while passing information to the CIA and to Bechtel.

With the assistance of Snodgrass and his similarly well-connected successors (including former CIA director Richard Helms, who joined the company as an "international consultant" in 1978), Bechtel's operations increasingly mimicked those of the CIA. The company drew up its plans and plotted its business operations with the same devotion to secrecy and clandestine intelligence-gathering as its governmental associate, much of them based on reports furnished by friends at the CIA and the Departments of State, Commerce and Defense. These reports in turn were compiled into confidential weekly summaries, broken into political, military, economic and technological categories. Typical of the intelligence flavor of the documents was an October 1, 1976 report on Africa entitled, "Objective: Develop new and expanded business throughout the African continent." "Rhodesia will go black in the very near future," the report began.

Major strife for black factional control will commence and continue ... South African whites will retain power with continuing guerilla action and civil strife. Look for regional partitioning and black local rule in the distant future. ... The U.S. and Soviet Union will continue to attempt to dominate the Horn of Africa (Somalia, Ethiopia, Afars and Issas) for military and political reasons ... Despite talk of Arab oil monies being used for development in black countries, no great rapport will develop between the Arabs and the Blacks in Africa.

The report then advised how to capitalize on the situation:

Increased attention should be paid to cultivating U.S. aid and to cultivating sources in the Departments of Commerce, Agriculture and State and to a lesser extent with the Corps of Engineers ... Maintain a presence with African representatives in Washington D.C. and at the U.N. in New York ... Have no B.D. [Bechtel Development] effort directed to the Horn of Africa ... Emphasize ability in the French language in future recruitment ... Maintain existing B.D. and technical efforts toward Sudan/Egypt, Algeria, Senegal and Nigeria.

Circulated to key Bechtel executives, reports like the one on Africa provided a battle plan for the company's operations, and at least partly explained why Bechtel seemed to have such a knack for being in so many places at precisely the right time.

The arrangement was beneficial for both parties, Bechtel and CIA. The company and The Company had prospered in their years together, and in the years to come they would prosper further. It was, as most such friendships were for Steve Bechtel, "good business."

CHAPTER 11

▲

THE SUCCESSION

C hristmas at the Bechtels' was always a special time—a moment to acknowledge accomplishments and count blessings; an occasion when Steve and Laura; their son and daughter, Steve junior and Barbara, their spouses and the growing brood of grandchildren all came together, no matter how far afield the family had wandered the rest of the year.

The ritual for the holiday seldom varied. On Christmas Eve, the clan would gather at Steve and Laura's apartment on Lakeside Drive, in the building that Dad Bechtel, flush with his first big profits as a builder, had acquired in the 1920s. In the afternoon, they would watch delightedly as the children raced to the big living room and the Christmas tree towering over the glittering piles of presents (perhaps yellow Bechtel hard hats for the boys, dolls for the girls) personally selected and wrapped by Laura. While the adults ferreted out their own gifts, and sipped at drinks served by Steve's driver, Mike, the children —Steven junior and Betty had five, Shana, Lauren, Gary, Riley and Nonie—would slip downstairs to the grand ballroom Dad had installed, and where the glistening polished floors were wonderful for sliding.

THE SUCCESSION

Promptly at 7:00, the squealing youngsters would be summoned up-
stairs, and the family, augmented by relatives and favored company
executives, would sit down at the big dining-room table, which had
been enlarged for the occasion by the addition of several card tables,
covered with Laura's finest linens. Steve would say grace, and the meal
would begin with a shrimp cocktail. Then, one by one, the children
would be called upon to stand on their chairs and sing a carol or recite
a Christmas verse. As they sang, the adults would join in, following the
words on the specially printed programs that Laura had placed with
party favors by each plate.

Finally, with everyone ravenous, the Bechtels' maid would bring in a
turkey the size of a bass drum, basted golden brown. While Mike
served Lancer's rosé—the favored wine in the household of one of
California's great family dynasties—servant girls hired for the evening
passed sweet potatoes, giblet gravy and cranberry stuffing and for des-
sert, ice cream snowmen frozen so hard that one once slipped from a
serving spoon and shattered one of Laura's prized Dresden plates.

After dinner, as the men loosened their belts a notch or two and the
women joked about having to start a diet in the morning, the stuffed
revelers would get up slowly from the table and drift into the living
room to admire the tree a final time or exchange a word with a cousin
they'd missed talking to earlier in the day. Exactly at 10:00, Steve, a
habitually early-to-bed man, would rise and announce, "Well, boys
and girls, it's ten o'clock. Time to go home." There would be embraces
and "thank-you's" and "goodbyes," and another Christmastime at the
Bechtels' would come to an end.

So, with little deviation, it went every year—except for 1960. For
Steve Bechtel, his only son and the Bechtel Corporation, that
Christmas was a special one indeed.

It was twenty-seven years now since Steve Bechtel had taken over the
family business—more than two and a half decades of sweat, toil and
unprecedented growth. The company had become a corporate colos-
sus, with projects stretching around the world, and revenues topping $1
billion every year. Steve Bechtel, whose energy and enterprise had
made it possible, was proud of his labors—and at the age of 61, increasingly worn out by them as well.

He had never been a man with much time or use for rest. When he
golfed or hiked, it was in the company of business associates or clients,

the customers who made his company grow. His one nonbusiness hobby—stamp collecting—was no more than a minor diversion, and though his collection was valued in the millions, he entrusted its ongoing upkeep to one of his employees. Despite his vast fortune—in 1958, *Fortune* estimated his net worth at $250 million, making him one of the richest men in the United States—he lived simply. The Lakeside apartment, for instance, though spacious and comfortable, and adorned with knickknacks from his travels (including, over the fireplace in the den, a silver sword presented to him by King ibn Saud), was no more luxurious than that which might belong to a middle-ranking insurance executive. Except for his charities,* he was, in all, a confirmed penny-pincher, who hated to shop and regarded consumerism generally as wasteful indulgence. The one time he allowed himself some luxury was while on the road. If only for the sake of conducting meetings conveniently, he and Laura, his constant traveling companion, stayed in the best hotels in every city, including New York, where he maintained a permanently rented suite on the thirty-third floor of the Carlyle, and in Vienna, where the Bechtels favored the luxuriously grand Imperial,** at home in San Francisco, there were no frills. To go to and from the office and the airport, Steve had himself ferried in an aging Cadillac sedan.

Save for a collection of fine jewels, which spent most of their time in the company safe, his wife, Laura, was equally frugal. Partly to save

---

* The Bechtel family's numerous and generous charitable contributions are with few exceptions tied in one way or another to business. Among the recipients of Bechtel's beneficence are Oakland's Merrit Hospital (which the family refers to as "Bechtel Hospital"); the University of California at Berkeley (where Steve senior, who failed to graduate, contributed most of the money that built the Stephen D. Bechtel School of Engineering); Stanford University's International Student Center, The Ford Foundation and the American University of Beirut. Bechtel has also contributed millions to various programs around the world designed to turn out engineers and technicians, teaching them the skills necessary to operate Bechtel facilities. In addition, the Bechtel Foundation was the vehicle for the Bechtel Corporation's philanthropic efforts, while the family-run Lakeside Foundation supported many of Steve and Laura's Bay Area charity projects.

** Though he enjoyed the Carlyle and was considered a generous tipper, Bechtel was not happy about paying the annual rent, which in the early 1970s came to $17,000. At one point, when the hotel raised the rate to what Bechtel considered an extortionate level, he and Henry Ford II, another unhappy Carlyle guest and a fellow Ford Foundation director, seriously discussed buying the hotel. The idea passed; Bechtel's unhappiness didn't.

money, for example, she waited to buy Christmas cards until the postholiday sales. She would then take cards with her on all her husband's travels, passing her time while Steve was in meetings carefully inscribing each of the thousand in her luggage according to precise routine. To recipients on her "A" list—relatives, close friends, important company executives—went a card with a photo of the Bechtel clan and a long, expansive message, signed by Laura and Steve. The most special of all also received a gift: a bouquet of Bechtel-grown orchids arranged in an empty Lancer's bottle. Meanwhile, those on the "B" list—acquaintances, distant cousins, Bechtel lower-downs—had to settle for off-the-rack Hallmarks.

The precision of Laura's Christmas-card writing, like Steve's battered Cadillac and their unostentatious apartment, were symbols of how a no-nonsense family ran a no-nonsense company. The same quality was evident in the way they had raised their offspring.

Children were important to Steve Bechtel, both in themselves and as a measure of the men who fathered them. "A good man," he was fond of telling his executives, in tones suggesting an order, "gets married. A good man has children."[1]

Steve's own children, no less than his wife, set the corporate example. As adolescents, neither had attended private school, gone to cotillions, been treated to anything the least bit extravagant. After graduation from high school, daughter Barbara had become a surgical nurse—Bechtel women weren't doctors—married well (her husband was Paul Davies, Jr., an attorney with the prestigious San Francisco firm of Pillsbury, Madison and Sutro; his father was chairman of the FMC Corporation and a colleague of Steve's at the Business Council, the Export-Import Bank and the Bohemian Grove) and settled down to a life of good works and raising children. She was, said her beaming father, "the salt of the earth."

The same characterization could apply to Steve's son. More, however, was expected of Steve junior than of Barbara. Bechtel men were meant to work. Moreover, this particular Bechtel man was born to succeed. How that succession would be accomplished, when and in what form was a subject which as the turn of the decade approached was increasingly on his father's mind.

There had never been any doubt that one day, someday, Stephen D. Bechtel, Jr., would take over the company Steve senior had built. Besides Bechtel blood, he had all the other requisite qualifications. As a child, he had traveled like his father before him, from jobsite to jobsite, the only difference being that where Steve senior had lived in a tent, his son found shelter in a private railway car. After attending grammar and junior high school in Oakland, he had gone to high school in the affluent suburb of Piedmont. Steve senior, though, had taken precautions lest the good life become too alluring. Most of all, he insisted that Steve junior work, and work hard. As a result, while his classmates were spending their summers lazing at the beach or cruising in convertibles, young Bechtel, richer than all of them, was laboring on a survey crew at the Oakland Port of Debarkation Bechtel-McCone was building for the Navy.

The few free hours he had were spent either sailing or hiking; and even then, there was a purposefulness to his leisure. Speaking of the sailboat racing in which he excelled, he said years later: "You've got to look ahead and plan your maneuvers and tactics. It teaches you to order your thinking and figure out what is going to happen and how to get where you are going at the right time."[2] He was likewise intense about his hiking. As he used up provisions and his backpack grew lighter, he would load it with rocks to demonstrate his self-discipline. *

To demonstrate it further, Steve enlisted in his senior year of high school in the Marine Corps Reserve, which, eager for officer material, especially engineers, sent him to the University of Colorado. There Steve distinguished himself principally by his diligence. "In college particularly," he admitted later, "I learned early on I wasn't as smart as some of the other kids. I had to work at it. The only way to do that was to organize my time."[3]

Fortunately, Steve junior had inherited his mother's aptitude for organization, and with it he managed to get through freshman year. He also managed to survive the following summer, spent at the Marine Corps's Parris Island boot camp. By the time classes resumed in the fall—at Purdue, to which the corps sent him after the Colorado program had shut down for lack of volunteers—he could march all day in the sun, make a bed from which a dime could be bounced six inches and press his trousers with a crease as sharp as a knife edge.

That—and toughness—was what the corps was looking for; but by the time Steve junior graduated and was commissioned a second lieu-

---

* Similarly, since becoming head of the company, Steve takes the elevator to the fourteenth floor of his office building each morning and then methodically climbs the remaining nine floors to his office. The stair-climbing is intended less as exercise than as a form of self-discipline.

tenant, World War II was over. The service offered him a choice: he could take up a career as an officer or without serving a day of active duty, continue in civilian life. Steve, who would later make much of his "service" in the corps and design a corporate logo similar to the Marines globe-and-anchor emblem, opted for the latter.

Whatever regret Steve may have felt at missing out on combat and Marine Corps life was offset by a girl he had met in high school who, in the summer of 1945, became his wife.

Her name was Betty Hogan, and she was everything a Bechtel wife was expected to be: ever-supportive, low-keyed (her hobby was collecting twine), pleasant-mannered. Steve senior and Laura adored her.

They also approved of Steve junior's enrollment in the MBA program at Stanford, where he came under the tutelage of Paul Holden, one of the leading business consultants of the day. They were less enthusiastic, however, when, following graduation from Stanford in 1947, Steve announced he was going into business for himself, building houses on the Menlo Park peninsula. Rather than confront his son directly, Steve senior set out to change his mind by subtler means—namely, by taking Steve junior and his bride along on a three-month round-the-world cruise. It would be a belated honeymoon, Bechtel senior promised—a chance to visit the Philippines, Tokyo, Shanghai, Hong Kong, India, the Middle East and the major capitals of Europe. Though he did not say so, it would also give his son a chance to see the Bechtel Corporation at work around the globe.

By the time the Bechtels' ship docked in the United States, all thoughts of house-building and 9:00-to-5:00 days had disappeared. Steve junior had seen the world of Bechtel and he wanted to be part of it. Conveniently, one of Bechtel's senior executives was waiting with a job offer. There was a pipeline down in Texas, he said. Was Steve interested? "Hell, yes," he exclaimed.

The conditions in Texas and the other pipelining sites where Steve junior worked the next several years were nearly as difficult as those at Boulder twenty years before. Gradually and determinedly, though, Steve junior worked his way up—assistant superintendent, then spread supervisor, then division manager—never complaining, earning every raise and promotion. When, eight years after he joined the company, a Bechtel engineer was needed in New York, Steve, who was simultaneously handling projects in New England and Michigan as well, went off without a whimper, not only doing the job, but getting his New York State engineer's license in the bargain. "Everybody in the outfit knew I was sitting for the goddam thing," he recalled, after the months of after-hours studying were over and the license won. "If I hadn't passed it, I might as well have never come back."[4]

His comment was good-humored, but he could also be hard when the occasion demanded. That was demonstrated in Texas, where one of his early supervisors, a man who had been good to him and to whom he had become especially close, was running into trouble on a rush job. Steve did not interfere when his mentor was replaced and exiled to corporate limbo for the remainder of his career.

Pleased as he was with his son's performance, Steve senior was growing impatient. He had wearied of supervising Bechtel's day-to-day business and was anxious for his son to take over the administrative load, freeing him to concentrate on deal-making. Moreover, he was growing concerned about the changing nature of the construction business. Long past were the days when a man like himself could do nearly anything he pleased—put up a bridge, open a mine, drill for oil— wherever it looked promising. Now there were rules to be followed, procedures to be adhered to, thickets of red tape through which to pass. Everything, in short, had become immeasurably more complicated. The construction business had also gotten vastly larger. When Steve senior started out, a million-dollar deal had been counted as a major project; now Bechtel was taking on jobs budgeted in the hundreds of millions. The stakes were higher and there was less latitude for error. The construction business called not just for toughness, imagination and connections, but for disciplined analytical planning and thinking. In one of his earliest managerial jobs, as a member of John Simpson's finance committee, Steve junior had shown a good grasp of the business, and equally important, a willingness to make hard decisions. All the same, he needed more experience, and the time to give it to him, his father decided, had arrived. There were, however, two problems: persuading Steve junior, who had become enamored of pipelining, and, trickier, devising a way to vault him over more seasoned executives who, if miffed, could touch off a palace revolt.

In mid-1957, Bechtel discussed the situation with two of his closest confidants: his financial advisor, John Simpson, and his attorney, Bob Bridges. Neither had any desire to run the company, but both agreed that Steve junior's elevation had to be handled delicately. Their particular concern was the sensibilities of three senior executives: Perry Yates, the longtime head of the company's Power Division: Bill Waste, the equally longtime chief of the Refinery and Chemical Division, and

George Cooley, Steve senior's friend since childhood and the boss of International. All were men with considerable egos, and just as considerable ambition. As long as they remained in their positions, there was no room at the top for Steve junior.

Accepting Simpson and Bridges' recommendation to temporize, Bechtel contented himself by naming Steve junior head of the Pipeline Division. Then, in 1958, tragedy provided an opening: George Cooley was murdered by an Iraqi mob. "When George died," Bridges recalled, "the first thought was to make Perry Yates the head of International. But John [Simpson] and I went to Steve senior and said, 'Look we're bringing Steve along. You want him to get control of each of these divisions ultimately. Make him the head of International now and make Jerry Komes [who had been Cooley's deputy] report to him.'"[5] Bechtel took the advice. He also used the opportunity to appoint his reluctant but dutiful son chairman of a newly formed three-member executive committee, giving him the bureaucratic edge on his putative rivals, Waste and Yates.

The creation of the executive committee, which reported exclusively to Steve senior, cut deeply into the power of Yates and Waste, who had run their divisions as self-described "little kings." It also provided Steve junior with the chance to observe at close range the company's other operations. The more he saw, the more he apparently liked. There was still, though, the problem of easing him past Waste and Yates.

Of the two rivals, Waste was the decided lesser concern. Though hardworking and good with detail, right down to personally selecting the color photographs of Bechtel projects that decorated the company headquarters, Waste was fundamentally a deskman, lacking both in field experience and in the stuff of corporate command. "I'm the feet-on-the-floor man," he said of himself, "while Steve does the flying."[6] Yates, however, was a different story—a highly competent, hard-charging executive, with twice Steve junior's experience, and possessed of an abundance of savvy and skill. Around the company, it was assumed that he would move into the top slot when Bechtel retired. Steve junior was only in his mid-30s, the speculation went; he could afford to wait his turn.

But in 1959, tragedy struck Yates, just as it had Cooley the year before. He contracted polio, and he soon retired, clearing the last obstacle to Steve junior's succession. The following year, shortly before Christmas, Steve senior called a meeting of the board to propose a corporate reorganization. He moved that Steve junior be appointed company president, while he continued the next five years as chairman and chief executive officer. To no one's surprise, the motion passed unanimously.

In the Bechtel household, the traditional Christmas feast was over, many of the guests departed, the dishes all put away. It was after 10:00, past Steve senior's bedtime, when the old man motioned his son and Betty into his study. He wanted to tell them how proud of them he was. They were an exemplary couple in every respect, a living representation of everything for which the Bechtel family and company stood. And as a token of his esteem, he would give them a special gift—a big house in Piedmont with a swimming pool, a tennis court and a dining room that would seat fifty—a room in which Steve junior and Betty could themselves host the family Christmas dinners someday. "Merry Christmas, you two," he told them. Steve senior had never been given to sentimentality or displays of emotion, but tonight there were tears in his eyes.

CHAPTER 12

▲

TAKING COMMAND

I n taking over as Bechtel's president, Steve Bechtel, Jr., sounded a brave note. He would run the business, he told his executives, with the same vigor and vision with which it had always been run. Nonetheless, there would be changes. He was a different man from his father, with a different background and different personality. From now on, Steve junior asserted, he would impose "my style of doing things."

They were fine words; but if Steve Bechtel, Jr., expected his father to fade into the background, he soon found he was mistaken.

Freed from the administrative chores he so detested, Steve senior was, if anything, even more dominant than before—and as his pile of used air tickets attested, just as much in motion. He spent fully six months of the year on the road, popping up one day in London, the next in Toronto, a third in Beirut, Seoul, Sydney or Rome. In his wake, he left a lengthening string of deals: phosphorous, zirconium, iron and nickel mines in South Africa; copper mines, mills and smelters in Chile, Mauritania and Ireland; pipelines in Germany and Switzerland; nuclear plants in Spain and India; hydroelectric complexes in New Zealand and Newfoundland, and, in the Canadian province of Quebec, a giant hydroelectric project that, when complete, would generate 5.25 million kilowatts of power and create a reservoir nearly half the size of Lake Ontario. So boundless was his energy that by the middle 1960s the Bechtel Corporation had operations in 22 countries on five continents, which together were bringing more than $3 billion per year.

To be sure, there were some miscues along the way. In Saudi Arabia, Bechtel had a temporary falling-out with its old partner Aramco over what Aramco considered cavalier treatment by Bechtel. "There was a period," explained former Aramco chairman Frank Jungers, "when Bechtel took its Aramco dealings for granted, and we phased Bechtel out and replaced them with another construction company, the Fluor Corporation. From the late 1950s to the mid-1960s our relations with Bechtel were at low ebb."[1] And then there was the great Indian fertilizer fiasco.

The Indian misadventure had begun in April 1964, when Steve senior, in the company of several members of the Business Council, visited New Delhi on a State Department–sponsored tour to drum up business.[2] Included in the American delegation was Bechtel's friend General Lucius Clay, whose presence cannot have been reassuring to the Indians. Seven months before, it had been largely his testimony to Congress which had doomed a provision of a foreign aid bill that would have underwritten India's construction of a badly needed steel mill. Clay had opposed the grant on the ground that building things like steel mills should be done by private companies (such as, notably, Bechtel), not by governments. The Indians had been infuriated, and along with them, U.S. Ambassador John Kenneth Galbraith, who charged that "for blatant ideological reasons [Clay] is going back to the policies of the Eisenhower Administration."[3] The ones left happy by the whole affair were the Russians, who, having no scruples about a government's doing anything, had built the steel mill for the Indians.

In any event, there Clay was, sitting alongside Bechtel, as Steve, who was interested in building nuclear plants in India, tried to smooth things over by telling Indian officials that he would like to relieve their food shortages by building several massive fertilizer plants. It was an idea that everyone liked: the Indians; the new American ambassador, Chester Bowles; the State Department and, not least, Bechtel, who saw the fertilizer plants generating hundreds of millions in additional business, not merely in India but across the Third World. Initially, the Indians had only one reservation: they wanted a feasibility study undertaken to confirm that the outlook for fertilizer was as rosy as Bechtel claimed. Fine, replied Steve; he'd have the Stanford Research Institute produce one. The $400,000 study (paid for by the Indians) came back confirming Bechtel's opinions, and then some: not only would one fertilizer plant be good for India, it said, but five—all to be built by Bechtel—would be even better.

From there on, things moved quickly. Returning to the United States, Bechtel rounded up support for the project from his friends at Texaco, Gulf, Hercules, Esso, Mobil, Shell, FMC, Allied Chemical and the investment-banking firm of Lehman Brothers, where Clay, who'd recently become a partner in the firm, promised to arrange the financing. He also stayed in touch with the State Department and the U.S. embassy, both of which were lobbying furiously for the project in hopes that it would generate $1 billion in U.S. investments in the country. During a trip to the subcontinent, even Averell Harriman got an oar in, by urging Indian officials to give a prompt go-ahead. When the Indians, because of bureaucratic conflicts, began foot-dragging, State turned up the pressure a notch, by warning that unless approval was soon forthcoming, the United States might undertake a review of its aid policies toward India. That, in turn, produced a blast from the *Financial Express* of New Delhi, which editorialized: "What is so shocking is that U.S. officials should identify themselves so much with the Bechtel proposal as to even hold out a threat of change in American attitude towards aid in this country."[4]

Nonetheless, the threats appeared to work, and by early September 1964, Bechtel and Clay were ready to return to India to close the deal. They spent five days in New Delhi haggling over details; all, however, seemed to be going well. Then, just before departing for the United States, Clay availed himself of an airport press conference to lecture the Indian government on its responsibility to approve the project, since he and Bechtel had gone to all the trouble of raising funds. That, alone, might have been enough to kill the deal. But there was more. In return for their participation in the fertilizer project, it developed, the American companies wanted certain concessions. Allied Chemical, for instance, made its commitment contingent on India's granting the company rights to its potash reserves, while the oil companies were insisting on similar access to the country's petrochemical resources. Bechtel's own demands were more modest: it wanted in on building a big refinery. Fed up, finally, with their high-handed treatment, the Indians told Bechtel to peddle his fertilizer elsewhere.

Which, as it happens, is precisely what he did, later selling a virtually identical plan to the government of Algeria.

Nothing, apparently, could stop him—not nettlesome governments
("to hell with both governments," he said to a partner, when they were
experiencing difficulties in getting U.S. and Soviet approval for a proposed pipeline in Siberia. "We'll find a way to build this pipeline some-
how"),[5] not the vagaries of airlines (once, when engine trouble on a
Pan Am flight to Tokyo grounded Bechtel in Alaska, he merely called
the president of the airline and had another 747 diverted to pick him
up), not other people's schedules (informed on one occasion that San
Francisco mayor Joseph Alioto would not be able to attend an impromptu dinner party he was hosting for Charles Lindbergh because of
a prior commitment, Bechtel "ordered" him to come; he did), not
age—and certainly not the coming to power of John Fitzgerald Kennedy.

Bechtel hadn't been pleased by the defeat of his friend Richard
Nixon; but the pain was lessened when the new president appointed
another old friend, C. Douglas Dillon, secretary of the Treasury, and,
later, an even older and better one, John McCone, as director of the
CIA. Such friendships—and there were others in the Kennedy administration, including General Clay, who was dispatched as the president's special representative to Berlin—gave Bechtel assured entrée to
the new administration. Not that he particularly needed assistance;
such was Bechtel's personal clout that the president himself was inviting him to call.

Still, the presence of all those Democrats in Washington seemed to
make Bechtel uneasy, and during the Kennedy years he spent more and
more time in New York, where, in his suite at the Carlyle, he regularly
gathered for dinner corporate cronies like Juan Trippe, Texaco chairman Augustus Long, Lucius Clay, FMC chairman Paul Davies and
Morgan Bank chairman and former Defense secretary Thomas Gates.

These Carlyle get-togethers followed an invariable script. After dinner in the Versailles Suite, Laura and the other wives would retire to
another hotel room for liqueurs and coffee, leaving the men to their
brandy and cigars and the business of the evening. At the start, Steve
would always appoint a discussion chairman—usually Juan Trippe,
because Trippe liked the role and was good at it. Then the guests
would talk in turn about their political concerns and the trends and
opportunities they saw developing that might have a bearing on their
operations. Gus Long, for instance, usually offered a reading on oil

prices, while Steve might tell the group of his latest visit to Saudi Arabia or of a recent tête-à-tête in Washington with John McCone. Gates, who frequently visited Europe and still had high-level contacts in the Pentagon, often voiced concern that NATO was not up to deterring the Russians. Davies would follow up with an even more pessimistic assessment of the worsening situation in Southeast Asia, where his company had major interests. As the talk wore into the night, plates became countries, napkins mountain ranges, salt and pepper shakers armies. Huddled over the dinner table, eyes gleaming like schoolboys, Steve Bechtel and his aging friends pushed them to and fro.

While his father was planning the future of the world and Bechtel's role in it, Steve Bechtel, Jr., was not having an easy time. He was just as energetic as the elder Bechtel, routinely working sixteen-hour days six, even seven days a week, and traveling just as extensively, racking up, on average, 250,000 air miles per year. He did his homework, informing himself on the details of each and every Bechtel project; he went into the field, peppering his employees with pointed, well-thought-out questions; he demonstrated he was tough, "taking a man's head off," as one executive put it, if he failed to deliver a sufficiently succinct presentation.* But unlike his father, who had taken over a relatively small company without the family patriarch watching over him, Steve junior was in nominal command of a giant corporation, with tens of thousands of employees, many of whom still looked to Steve senior for leadership.

Comparisons were inevitable, and at least at first, the slightly built (5 feet 10 inches, 155 pounds), reclusive "Junior," as his enemies derisively called him, was found wanting. Some Bechtel employees thought him cold and arrogant; others found him charmless and plodding; still others faulted him for failing ever to follow his father's practice of inquiring after Bechtel employees, their lives, wives and children, many of whom Steve senior knew by name. He was also, said his critics, utterly lacking in humor. Once, when one of the company's brightest wits, a sophisticated businessman who had traveled the world over, handling Bechtel's most delicate problems, was preparing to make a presentation for Steve and other senior executives, he jocularly cautioned that what they were about to hear "might be too deep for the

---

* At home, Steve could be equally stern. He laid down a strict rule that none of his five children could cry in his presence and if they disobeyed him would punish them by sending them to their rooms.

engineers in the room." All those present—engineers to a man—exploded in laughter. All, that is, except Steve junior, who stormed out in a huff.

The basic problem was that Steve junior was Steve junior—not his father. Said one sympathetic Bechtel observer: "He was in a terribly difficult position, taking over from the largest builder in the world, and it had to leave scars. Around the company, he was regarded as the not-so-smart, not-so-great, not-so-dynamic son of Steve senior. He could run a tight ship, be an excellent businessman and a good builder, but he didn't have his father's flair."[6]

As his father had with the Broadway Tunnel, Steve junior also ran into trouble, though the difficulties he encountered lay not with a particular project but with corrupt politicians.

The situation involved a 90-mile pipeline Bechtel was building for Texaco in 1964. Part of the line was to run from the Delaware River through Woodbridge, New Jersey, a suburban hamlet that had recently been honored by *Look* magazine as an "All American City." When the pipeline managers sought a building permit from Woodbridge mayor Walter Zirpolo, though, the response was anything but All-American; to grant the permit, Zirpolo wanted a bribe of $60,000.

Not wishing to become involved in what was, after all, a felony, but still eager to build the pipeline, the managers kicked the problem to Bechtel vice-president and pipeline manager Harry Waste, a son, as it happened, of Steve junior's key executive Bill Waste. Young Waste found himself in something of a bind, for Bechtel was still in the process of negotiating the pipeline process with Woodbridge officials. If he turned down the request, the deal might be blown, which would not stand him in a good stead in San Francisco. If he acceded, and was caught, he faced a jail term. He resolved the dilemma in time-honored corporate fashion, by telling the pipeline managers he needed a few weeks to arrange the payoff, then passing along the dirty work to a subordinate named William L. Fallow. Shortly thereafter, Bechtel's contract with the pipeline company went through, renegotiated upward by $1 million.

Fallow, meanwhile, was arranging the details of the bribe. With the complicity of Harry Waste and several other senior Bechtel executives, including the company treasurer, he drew a check on the company's account at the Morgan Guaranty Trust Company of New York for $20,000, made out to "cash." This was to be the first of three payments Bechtel promised to make, and Fallow delivered a manila envelope stuffed full of $100 bills to the mayor in his private office at a nearby shopping center.

Steve junior hadn't known about the first payment, but several days before the second was to be made, he learned of it and exploded. In a rage, he summoned Waste to San Francisco and instructed him to secure from the pipeline managers a letter stating that they, not Bechtel, had authorized the payments, and a promise from the managers to reimburse Bechtel in full. Unless both were soon forthcoming, Bechtel said bluntly, Waste and Fallows would find themselves on the street.

Waste returned to New Jersey and did as ordered. He also arranged for the remaining two payments to be made to Zirpolo by a small local subcontractor called Gates Construction. The Bechtel Corporation, he assumed, was in the clear.

For a time, it seemed to be. Zirpolo delivered the permit, and the pipeline was built without further incident. Then, in May 1966, an FBI agent working on another New Jersey case stumbled across bank records stating that Bechtel had drawn a $20,000 check made out to cash. Large companies, the agent realized, did not use cash unless they had something to hide. He began probing further and eventually a federal grand jury was called. On February 24, 1967, it handed up a nine count indictment charging Zirpolo, the Bechtel Corporation, Gates Construction, the pipeline managers and several other firms that had become involved with two conspiracies to use interstate mails for the purposes of bribery. Each of the accused parties "passed a dirty job down to the next one because each knew what they were doing was unlawful," the federal prosecutor said in summary. The jury concurred and convicted all the defendants except for Zirpolo, who was convicted later in a separate trial but then won a retrial.*

Steve junior personally was not charged with anything. His penalty was merely severe embarrassment.

Though the pipeline episode had been a fiasco, just as the Broadway Tunnel had been thirty years before, Steve, like his father, had learned from it. He would be wary from now on of the company old guard and the traditional Bechtel way of doing things. Soon he would establish a mandatory retirement age in order to ease out his father's old pal Bill Waste, whose operations, obviously, demanded closer scrutiny. He

* The defendants were fined, but the trial judge, Reynier J. Wortendyke, Jr., did not impose prison sentences, on the ground that their crime had not been one of violence.

would give them that scrutiny, and as he did, he would begin to put his mark on the company.

In 1965, with his father's formal retirement and his own elevation to chairman and chief executive officer, Steve junior demonstrated just how independent he meant to be. He presented that year for his father's inspection a plan for a new corporate headquarters, a twenty-two-story, aluminum-skinned monolith that would rise at the intersection of Mission and Beale Streets. As he described the project, explaining the need to consolidate Bechtel's 10,000-member office force—now tied with Pacific Bell as the largest employers in the city —extolling the building's Skidmore, Owings & Merrill design, detailing how it would be equipped with satellite receivers and the latest Univac mainframes, the old man sat in stony, disapproving silence. To the other Bechtel executives in the room, the tension was almost palpable. For the first time, Steve junior was defying his father, and he was doing it in a way that no one could miss. He wasn't asking for approval, and he didn't need it. Junior was the boss.

When the building was finished, in 1968, it provided a home for virtually all of Bechtel's operations. Steve senior, however, remained behind in his old office at the former headquarters on Sansome Street.

The break with his father didn't trouble Steve junior. There was a saying at the Bechtel Corporation he liked to repeat: "A builder is measured by the length of his shadow." Steve Bechtel, Jr., had begun to cast his. With the help of a curious man named Armand Hammer in a curious place called Libya, it would lengthen even further.

CHAPTER 13

LIBYA

O f all the business relationships the Bechtel Corporation entered into over the years, none was stranger—and a few more lucrative—than its alliance in Libya with the international entrepreneur who shared his name with a baking soda.

Armand Hammer was unique: a multimillionaire capitalist who had made a fortune doing business with the Russians (among his best friends, he claimed, was Lenin, whom he had met in October 1922 and had struck deals with); a New York Jew who wheeled and dealt with (and was beloved by) Israel's bitterest enemies; a financial genius who looked, talked and acted like the cartoon character Mr. Magoo.

Yet this improbable, walnut-faced man, would, over the years, bring the Bechtel Corporation billions.

The means by which he would do it was, perhaps, the most improbable thing of all: through oil, and in, of all places, Libya.

The saga had its beginnings during the winter of 1957–58, when Hammer, who until then had made his money by importing and exporting items like cattle, Russian furs and art, invested $120,000 in a little-known, nearly bankrupt California oil company called Occidental

Petroleum. Hammer didn't claim to know much about oil—"I wouldn't have known a barrel of oil if I fell in it," he said later—but Occidental seemed promising, if only as a tax shelter. It turned out to be considerably more than that.

With Hammer's cash, Occidental began drilling wildcat wells in an abandoned Socal field in the San Joaquin Valley, east of San Francisco. Three years and more than a million dollars in additional Hammer money showed no notable results. Then, in 1961, the company made a major gas strike. Oxy and Armand Hammer were on their way.

The same year as the gas discovery, Hammer visited Libya as a member of a quasi-official trade delegation for the Kennedy administration. The trip didn't produce much commerce, but the sight of all those oil companies, pumping the Sahara, inspired Hammer. On his return to California, he dispatched a team of Occidental engineers to begin scouting for a supply of his own.

The search was prolonged and painstaking, and nearly five years went by before Hammer's engineers found a promising site. Before drilling could begin, however, Hammer had to secure a concession from the Libyan government, which, in turn, necessitated making certain financial arrangements with well-placed members of King Idris al Sanussi's entourage. In due course, a facilitator appeared: a self-styled Spanish "general" and international con man named Pegulu de Rovín. For $400,000, a fourth of which was to be placed in advance in a Swiss bank, de Rovín told Hammer, the fields could be his. Hammer paid.[1]

With financing from Allen and Co., a Wall Street investment bank, Hammer agreed as well to pay a group of Libyan officials, led by court minister Omar Shelbi, who offered to smooth the way with King Idris. Their fee: 3 percent of the sale price of every barrel of oil Hammer shipped out of the country. Between the officials and de Rovín—not to mention the cost of the five years Oxy's engineers had spent wandering in the Libyan desert—Hammer had made an expensive commitment. The investment, however, soon paid off. Awarded drilling rights to several supposedly worthless plots formerly owned by Mobil, Oxy drilled two miles into the earth and struck a pool of oil yielding a phenomenal 70,000 gallons a day.

Before Hammer could begin cashing in on his gusher, however, he had to resolve a host of problems. One was dealing with de Rovín and Allen and Co., both of whom he had abandoned when the well came in, and who had just as quickly filed lawsuits against him. Another was finding a way to cope with the battalions of Libyan contractors, sup-

pliers and government bureaucrats who had been besieging his offices
since news of the strike. Then there was the small matter of transporting the oil he had discovered 130 miles to the nearest port. A pipeline
would have to be built, costing tens of millions—money that Hammer
at the moment did not have. Moreover, the line would have to be built
quickly, since, under Libyan law, Hammer could not begin writing off
his exploration expenditures until he began exporting crude. As if all
this were not enough, rumors were spreading of an impending revolt
against the aged and decadent King Idris, who was now spending most
of his time with Queen Fatima vacationing on Turkey's Marmara coast.

When everything was put together, it was apparent that Hammer
needed assistance—and fast. Enter the Bechtel Corporation. Bechtel's
people knew oil, and they knew Libya: how to do business there, how
to build there—and how to pay the *baksheesh* that made both possible.

The company had been working in the country since 1958, when it
built a pipeline for the French government, then owner of a 10,000-
square-mile concession in Libya's western desert. The pipeline was a
relatively minor affair, as, at the time, was oil exploration in Libya
itself. Since gaining its independence in 1952, the country had been
struggling to overcome the devastation wrought by World War II, as
well as decades of Italian colonization. Port and refinery facilities were
meager; the most notable modern enterprise in the country was
Wheelus U.S. Air Force Base outside Tripoli, where nuclear-laden
Strategic Air Command bombers were ever on the alert.

The situation might never have changed, but for the Suez Crisis of
1956. With the canal temporarily blocked, oil shipments from the Persian Gulf had slowed to a comparative trickle. Much of the oil that was
getting through had to be shipped around the Cape of Good Hope,
making it vastly more expensive. Eager to develop a new supply of
cheap petroleum closer to Europe, the oil companies began moving
into Libya in droves.

One of those companies was Standard Oil of New Jersey (Esso),
which in 1959 contracted with Bechtel to build a 130-mile pipeline
from its fields in Zeltan to the Mediterranean port of Mersa Brega.
When IBI executive vice-president Jerry Komes arrived in Tripoli to
begin lining up the job, he was informed that contract or no, things
didn't get done in Libya unless "special arrangements" were made with
the king's chief advisor, Mustafa ben Halim. Without Halim's backing
on the Esso project, Bechtel experienced delays and frustrations.

Born in Tripoli and trained as an engineer at the Egyptian University in Alexandria, Halim had begun his career working for an Egyptian engineering firm. It was in Libyan politics, however, that the short, roly-poly Halim made his fortune. Returning to his native land, he became enmeshed in palace intrigues, and quickly rose to become minister of the oil-rich province of Cyrenaica, where he gained a reputation as a shrewd—and avaricious—politician. So much graft did Halim extort during his tour in Cyrenaica that he was eventually compelled to leave the province for fear of physical injury. Halim, however, had taken care to share his booty with the king and his courtiers, and with their backing he was named prime minister in 1954.

In his new post, Halim enriched his king and himself with a series of spectacular deals. The first was with the French government, which paid handsomely for its oil concession. The second was with the U.S. Air Force, which, according to former CIA officials,[2] paid Halim a $1 million fee for arranging the lease for Wheelus. It was the oil companies, though, which paid most of all.

Unlike the Iranians and Saudi Arabians, who awarded their countries' drilling rights to a single company or consortium, Halim divided Libya into dozens of grids or sectors, and gave out separate concessions to different oil companies, both the majors, like Esso, and the smaller independents, like Occidental. Halim was thus able to constantly play the oil companies against each other, sending the bidding for individual concessions higher and higher. The more oil companies were involved, the better it was for Halim, not only in bribes to gain concessions, but in kickbacks and contracts the companies were compelled to give, either to Halim directly or to Libyan companies controlled by him.

But Halim didn't restrict his demands to the oil companies. After leaving the government in 1959, he was soon putting the squeeze on Bechtel as well. His proposal was a simple one: if Bechtel wanted to work on a second pipeline project, this one for Oasis, the company would have to pay Halim a "retainer" of $2,500 a month—"walking-around money," as a former Bechtel director described it—and give his engineering and construction firm, Libeco, 10 percent of its net profits on all projects. According to former CIA officials, funds allocated for Libeco were to be paid to a London account controlled by Halim. Assuming all went well on the Oasis pipeline, Bechtel would then be rewarded with additional construction contracts. There was, in fact, no end to the work Bechtel could do in Libya—provided it cooperated with Halim.

Despite the millions of dollars that were conceivably at stake, Jerry

Komes and his superiors in San Francisco were uneasy. It was one thing to build a palace or two for a Saudi prince; it was quite another to enter into a formal business arrangement with someone the likes of Halim. Komes's reservations were evident in a November 25, 1960, memo he sent to Steve Bechtel, Jr. Under a "strictly confidential" heading, Komes wrote:

> I am convinced that our joint venture with Libeco is the only answer on a short-term basis. For the longer view, however, I think we should take steps to protect ourselves. There is no doubt that Libya is a volatile, explosive situation, and when the as-it-now-seems inevitable blow up occurs, many could be hurt.

To deal with the danger—and to buffer Bechtel from it—Komes proposed that Steve junior adopt a four-point plan:

1. Through your father's friends at the State Department, try to get a confidential briefing on Libya and Ben Halim.
2. The same effort should be made at the CIA.
3. Play our hand cautiously in Libya and be most circumspect in our acts and associations.
4. Consider some local publicity as the project progresses. Take advantage of the fact that we were urged by the oil companies into this joint venture and tie the oil companies into the picture as much as possible so that we may look to them for help in the future.

Whatever reservations Steve junior may have had about Komes's recommendations disappeared a few months later when, on a flight to Libya, he found himself sitting next to William Crane Eveland, a veteran Middle East CIA agent, then being given "cover" employment by the Vinnell Corporation, an Alhambra, California–based company that did petroleum-related construction work in Saudi Arabia and Iran as well as Libya. Eveland, who was about to leave the agency to join Vinnell full time, was well acquainted with Halim, and he gave Steve junior a blunt piece of advice: if he wanted to work in Libya, his company had better play ball. "The formula," he said, "is straightforward and simple. Ben Halim or one of his brothers shares in the contract, and the payments for their 'services' are made in a foreign bank account." That was the way the oil companies did business in Libya, Eveland counseled;[3] if the Bechtel Corporation wanted to join them, it should get on board.

Bechtel did, and wound up going Vinnell and the other oil companies one better. Not only did it agree to Halim's participation in the construction of the Oasis pipeline—and later, one for Mobil as well—it became, in time, Halim's principal intermediary with the oil companies. Whatever the companies problems—from engineering services to importing fuel to building refineries and roads—Bechtel took care of them, and in the process, ensured that Halim and other local businessmen got their cut. In exchange for these services, Bechtel tacked a fee of up to 18 percent onto its operating charges. Freed from the bother of dealing with Libeco or other local businesses, the oil companies were happy to pay.

And as it turned out, so was Armand Hammer.

Bechtel was well aware of Hammer's operations in Libya, as well as how desperately he required a pipeline. It had also learned that the contract for the Occidental pipeline job was about to go to another American contractor, Williams Brothers. However, the deal had not yet been sealed, largely because Hammer was still lining up the necessary financing. Hammer's apparent lack of cash troubled Bechtel's executives, who were further worried that doing business with Occidental would offend the company's longtime clients among the oil majors, none of whom were fans of Occidental. Steve junior possessed some doubts as well. "Watch out for Hammer," he warned. "We don't want him to cross ways with our regular clients." Steve senior, however, saw only opportunity in dealing with Hammer, and ignoring the counsel of the Bechtel executive suite, he dispatched one of the company's top emissaries, Raphael Dorman, to Paris, where Hammer was then laying over while on a European business trip.[4]

Meeting in Hammer's suite at the George V, Dorman laid out a proposal hard to resist: Bechtel would build the Occidental pipeline on a cash basis for $49 million plus bonus incentives—an all-or-nothing gamble, since $48 million at the time was Oxy's total net worth. Moreover, Bechtel would agree to defer all payments until the line was in operation and Occidental began pumping crude. After forty-eight hours of marathon negotiation, the deal was set in early December 1966.

Bechtel had promised to build quickly, and build quickly it did, completing a job that normally would have taken a year in eleven months. Just as quickly, Occidental began pumping and shipping oil in prodigious amounts. By 1968, its daily crude total had reached 500,000 barrels, and what had once been a nearly bankrupt enterprise had become one of the ten largest oil companies in the world—thanks largely to Bechtel. "We made Hammer's fortune for him in Libya," boasted Bechtel's pipeline chief John L. "Jack" Lynch.[5]

Hammer, understandably, was delighted—and not about to quibble when the Bechtel Corporation presented him with a bill for $153 million—the cost of the original pipeline plus an additional pipeline and terminal the company had built for Oxy. Nor were Halim and Libeco complaining. They too had made millions.

Not everyone in Libya, though, was happy. There were complaints that Occidental and other oil companies, in their haste to sell as much oil as possible before the expected overthrow of the Idris government, were posting prices for Libyan crude 10 to 15 percent below the international level—thus cutting into Libyan royalties. There were further complaints that the companies were habitually late in paying Libyan taxes, as there were also complaints that the companies, Occidental in particular, were overproducing and thus ruining the Libyan fields. The major bone of contention with Occidental, however, was over a promise Hammer had made in order to secure his original concessions. If the Libyans granted him the right to search for oil, Hammer had said, he would build the country a badly needed ammonia-fertilizer plant. Since then, the world price of ammonia had collapsed, and largely as a result, Hammer had reneged on the commitment. He had tried to smooth things over by offering to build, with Bechtel, a major liquid-natural-gas plant, but feelings were still bruised. Thus far, however, the Libyans had done nothing about it.

Then, in August 1969, a Bechtel electrician named John Maguire went to Libyan under-secretary of petroleum Ibrahim Hangari with several startling accusations. In abetting Occidental's efforts to get as much oil out of Libya as possible, Maguire maintained, Bechtel had taken a number of dangerous shortcuts.[6] Specifically, Maguire, whom Bechtel characterized as a disgruntled ex-employee it had fired, claimed that the Oxy pipeline had sprung numerous leaks because of corrosion, that a vent had ruptured in a poorly constructed storage tank and that the Bechtel-installed wiring and metering mechanisms in the fields were substandard. Safety precautions were so lax, Maguire went on, that a Palestinian welder had recently died in a fire after being sent into the fields without a protective gas "sniffer." But Maguire's most sensational charge was that Occidental, with Bechtel's complicity, was moving unmetered oil out of the country—in effect stealing from Libya.

He had no documentable proof for his last claim, Maguire admitted, but he suggested that the Libyans stage a surprise raid on the fields to catch the Americans in the act. He added that he was in fear for his life: when he had gone to his Bechtel supervisor with his charges, the supervisor had told him to leave the country or he would be killed.

Hangari had special reasons for believing Maguire's tale: it was to him that Hammer had made the promise to build the fertilizer plant. The nonfulfillment of that pledge had caused Hangari to lose face and had stalled his career; it had also instilled a burning dislike of Armand Hammer.

After taking Maguire's statement, Hangari had the American placed under protective custody in a Tripoli hotel. Several days later, after Maguire had been secretly flown to Italy in the care of a Libyan plain-clothes officer, Hangari launched a confidential investigation. His aim was to put Armand Hammer in jail.

But before anything could come of Hangari's probe, Libya was over-taken by the "inevitable blowup" Jerry Komes had predicted to Steve junior nine years before. On the night of September 1, 1969, a group of young colonels—preempting a similar move about to be made by court minister Shelbi—overthrew the regime of King Idris and pro-claimed themselves Libya's masters. The new "Revolution Command Council," as it was dubbed, was headed by a then-obscure young of-ficer from the area where the French had gained their oil concessions. His name was Muhammar al-Qaddafi.

Tipped by the CIA that a coup was imminent, Mustafa ben Halim and the executives of most American companies, including those of Occidental and Bechtel, had by then left the country to take refuge in Rome.* Senior U.S. officials soon assured them there was no cause for worry. The young officers, the U.S. embassy cabled Washington would prove to be important assets in the struggle to keep Soviet influence and Communism out of the Arab world. Already, the cable continued,

---

* According to U.S. government sources, Halim left Libya on a Saudi passport pro-vided him by Bechtel and the CIA. Eventually, he settled in London, where he be-came a financial consultant to various Saudi Arabian interests, as well as paymaster for anti-Qaddafi exile groups. In 1976, while on a business trip to Beirut, Halim was kidnapped by Palestinians in Qaddafi's employ and stuffed into the trunk of a Mer-cedes, which the Palestinians then proceeded to push off a cliff. Luckily for Halim, the car got stuck on a promontory and did not crash and burn as planned. After several days of being trapped in the trunk, Halim was finally rescued and returned to London, vastly amused by the incident. His humor began to wane during the middle 1980s, when Qaddafi dispatched assassination squads to various European capitals, intent on eliminating exiles like himself. Eventually, Halim fled to an affluent suburb of a major U.S. city, where, guarded heavily, he continues to reside today.

Qaddafi had promised to protect "all Western interests, including the pumping of oil."[7]

Taking the State Department at its word, Bechtel and Occidental returned to Libya, and within a month, crews from both companies were back at work. They would remain there doing business, at least until 1971, when Libya nationalized the assets of foreign oil companies. They would build more pipelines, more refinery facilities, more of everything connected with oil. It was a profitable enterprise for all of them.

CHAPTER 14

▲

A FRIEND
IN THE WHITE HOUSE

W hile the Bechtel Corporation was making the most of its opportunity in Libya, Lyndon Johnson had been having a rather
more difficult time in the White House—all of which was fine with
Bechtel.

Despite the posts and contracts that had occasionally come their way,
Steve junior and his father had never much cared for Johnson, who
was a Democrat, sometimes confused which of them was who and,
worst of all, was bound body and soul to their chief business rivals, the
Texas-based construction giant Brown and Root. It was Brown and
Root that had gotten most of the choice projects during LBJ's administration, from constructing the Space Center in Houston to building the
infrastructure for the Vietnam War. Bechtel, by contrast, had come
away with only comparative crumbs, and in one instance, namely
Libya, had been pressured by the White House to take on Brown and
Root as a partner.

Now, though, the situation was about to change radically. Richard
Nixon had been elected president, and for the Bechtel Corporation and
its proprietors, he would prove to be a very good friend indeed.

A FRIEND IN THE WHITE HOUSE

The ties between Bechtel and the new president were part the result of friendship (Steve senior had known Nixon since his days as a California congressman), in part a consequence of geography (both had a native-born chauvinism about California and the West), but mostly a matter of mutual interest. Like the Bechtels, Nixon was pragmatic, internationalist and, as events would amply demonstrate, not above doing an occasional shady deal. He was also very much interested in boosting American exports, improving relations with the Soviets and developing new sources of energy—all goals that dovetailed neatly with Bechtel's business interests.

Just how helpful Nixon could be to those interests was demonstrated six weeks after the inauguration, when the president's mentor and former law partner Attorney General John Mitchell announced that the Justice Department was dropping its eight-year-long prosecution of El Paso Natural Gas on antitrust charges. The decision was significant on several counts, not least of them the fact that in defending itself against the charges, El Paso had paid a total of $770,000 to Mudge, Rose, Guthrie & Alexander, the New York law firm where both Mitchell and Nixon had lately been senior partners. For Bechtel, which, like El Paso, had been a major contributor to the Nixon campaign, the decision was welcome as well. In one stroke, the administration had cleared the way for the company to contract with El Paso for a number of major projects, most notable among them a $235 million natural-gas facility in Algeria.

The El Paso decision, however, was only a foretaste of favors to come. During the Nixon presidency major government projects, from the Alaska pipeline* to the Washington Metro to a raft of nuclear

---

* When in February 1974, Bechtel won the contract from the Alyeska Pipeline Service Company to serve as the prime management contractor for the $8 billion, 789-mile-long Alaska pipeline, the project was heralded by Bechtel as one of the most important in its history. However, Bechtel soon became involved in a bitter battle with Alyeska, which became increasingly critical of Bechtel's performance in Alaska. It claimed that Bechtel was overstaffing with senior-level people to increase its fees on the cost-plus contract and overbilling Alyeska for many of its 1,800 pipeline employees. Under Bechtel, Alyeska claimed, the pipeline project was plagued with low productivity, featherbedding, on-site thievery and glaring supply problems. In addition Bechtel was accused of ordering its quality-control staff deliberately to falsify X-rays of thousands of pipeline welds in order to expedite construction. Bechtel, in turn, claimed that Alyeska had dragged its feet in awarding the prime management contract and was so slow in paying its bills that Bechtel's relations with its subcontractors were jeopardized and performance suffered as a result. Bechtel managers in Alaska said Alyeska person-

power plants, fairly rained on the Bechtel corporation, which saw its gross annual revenues go from $750 million in 1968 to nearly $2 billion in 1974—an increase of more than 150 percent.

With the contracts came appointment of both Bechtels to an array of prestigious posts, including, in the case of Steve junior, membership on the Treasury Department's Labor–Management Advisory Committee. "Bechtel is one of the elite group around here," a White House aide told a reporter after Steve junior's designation. "Anyone on that committee had no trouble getting his views to the President."[1]

It was Steve senior, though, who got the choicest plum: appointment to the advisory committee of the U.S. Export-Import Bank, a job that during the Nixon years added billions to Bechtel's bottom line.

The credit—or blame—for this development rested with the bank's Nixon-appointed president, an ebullient, pudgy 59-year-old former car salesman named Henry Kearns.

That Henry Kearns would play so central a role in Bechtel's financial fortunes—not to mention those of the countries in which it operated —was, to put it mildly, an improbable happenstance: nearly as improbable as Henry Kearns himself.

He had been born in Utah, where he studied engineering for a time at the state university before dropping out to move to Southern California. There, armed with a business degree obtained through a correspondence course, he tried his hand at various odd occupations (none of them related to banking or international finance) before discovering his true talent, selling—selling, in fact, almost anything, from real estate to gasoline to, best of all, cars, which he did with conspicuous success for the Loesh and Osborne Motor Company of Pasadena.

Kearns's career attainment might have ended there, but for the fact that in addition to being a supersalesman, he was also a fervent anti-Communist, a trait he had in common with an ambitious young California politician named Richard Nixon. The two became friends, and when Nixon ran as Dwight Eisenhower's vice-president in 1952, Kearns served as chairman of the Eisenhower-Nixon campaign in Southern California. Following the election, and a stint spent as vice-chairman of the Republican National Finance Committee, Kearns, at

nel insisted on duplicating Bechtel efforts and generated unnecessary red tape. The dispute culminated in May 1975 when Alyeska fired Bechtel from the project. Steve junior was reportedly enraged and embittered and rarely spoke of the project again. What should have been the crown jewel in his career as a builder proved to be severely flawed.

Nixon's recommendation, was appointed by Eisenhower as assistant secretary for international affairs at the Commerce Department.

During his years at Commerce, Kearns traveled frequently, especially to Asia, where he developed a network of contracts with many of the region's leading businessmen. In 1961, following Nixon's defeat at the hands of John Kennedy, Kearns moved to Tokyo, and there became a consultant to Mitsui, the giant Japanese trading company. Operating out of an office in Mitsui's corporate headquarters, Kearns set up a number of businesses in Southeast Asia, including Thailand, where, in the company of a Pasadena lawyer named Maurice Stans—later to be Nixon's secretary of Commerce and chairman of his reelection committee—he made what would turn out to be a fateful investment in a Bangkok pulp and paper mill, Siam Kraft.

While Kearns saw to his business interests, he also maintained his relations with Nixon. In 1967, when the former vice-president came to Japan, hunting clients for his New York law firm, Kearns served as his guide and door-opener, introducing Nixon to the principals at Mitsui (which wound up hiring Nixon's firm to handle much of the company's American legal work), putting him together with such notables as former prime minister Kishi Nobosuke and arranging for him to be entertained in the capital's Ginza district.

Kearns's efforts were rewarded two years later, when now President Nixon named him head of the Export-Import Bank.

The appointment did not go down well with everyone—"What we need here," said one State Department official after meeting him, "is fewer snake-oil salesmen"—and Kearns himself was highly defensive about his limited background and even more limited qualifications. It was not true, he insisted, that he had sold used cars; he had sold only *new* cars. But whatever others in the administration might think of him (including White House chief of staff H. R. Haldeman, who treated him with special condescension), Kearns had Nixon's full confidence, and was one of the few administration officials able to drop by the Oval Office without prior clearance from Haldeman. During one such visit, Nixon revealed to Kearns that for foreign-policy and economic reasons, he wanted to greatly increase U.S. exports. Accordingly, Kearns by 1972 was to boost Eximbank loans to $10 billion.

It was a staggering sum, more than three times the total of all the bank's outstanding loans, when Kearns assumed office—more, in fact, than the bank had lent in its entire thirty-three year history. If he was going to meet Nixon's goal, Kearns, who had no lending experience, needed advice. He decided to seek it from Steve Bechtel, Sr.

The two had met in 1955, when Kearns was serving on the Hoover Commission on Intelligence, and Bechtel, a longtime friend of the intelligence community, had flown to Washington to kibbitz. Kearns came away from the experience impressed—indeed, nearly awed—and since then, he and Bechtel had stayed in frequent touch. When, in May 1969, Kearns asked Bechtel to serve on the bank's six-member advisory committee and Steve accepted, Kearns could not conceal his delight. In signing on Steve Bechtel, Kearns boasted to friends, he had acquired not just an advisor, but instant credibility.

Bechtel, for his part, had acquired entrée into the U.S. vault. Through the years, below-market, federally guaranteed loans like those provided by the Export-Import Bank had been one of the keys to his company's overseas success—and Bechtel had been a master in securing them. "The South American general who needed $60 million to build a pipeline usually didn't have any idea where to go for his financing or what elevator button to push when he got there," said one former Bechtel director. "[Our] job was to point the way and help him put together all the necessary paperwork."[2] But for all of Bechtel's financial finesse—and the billions that accrued because of it—never had the company enjoyed such free access to no-risk, low interest capital as Kearns was offering now. It was a unique opportunity, and while it lasted, Bechtel made the most of it.

He began by flattering Kearns's ego—congratulating him on the fine job he was doing, and offering to help in any way possible. Knowing of Kearns's thirst for publicity (one of his first moves at the bank had been to launch a splashy public relations campaign), Bechtel also began sending along newspaper clips about the bank's activities, attaching to them complimentary notes. He ingratiated himself further by suggesting to Kearns that he commission a film about the bank, in which its president, naturally, would play a starring role. To make it possible, Bechtel personally undertook some low-keyed lobbying with Congress that resulted in an increase in the bank's public relations budget.

A great believer in the value of favor-doing—"It's more effective to do a man a favor than to ask him for one," Steve senior told his executives—Bechtel provided more and more as the months went by. When, for instance, a traveling Eximbank official sought an introduction in Jakarta or accommodations in Manila, it was Bechtel employees who arranged it. Similarly, when Kearns or his vice-chairman, Walter C. Sauer, decided that the bank should prepare a study on a particular industry, Bechtel brought in the Stanford Research Institute or provided Bechtel's own research. He was just as gracious in offering to fill in for former Texas governor Allen Shivers when Shivers, the advisory committee's chairman, couldn't make a quarterly meeting. Ever-obliging Steve senior also helped Kearns fill vacancies on the bank's advisory committee, with the result that before long it was dominated by Bechtel friends and customers, including investment banker and former FMC corporation head Paul Davies.

There was nothing, apparently, that Steve Bechtel, Sr., wouldn't do for Henry Kearns and his bank, including flying to Washington to testify before Congress in their behalf—and doing so with such effectiveness that Congress increased Eximbank's lending authority to $20 billion, double what Nixon had requested. In turn, there was very little, if anything, that Walter Kearns wouldn't do for the Bechtel Corporation.

That became clear in 1970, when Kearns stepped in to assist Bechtel with a project that was having troubles in Indonesia. The project in question was the mining of a 586-foot-tall mountain of copper ore, high in the remote and rugged jungles of Irian Jaya. The job, which was being undertaken for a company called Freeport Minerals, had not been going well, a source of considerable distress for Texaco, a major stockholder in the venture, and its chairman, Gus Long, Steve senior's oldest and closest friend in the oil industry. At one point, when it appeared that the entire project would collapse, Freeport's president, Forbes Wilson, stormed into Steve junior's office, charging that Bechtel had vastly underestimated the complexity of the mining. Either Bechtel allocate its full resources to the project and replace the project manager, or, Wilson threatened, Freeport was going to bring in another construction company.[3]

Steve junior immediately sent one of his best men to Irian Jaya and gave the project his top priority. He also assured Wilson that his father would guarantee the project's proposed $20 million funding, which was then before the Export-Import Bank. What Steve junior didn't foresee was the recalcitrance of Eximbank's chief engineer, who, after reviewing the loan application, refused to believe that high-grade copper ore could be extracted from such a remote site at a commercially viable price. With that, the loan was dead.

It was, that is, until Steve senior put in a complaining call to Henry Kearns, who thereupon overrode his own engineer and personally cleared the loan.[4]

Under Kearns's direction, Eximbank was even more generous in financing Bechtel's dealings with Pertamina, the Indonesian government's corruption-riddled oil company, for which Bechtel was building a number of refineries and pipelines.

The Pertamina work was especially important to Bechtel not only because of the size of the contracts involved (they totaled in the billions), but because of the lengths to which the company had gone to get them. In some cases, Bechtel had been nurturing friendships for years. One such relationship was with Julius Tahija, a famed Indonesian war hero (during one World War II battle, Tahija was said to have killed 250 Japanese single-handedly), who when Steve senior met him for the first time in 1952 was a middle manager for Caltex. By the 1960s, Tahija was managing director of Caltex in Indonesia, and sufficiently wired with the government that he was able to operate Caltex (and to award Bechtel contracts) even after Sukarno expropriated most foreign interests in 1963. Another crucial Bechtel contract in Indonesia was Ibnu Sutowo, a flamboyant, golf-playing army general and one-time surgeon who was serving as minister of Mining and Petroleum when Steve senior began dealing with him in the early 1960s. Sutowo subsequently became chairman of Pertamina, and it was through him that Bechtel became the state-owned oil company's chief contractor, building not only all its oil projects, but its liquid-natural gas ones as well. Still more friends were made for Bechtel by Harold Wilson, the head of the company's Indonesian operations, married to the widow of a prominent Indonesian Air Force general who, fortuitously, was the best friend of Tien Suharto, the wife of Indonesia's President Suharto.

But the Bechtel Corporation had done more than make friends in Indonesia. According to former company executives, it had also spread prodigious amounts of cash, rumored to exceed $3 million to senior government officials in the early 1970s.* Bechtel denies these allegations.

---

* According to senior-level sources at both Bechtel and Pertamina, these payments were channeled to Indonesian officials through Bechtel's Japanese subcontractors in Indonesia, who deposited the funds in the Bank of Hongkong on behalf of the recipients. In addition, these sources charge that Bechtel underwrote many of the high-living General Ibnu Sutowo's expenses and made at least one more payment of $300,000 to government officials in Indonesia.

When reporters Mark Dowie, Tim Shorrock, Lyuba Zarsky and Peter Hayes revealed in June 1984 that a Bechtel consultant in Korea named Yoon Sik Cho had been

Much, then, was at stake for Bechtel in Indonesia, which Steve senior described to Kearns and his fellow advisory board members as possessing the potential for "hundreds of millions in U.S. exports." It did—at least, for Bechtel—and thanks to Kearns, a $160 million loan for Pertamina sailed through.

With so much money available, and Kearns seemingly so willing to dispense it, the friendship between the builder and the banker deepened. They talked by phone at least once a week, Kearns passing along such helpful information as which countries the bank considered credit risks, and ever soliciting Bechtel for ideas about new loan possibilities. Bechtel was never shy in providing them. He had, in fact, all manner of notions where the bank could put its cash: the Philippines, where Eximbank provided $13.5 million to a Bechtel customer building a nickel-production facility; Egypt, where Eximbank offered $100 million so that Bechtel could build the Sumed pipeline, and especially, Algeria, where Eximbank put up $145 million to construct fertilizer plants (the same ones Bechtel had been unable to sell to the Indians) and a total of $294 million to finance Bechtel's building of liquid-natural-gas facilities ("an extremely important" project, Bechtel told Kearns) for Sonatrach, the state-owned oil company, which during Kearns's tenure became the bank's largest single customer.

Kearns also opened doors for Bechtel with important members of the Nixon administration. At Kearns's invitation, Treasury Secretary John Connally, Commerce Secretary Maurice Stans, Labor Secretary George Shultz, Office of Management and Budget Director Caspar Weinberger and Peter G. Peterson, executive director of the president's cabinet-level Council on International Economic Policy, all dropped by the bank for lunch and the chance to meet the remarkable Steve Bechtel.

Nor was that the end of Kearns's helpfulness. When Bechtel complained about the slowness of the bank's lending procedures, warning that such delays might cost U.S. companies valuable business, Kearns persuaded the administration to drop the requirement that loans be

---

providing expensive gifts to Korean officials in an effort to help Bechtel gain major nuclear contracts there, the company flatly denied the charges. According to Bechtel, a federal grand jury investigated the charges and failed to return an indictment.

approved by a committee consisting of the head of the bank and the secretaries of State, Treasury and Commerce. From here on, Kearns proudly told Bechtel, he could personally approve any request of $30 million or less.

Under Bechtel's careful tutelage, Kearns also became an apostle and financial backer of international nuclear power. "The United States would benefit highly by offering financial assistance to the construction of [nuclear] energy-producing facilities," Steve senior announced at one of the first meetings of the advisory committee, adding that "huge capital expenditures will be necessary."[6] Within months, Kearns was echoing the refrain, emphasizing "the desirability," as he put it, "for the United States to be involved in as many nuclear plants as possible." He went on: "Any company which purchases U.S. equipment and services for a nuclear power plant should be able to obtain financing for the fuel required to operate that plant."[7]

Within two years, the bank had passed the $1 billion mark in nuclear financing, much of it allocated to Bechtel-built plants around the world. The loan that pushed the bank over the $1 billion threshold was earmarked for a Bechtel nuclear plant in Brazil, the country's first. While Steve senior orchestrated the project's financing, getting his old friends at Morgan to put up $33.5 million and Eximbank the remaining $107 million, Kearns himself traveled to Brazil and sold the deal to the country's minister of Mines and Energy, Dr. Antonio Lias Liete.

The Brazil financing was a milestone for the bank, and Kearns threw a party to celebrate. At the bank's expense, 150 of the world's top energy and nuclear officials were flown to Washington for a black-tie dinner presided over by Vice-President Spiro Agnew. The next day Kearns told a press conference, "We welcome the opportunity to play a part in this important endeavor. And the prospect is now that we may be called upon to assist in financing $1.5 billion to $2 billion of U.S. exports in the nuclear field each year over the next five years." No one welcomed Kearns's announcement more than Steve Bechtel, Sr., whose company got the lion's share of the work.

With Nixon's reelection in 1972, it appeared that Bechtel would be tapping the bank's coffers for even more funds. Shortly after beginning his second term, Nixon declared his intention of boosting U.S. exports from their current level of $30 billion to $50 billion by 1976. The principal means of accomplishing that goal, the president stated, would be loans granted by the Export-Import Bank.

Given the presidential green light, Bechtel, in partnership with Armand Hammer, who had cemented his own ties with the administration with a recent (illegal) $100,000 campaign contribution,* began laying plans for spending a goodly chunk of those loans in the Soviet Union. The centerpiece of their plans was a projected World Trade Center in Moscow, and nearly all of its $55 million cost was to be financed by loans granted by Henry Kearns. The partners sought an additional $180 million in Eximbank financing to build a series of fertilizer plants astride the Volga River. But by far the most ambitious and expensive venture was the development of the Yakutsk natural-gas fields in western Siberia. Working in partnership with the Russians and El Paso Natural Gas, Bechtel and Hammer foresaw a development worth up to $11 billion, of which Kearns promised $10 billion in financing.

The Russians were enthusiastic—"I am a supporter of contracts, contracts, contracts that lead to more contracts, contracts, contracts," proclaimed Soviet Trade Minister Nikolai Patolichev in a meeting with Hammer and Bechtel executives—and so was the White House, which announced its readiness to do everything in its power "to help U.S. firms crack the Soviet market." With the signing of a trade agreement by Nixon and Soviet party chairman Leonid Brezhnev during a 1974 summit conference in Moscow, and the grant by Kearns of an initial $185 million in funding, it appeared that billions for Bechtel were in the offing. So confident was Steve senior of the company's Soviet prospects that after a personal inspection tour of the Yakutsk fields, he ordered up a program to teach Bechtel's engineers to speak Russian.

All that remained was persuading Congress to grant the Soviets most-favored-nation trading status—that is, offering them repayment terms equal to the best offered any nation. And that, it turned out, was the rub.

"You must be out of your cotton-pickin' mind to dream up something like that," an astonished Senator Henry Jackson told an administration official after he heard of the financing for the Russian deal. With that, Jackson began drafting legislation—the "Jackson Amendment," it came to be called—tying approval of most-favored-nation

---

* Of Hammer's $100,000 donation to the Nixon campaign, $54,000 was given after the new campaign-financing law requiring full disclosure went into effect. When the Watergate special counselor discovered Hammer's contribution, he brought the matter before a grand jury. On March 4, 1976, Hammer was found guilty of a misdemeanor, fined $3,000 and given a year's probation.

trading status to Soviet willingness to allow Russian Jews to emigrate. Jackson's congressional colleagues, including a number of Nixon's Republican allies, were also outraged by the "U.S. giveaway," as several of them called it, and vowed to bottle up the trade legislation in committee. In March 1974, Bechtel received more bad news when the General Accounting Office, the investigative arm of Congress, unexpectedly announced that $315 million in pending Eximbank loans and credits for the Russian projects were illegal, since the president had failed to stipulate that each of them was in the national interest. The result, until the Justice Department reviewed the GAO's finding, was that the loans were held up. Despite these developments, the Bechtel Corporation announced it would go forward, congressional approval or no. "We are going ahead with the negotiations aspect [of the Yakutsk deal] so that when resolutions are reached, we will have made as much progress as possible," a senior Bechtel executive, Raphael Dorman, told a reporter. "Although this development could seriously affect the use of goods and services from the U.S., it doesn't affect our participation since we will probably be forced to use export credits from other sources of financing from countries other than the U.S."8*

Bechtel's bravado served only to enrage the lawmakers all the more. At a hearing called by the Senate subcommittee on multinational corporations to investigate the deal, chairman Frank Church of Idaho told his colleagues:

> What bothers me about this process is how things germinate. We start with large multinational corporations that are looking for profitable investments abroad. They are the initiators of these proposed projects, and, having worked out an arrangement that is to their satisfaction, they come to the U.S. government and apply for a large federal subsidy through the Export-Import Bank or federal guarantees of private capital outlays. It is at this point that the government is asked to make a decision, and if the project is not already *fait accompli*, it is at least sufficiently well advanced and worked out by the companies and the Soviet government that a very plausible case can be made for it.

* Despite Raphael Dorman's determination to finance the Yakutsk project from other sources, the deal was shelved after Dorman died suddenly in early May 1974 and Richard Nixon, the prime architect of U.S.–U.S.S.R détente resigned from the presidency that summer.

The companies say this is a splendid deal because they don't have to assume any risk; they don't have to put out much capital. That is all done by the federal government, our government, which comes in well along in the process when a lot of vested interests are already behind the proposal . . . Now is this really a wise way to formulate a national economic policy?

The Eximbank's policies were also drawing fire from European suppliers, who were finding it hard to get contracts, not to speak of making a profit, given the edge the bank's low-interest loans gave companies like Bechtel. As one West German official put it: "Our most tenacious competition isn't [U.S. industry], but the Export-Import Bank."

The controversy over the Eximbank was still mounting, when, on October 8, 1973, Kearns suddenly resigned.

The reason for his departure became apparent a few weeks later, when the GAO revealed that during Kearns's administration, the bank had made a number of loans to Siam Kraft, the Bangkok, Thailand–based paper company in which Kearns, his executive vice-president, Donald T. Bostwick, and Nixon reelection official and former Commerce secretary Maurice Stans all owned substantial blocks of stock. The GAO further disclosed that during the same period the bank had also made thirty-seven separate loans to Mitsui, the huge Japanese trading firm with which Kearns and Nixon had done business in the late 1960s. But what really raised eyebrows at the GAO and subsequently in Congress was the revelation that while Kearns was running the Eximbank, Mitsui had purchased his stock in Siam Kraft at nearly ten times its market value, a transaction that netted Kearns $500,000.

"This is the worst conflict of interest in the seventeen years I have been in the Senate," said Wisconsin's William Proxmire, who during Kearns's confirmation hearings had pressed him to sell his Siam Kraft holdings. Ultimately, the Justice Department came to a similar conclusion and launched an investigation to determine whether Kearns and Bostwick had violated any criminal statutes. *

* The investigation of Kearns and Bostwick took place only after Senator Proxmire brought pressure on U.S. Attorney General William Saxbe. He in turn referred the case to Assistant Attorney General (and later governor of Pennsylvania) Richard L. Thornburgh, who eventually concluded that there was "insufficient evidence" to charge either man with a criminal offense. Proxmire, not mollified, blasted the decision in a letter to the attorney general. Wrote Proxmire: "Kearns obviously feathered his own nest at a time when he was President of the Bank and openly solicited the pur-

While Steve Bechtel senior had had no connection to either the Mitsui or the Siam Kraft loans, Congressman Les Aspin of Wisconsin charged that he had been guilty of other interest conflicts during his tenure on the Eximbank's advisory committee. In particular, Aspin singled out the Sonatrach LNG loans, as well as the loans for the Sumed pipeline, which had been approved after Bechtel's term on the committee expired in mid-September. "Obviously, Bechtel's firm benefited while he was on the committee and since he left," Aspin asserted. "Bechtel's conflict of interest raises questions about the integrity of the bank's entire fiscal operations."[9]

When the reporter from *The Washington Post* called Bechtel for comment, the 73-year-old family patriarch pleaded ignorance. He had no knowledge of questionable Eximbank loans, he said; in fact, he was even unaware that there was an LNG project in Algeria. As for his role as a member of the bank's advisory committee, Bechtel said, "We had no regular duties and no regular meetings. I haven't heard anything from that committee in six months."[10] So remote was he from the bank's operations, Bechtel insisted, that he didn't know until the reporter's call that his advisory term with the bank had expired. Affable as ever, Bechtel apologized for not being able to help the reporter more. He was an old man, he explained, and had not played an active role in the Bechtel Corporation's operations since 1960.

It was a vintage Bechtel performance. He'd been charming and avuncular, and ringing off, the *Post* reporter felt a little sheepish for troubling such a kindly old gentleman. What he didn't know—because Bechtel hadn't told him—was that just down the hall from Steve's office, ensconced in a new consulting firm which "old" Steve Bechtel, Sr., had personally helped to finance, were none other than Henry Kearns and his deputy, Don Bostwick. Nor could the reporter know the identity of Kearns International's first big client: Sonatrach of Algeria, which would pay Kearns $350,000, plus $46,000 in expenses, to lobby on its behalf.[11]

Steve senior knew when to say nothing. Like helpful Henry Kearns, he also knew how to take care of his friends.

chase of his stock from a company with which he was dealing officially as President of the Bank and whom he was not only in a position to help, but did help." As a result of the decision not to prosecute, Proxmire went on, "It will appear to millions of American citizens that there is a double standard in the law, one for the ordinary citizen and quite another for those who hold high positions in government and make thousands of dollars in personal profit as a result of official actions."

CHAPTER 15

▲

SECRETARY SHULTZ

T he Bechtel method—win favors by doing favors—would, as it had with Henry Kearns, work many times during the course of the Nixon administration, and never with better results than in the case of the man who would eventually become the company's president, George P. Shultz.

The 49-year-old former Marine officer needed a favor just then, for since giving up his post as dean of the University of Chicago's business school to become secretary of Labor, he had not been having an easy time of it. He had not been a favorite of the president's (who, on the White House tapes, was heard calling him a "candy ass"), and he had had the further ill fortune of taking office in the midst of the greatest surge of labor militancy since the immediate post–World War II period. Barely, for instance, had Shultz begun his duties when he found himself embroiled in a six-week East Coast longshoremen's strike. That had been followed by a particularly acrimonious three-month-long strike at General Electric. But the most irritating thorn embedded in Shultz's flank, as well as that of the Nixon administration, was George Meany, the aging, irascible president of the AFL-CIO.

Meany made no secret of his distaste for Nixon, and since the inauguration he had seemed to go out of his way to seek confrontation. At the onset of the 1969 recession, for instance, Meany first criticized Nixon for doing nothing, then, when Nixon finally did do something —namely, initiate a ninety-day wage-price freeze—blasted the president's solution as being "patently discriminatory against labor." Later the same year, Meany clashed with Nixon again, this time over the Supreme Court nomination of South Carolina federal judge Clement Haynsworth. Claiming that Haynsworth was "antilabor," Meany had helped lead the successful Senate fight against his confirmation.

Those episodes, however, were minor compared with the explosion that occurred late in the summer of 1969 over Shultz and Nixon's attempt to correct racial discrimination in the U.S. construction industry, where out of 1.3 million workers, only 106,000 were black. Under pressure from the NAACP, which had filed suit against the administration, charging that it had failed to enforce the provisions of the Equal Opportunity Act, Shultz had persuaded Nixon to require builders with federal contracts to take affirmative action in hiring minorities. If they refused, the builders lost their contracts.

The "Philadelphia Plan," as it was dubbed, after its first application to a federally financed hospital project in that city, came under immediate fire. The NAACP branded it "tokenism," while the construction industry, then in a severe slump and already heavily burdened by a number of costly wage settlements, claimed that the administration's hiring target—a 26 percent minority work force by 1972—would be impossible to meet. The most withering assault, though, came from Meany. Recalled Nixon in his memoirs: "George Meany hit the roof, charging the Administration was making the unions a 'whipping boy' and trying to score 'brownie points' with civil rights groups."[1]

Under attack from all sides, Shultz was battle-scarred and weary. "I was tired of hearing problems," he later recounted. "So I finally said, 'Why doesn't someone be constructive and tell me what can be done about the problems?'"[2]

Someone finally did: Steve Bechtel, Jr.

The Bechtel family had been keeping a watchful and appreciative eye on Shultz since 1967, when Steve senior had heard the then dean of the University of Chicago's business school address the board of directors of the Morgan Bank. Bechtel had come away impressed. Though Shultz was an academic, with an undergraduate degree from Princeton and a doctorate from MIT, he was no dreamy socialist leaning professor. He was, in fact, deeply conservative, and entirely friendly with business. Bechtel was also heartened by the fact that Shultz, a very "clubbable" sort, also had a suitably businesslike passion for martinis and golf. Steve junior took a liking to Shultz as well, especially after he learned that the secretary of labor had been a Marine Corps combat colonel in World War II.

What impressed the Bechtels most, though, was Shultz's policies. Like Nixon and themselves, Shultz was a believer in the inviolability of U.S. trade, which, he held, "should not be turned on and off again like a light switch to induce changes in the domestic and foreign policies" of other governments. He was also a supporter of Bechtel's ongoing business dealings with the Soviet Union—and, indeed, with virtually any nation where the company thought it could make a profit. Taken together, these considerations were good reason for the Bechtel Corporation to lend the struggling secretary a hand.

In May 1974, Steve junior arranged a meeting with Shultz and flew to Washington, bringing with him an executive who would be the key to solving Shultz' problems. That was Bechtel's vice-chairman and labor chief, John O'Connell.

A bluff, backslapping Irishman, O'Connell, who, in addition to his labor responsibilities, appointed himself Bechtel's unofficial ambassador to Saudi Arabia, was nothing if not gregarious—too much so for some tastes. Referring to O'Connell's penchant for treating the Saudis to boisterous, lavish American-style entertaining, often at the expense of Saudi sensibilities, one senior Bechtel official shuddered, "I can't think of anyone who was more insensitive to the Arabs."[3] But "Mr. Full Charge," as O'Connell was known at Bechtel, also had his defenders, chief among them Steve junior, who, according to a number of company officials, regarded him almost as a surrogate father. Of more immediate importance, O'Connell enjoyed a longtime intimate relationship with George Meany.

The two men's friendship dated back nearly twenty years to the bitter strike at the Joppa, Illinois, atomic-energy plant. Ending the walkout, which centered on a jurisdictional dispute between local workers and the national labor federation, was a crucial test for Meany, who had only recently taken over as president of the AFL. The stakes were also high for Bechtel, which was just then entering the nuclear-power industry, as well as for O'Connell, who had just been named the company's first labor chief. Out of that shared self-interest, the two sons of Irish-Catholic immigrants fashioned a deal. Under its terms, Bechtel agreed to fire all the 1,500 workers who did not strike at Joppa, and rehire only those of whom the AFL leadership approved. In return, Meany agreed to enforce a no-strike pledge while Bechtel finished construction of the $830 million plant.

The agreement, which was enforced only after a number of violent incidents, paid off for both men, and they had subsequently become close. O'Connell had invited Meany out to his encampment at the Bohemian Grove, flown him to California for golf and gin rummy weekends with Steves senior and junior, vacationed with him at the Bechtels' fishing camp in Jasper, Canada. Meany, in turn, had introduced O'Connell to the whole of the U.S. labor establishment, which thereafter seldom, if ever, quarreled with affable John O'Connell's employer. "John dedicated himself to knowing George Meany," said a former Bechtel director. "As a result, Bechtel projects in the United States never experienced any real major problems. That was O'Connell's contribution."[4]

At the Washington meeting with Shultz, O'Connell contributed again by offering to arrange a golf get-together with Meany at the Augusta National Country Club in Georgia, site of the Masters Tournament. Shultz accepted at once, and so, after a friendly phone call from O'Connell, did Meany. Several weeks later, after a friendly contest on the same links where Dwight Eisenhower had spent so many vacations, the two enemies repaired to a cottage alongside one of the fairways and over cocktails and Cuban cigars, thrashed out their differences. "It was all done extremely discreetly," said Nixon aide John Ehrlichman. "George enjoyed the golf and the talk with Meany. He got a lot done and was extremely grateful."[5]

Under O'Connell's sponsorship, the golf weekends continued at a rate of one a month. Soon, Meany's vehemence about the Philadelphia Plan began to lessen. He also started to pare back his opposition to Nixon's price controls, agreeing to cooperate if the president appointed an independent three-member commission to administer them. With Shultz acting as go-between, Nixon accepted the suggestion, appointed Meany one of the commission's members and, at the same time, named him a member of the President's Productivity Commission. Before long, *Time* was hailing Shultz as "the only Nixon administration official trusted by AFL-CIO President George Meany."[6] In large part because of that relationship, Meany saw to it that the AFL-CIO refrained from endorsing Democrat George McGovern, thus all but guaranteeing Nixon's reelection. "It was a moment to ponder and savor," Nixon wrote of Meany's decision. "For the first time in 17 years the AFL-CIO was not going to endorse a Democratic candidate for President."

Following Nixon's reelection, Shultz moved up to become Treasury secretary, and played a leading role in the administration's continuing efforts to unlock the Soviet Union to American trade. Though frustrated by Congress, Shultz' efforts were appreciated by the Bechtels, with whom he developed an increasingly close personal friendship.

The company itself, meanwhile, was thriving, thanks in no small part to the efforts of a key executive named Raphael Dorman.

The son of an American diplomat and an art-loving Italian countessa who named him after her favorite painter, Raph Dorman was an oddity at Bechtel. For one thing, he was part Jewish. For another, Dorman, who had entered Stanford at the age of 14, after placing first in a national scholarship contest, was coruscatingly bright. He also flouted Bechtel's no-nonsense strictures by traveling openly—and by all accounts, most happily—with his mistress. But what truly set Dorman apart was his genius for doing deals.

It was Dorman, for instance, who had "opened" India for Bechtel in the middle 1960s, in part by presenting Prime Minister Jawaharlal Nehru with his favorite delicacy, yellow asparagus. It was Dorman as well who had landed the $500 million Sonatrach contract for Bechtel, and it was also Dorman who had persuaded Armand Hammer to give Bechtel its Libyan business. From Peru to Indonesia, from Saudi Arabia to Switzerland, if big money was on the line for Bechtel, then it was invariably Raphael Dorman, Bechtel's "secretary of state," who corralled it.

Then, in early May 1974, while on a business trip to the Soviet Union, where, with his old friend Armand Hammer, he had come to do yet another deal, disaster struck: Raphael Dorman suffered a fatal heart attack—ironically, in the same hotel where Dad Bechtel had died almost fifty years earlier.

The grief the Bechtels felt over Dorman's death was matched only by their anxiety over who would replace him. Steve junior and his father began considering outside candidates. What they required was someone with all of Dorman's skills, along with his sophistication and grounding in economics and politics. Whoever the replacement would be, he would also have to mesh well into Bechtel's inbred corporate culture. George Shultz, John O'Connell suggested, would be ideal for the slot. Aware that Shultz was eager to leave the collapsing Nixon administration, the Bechtels concurred. Induced by an offer of more than $400,000 a year, six times his government salary, and a stock-purchase plan that made him a millionaire several times over, Shultz promptly accepted. He became Bechtel's executive president in May 1974.

The appointment of Shultz to so senior a position broke all company precedent. As with the military, Bechtel executives, including Steve junior, worked their way through the corporate ranks, one painstaking rung at a time. All at once, however, an outsider—and a nonengineering outsider at that—was being catapulted to the top. The question—and the worry for Steve junior and his father—was whether Shultz would be accepted.

There turned out to be no cause for alarm. Low-key and avuncular, Shultz went out of his way to accommodate company sensibilities. "George would come into the office Saturday morning wearing a bow tie and a cardigan sweater and wander around smoking a pipe," Fred Jacobs, a former company executive, remembered. "He was nonthreatening, and he'd take time to sit down and ask people—secretaries, clericals, anyone who happened to be in the office—how things were going. You felt comfortable with him."[7]

Shultz' professorial style also served him well in conferences with his fellow executives. "It soon became clear that Shultz could outshine most people," recalled an admiring colleague, "but he did it in a way that was never offensive. Typically, management meetings are very volatile, with engineers letting off steam and shouting at each other. In contrast, George spoke beautifully. He was always logical and very much the calm, collected professor. He proved highly effective."[8]

Shultz, who pronounced himself delighted to be at Bechtel—"After shuffling papers for a long time," as he put it, "it's nice working for a company where you can point to results"—scored more points by downplaying his status, through such symbolic measures as choosing an Oldsmobile for his company car rather than the Cadillac to which he was entitled. With Helena "Obie" O'Brien, his wife of thirty years, and their five children, he lived unpretentiously in a modest, Colonial-style house on the Stanford campus, where he enhanced the professorial image by teaching courses in management and public policy. Shultz the teacher also showed himself willing to learn, particularly the ways of Mining and Metals, the division of which he had been put in charge. With Shultz' eager acquiescence, the division's senior engineers put their new boss through the equivalent of a crash course. "At least two dozen of the division's engineers," said one of his "instructors," "made presentations to Shultz over a period of several months. Even though Shultz was continually being called into other meetings or receiving important phone calls through all of this, he really took an interest in each presentation. In the end, we gave him a graduation certificate in the form of a shredded blueprint and his own hard hat. He thanked us all with a totally improvised speech that was delightful."[9]

Shultz faced a potentially more critical audience in Bechtel's finance committee, whose members—Jerry Komes, Bob Bridges, Bill Slusser and pipeline division chief Jack Lynch—had known and worked with each other for years. "The four of us were old buddies," as Lynch put it. "We could just look at each other and know what the other guys was thinking. And we knew exactly how far we could go with each other."[10]

Not so, however, with Shultz, the nonengineer, whose arrival from outside the company ranks had been unsettling to the committee, whose members now found themselves reporting to the former Treasury secretary. Before deciding whether or not to accept Shultz, they put him to a good-humored test.

On the Friday before the first committee meeting Shultz was scheduled to chair, the four friends gave him a Bechtel briefing book summarizing the company's monthly and year-to-date financial activities and told him to review over the weekend. "Did you read the briefing book?" Jerry Komes, the committee chairman, asked Shultz, as soon as the meeting got under way Monday morning. Shultz said that he had. "What did you think?" Komes inquired.

"I'm impressed," Shultz smilingly answered. "I never realized that a company could have so much cash."

"That's right," Komes said. "Now Bob has something to tell you."

Bridges tried hard to keep a straight face. He, Komes and the others had rehearsed this conversation and it was progressing exactly as anticipated.

"Well, George," he began, "what Jerry wants me to tell you is a couple of things we've all learned the hard way around here. Number one, we know how to make money. Number two, we know how to keep it. Your experience has been in the academic world, where maybe you didn't have to think about money. And you've been in government, where you've been giving money away. So, as Steve senior would tell you, whatever you do around here, George, *don't fuck with the money.*"

Momentarily, the man who only a few months earlier had been the Treasury secretary of the United States looked as though he had been poleaxed. "You could see his mind spinning around and Shultz thinking, 'My God, these guys are tough. They're telling me off,'" Lynch later recounted. Then Shultz, aware that he had been set up, roared with laughter.

From then on, Shultz was no longer treated with the arm's-length, formal deference accorded to a visiting dignitary. "George Shultz did everything right," Bechtel chief counsel Bill Slusser noted. "Here was a guy who had been secretary of the Treasury and held a post at Stanford. Yet he got down in the trenches and proved himself to a bunch of hard-hats. The fact that he did it, that he enjoyed doing it, that he did it with such goodwill—all of that impressed people."[11]

Including his bosses, the Bechtels. They too were pleased with their new charge's progress, and even more so by the skill he was showing as a negotiator. No less than Raph Dorman, Shultz was proving adept in handling the company's overseas clients, more and more of whom he was coming to know on a personal basis. Steve senior had helped smooth the way by introducing Shultz to old friends like Saudi Arabia's King Faisal and Algeria's Houari Boumédienne, but it was Shultz himself who had charmed them. Domestically the new recruit was having an excellent run too, thanks in part to the contacts Steve senior had provided. Through his intercession, Shultz was soon serving on an array of prestigious corporate boards, including General Motors; Sears, Roebuck; Dillon, Read; Morgan Guaranty and SRI International. Thanks to his patron, Shultz was also asked to join the Morgan International Council and the Business Roundtable, widely accounted the most influential corporate lobby in the country. One area where Shultz needed no help was in Washington: to Steve junior's occasional distress, he continued to keep in touch with the members of the new administration, including President Gerald Ford, whom he informally advised on economic matters. When Shultz first joined the company, Steve junior would grouse about his government dealings, worrying that publicity about them would damage Bechtel, but there was little he could do to stop them. Shultz had proved that when, in direct defiance of his new boss, he attended a testimonial dinner for his old friend and colleague Henry Kissinger. The incident had infuriated Bechtel (and Shultz, angry in turn, had briefly considered quitting); but if nothing else, it had demonstrated Shultz' grit.

Steve junior liked that quality in Shultz, and he was coming to increasingly admire him. Not long after the Kissinger dinner, he demonstrated his esteem by inviting Shultz to become a member of Mandalay, his personal lodge at the Bohemian Grove. Never before had such a gesture been made to any Bechtel employee, however long or devoted his service. Along "Mahogany Row," the Bechtel executive suite, the invitation, which Shultz immediately accepted, * was read as a portent of bigger things soon to come. The estimation was correct. In May 1975, Steve junior proposed, and the company's board of directors unanimously approved, Shultz' appointment as president of the Bechtel Corporation, the most important of Bechtel's three operating companies.

Only a year had passed since George Shultz, the outsider and former academic, had joined Bechtel. Now he was but one step away from the pinnacle of company power. It had been a dizzying rise, and in Washington, another cabinet member was about to attempt to match it.

---

* Shultz put his membership in The Grove to good and immediate use, inviting a number of former government colleagues to be his guests. One of the most notable occasions was during the 1979 encampment, when Shultz played host to former secretary of State Henry Kissinger, West German Chancellor Helmut Schmidt, former Nixon chief of staff and NATO commander Alexander Haig and computer magnate David Packard, who would eventually become Ronald Reagan's deputy secretary of Defense. After the encampment, Shultz flew the party to Steve junior's Pebble Beach vacation house aboard one of Bechtel's corporate jets. They remained there several days, talking and socializing in private.

CHAPTER 16

▲

CAP'S PERIOD
OF ADJUSTMENT

S ix weeks after George Shultz' designation as company president, another member of the Nixon cabinet arrived in San Francisco to take up duties as the Bechtel Corporation's general counsel. The new recruit was Caspar Weinberger, of late secretary of Health, Education and Welfare.*

Around San Francisco and Washington, it was assumed that the California-born Weinberger had been lured back to his native state by his onetime colleague and boss, George Shultz. It was also assumed that once he was in place, Weinberger's career at Bechtel would be just as glittering as that of his former cabinet colleague. Neither assumption was correct.

---

* A number of Nixon appointees besides Weinberger and Shultz wound up working for Bechtel in one capacity or another. They ranged from CIA director Richard Helms (who became a Bechtel Corporation consultant); to White House political advisor Peter Flanigan (who would become a senior partner in the Bechtel-owned New York investment house Dillon, Read); to the Atomic Energy Commission's general manager Robert L. Hollingsworth (who became manager of manpower services at Bechtel); to Treasury secretary William Simon, who became still another Bechtel consultant.

The truth was that Weinberger had come to Bechtel not because of Shultz, but in spite of him. They were different men, with different—and often conflicting—styles, and at Bechtel, their progress would be dissimilar as well.

That Weinberger had joined Bechtel was, in fact, rather odd. There were, in the first place, his origins. While his mother had been Episcopalian, as was Cap himself, his father, Herman Weinberger, was the son of immigrant Bohemian Jews—not a plus at a company with extensive dealings with the Arabs and more than a little anti-Semitism in its own executive suite. Moreover, while Weinberger had begun his career as a corporate lawyer, it had been years since he had practiced law, a subject that never held much interest for him. Nor did he claim to know much about business, especially the business of construction and engineering. His expertise was as a manager, a cost-cutter, a political doer and fixer, and through the years it had served him well. Indeed, if anything, the former cabinet secretary, OMB director and Federal Trade Commission chairman was overqualified for the post of general counsel.

Yet Weinberger had been recruited for the Bechtel job by the company's general counsel, Bill Slusser, who was planning to retire, and it appealed to him on a number of counts. With a $200,000-a-year-plus salary, he could afford a residence in one of San Francisco's most affluent suburbs and later acquire a summer place on Maine's tony Mount Desert Island. His wife, Jane, suffered from arthritis, a condition aggravated by the Washington climate, so the Weinbergers were eager to return to California. Finally, a move to Bechtel would put Cap on the same political fast track trodden by so many who shuttled between corporate America and government postings.

Government, and the politics that went with it, had been in Weinberger's blood since boyhood, when for a bedtime story, his father would recount the tale of the Constitutional Convention. His allegiance to the Republican Party began when, at the age of 7, he listened to the proceedings of the 1924 Democratic Convention on the radio. The 103-ballot struggle that produced the presidential nomination of John W. Davies was, Weinberger averred, "exciting," but, on the balance, "I thought the whole proceeding untidy and disorderly."[1]

Weinberger's fascination with politics continued through high school, where he read the *Congressional Record* every day, and as an undergraduate at Harvard, where he served as editor of the *Crimson*, writing editorials he later characterized as "heavily Republican in nature." Despite the prominence his position on the paper gave him, Weinberger experienced some unpleasant moments at Harvard, where he suffered from being a public-school boy, a Westerner and most conspicuously, the bearer of a Jewish surname. On more than one occasion, Weinberger, a practicing Episcopalian, found anonymously written anti-Semitic notes stuffed in his mailbox. In his senior year, he was also passed over for election to any of the college's socially prestigious "final clubs."[2]

Academically, however, his record was exceptional and, after graduating in 1938 *magna cum laude* and a member of Phi Beta Kappa, he was admitted to Harvard Law. Following wartime service as a member of Douglas MacArthur's intelligence staff, he returned to San Francisco, where he entered law practice and soon was involved in local politics. "I became interested in the new group that was formed in San Francisco to do something about the moribund state of the Republican Party," he recalled. "We formed a group that ultimately won . . . a little more than half the seats in the election for the Republican County Committee in San Francisco. Then I became increasingly active in that committee. Ultimately, one of the [state] assembly seats of San Francisco became vacant. . . . People asked me to run, and I agreed, and that's how it all began."[3]

Elected to the state assembly in 1950, Weinberger was originally counted as a liberal Republican and a comer in state politics. That reputation was enhanced when, with A. Alan Post, the state's legislative analyst, he orchestrated an investigation of California's corrupt liquor-licensing practices, then centered around a powerful political figure named William Bonelli. Largely as a result of Weinberger and Post's efforts, Bonelli and a number of his associates were indicted on charges of giving and receiving kickbacks. "It was real major corruption," Weinberger boasted. "Old-fashioned Tammany Hall–style corruption of a really major sort."[4]

Emboldened by his success as a graft-fighter, Weinberger in 1958 resigned his assembly seat to declare his candidacy for state attorney general. He seemed a formidable candidate on the basis of his assembly record. His primary opponent, however, turned out to be even more formidable, and after a lackluster campaign, Weinberger was swept to defeat. He showed no more political aptitude four years later by advising former vice-president Richard Nixon to challenge California governor Pat Brown. Nixon took the advice, ran and was clobbered, nearly ending his political career.

Meanwhile, Weinberger's own forays into politics were proving disastrous. An example of the latter came in 1964, when Weinberger favored the presidential candidacy of Nelson Rockefeller—thus infuriating the state's conservative Republican leaders. Two years later, he blundered again in the Republican primary for governor, a race that pitted Ronald Reagan against former San Francisco mayor George Christopher. Though Weinberger had known Reagan since 1958, and was, by his own accounting, "enormously impressed with his ability to communicate to audiences,"[5] he supported Christopher, and as a result, found himself on the outside looking in when Reagan was elected.

The miscalculation pained Weinberger, who badly wanted to be the state's finance director, a job second in importance only to the governorship itself. Instead, the post went to a Booz, Allen management consultant named Gordon Paul Smith. Fortunately for Weinberger, Smith lasted in the job only a year, and on his resignation, Reagan named him Smith's replacement.

As finance director, Weinberger, the former liberal, experienced a political conversion. "He became a very skillful apologist for what Ronald Reagan wanted," said Post, reporting that Weinberger tailored policies to fit Reagan's views. "He acted like a good lawyer taking the side of his client."[6] "Cap the Knife," as he came to be called, in tribute to his budget cutting, had a rather more difficult time straightening out his client's finances. Despite his promises of fiscal restraint, Reagan in his first year in office had gotten the California legislature to enact the largest state tax increase in U.S. history. Confronted with a huge and embarrassing surplus, Weinberger was then given the task of getting rid of it through massive rebates. As a direct consequence, the state plunged once more into the red. Weinberger solved that problem in turn by recommending another tax increase, which produced another surplus, which eventually gave birth to the Proposition 13 taxpayer revolt.

By then, however, Weinberger had departed Sacramento for Washington and an appointment by Richard Nixon as chairman of the Federal Trade Commission. In six months on the job, Weinberger streamlined the FTC and made it such a watchdog of consumer interests, particularly in the area of auto safety and reliability, that he was congratulated by no less than Ralph Nader. Weinberger also won plaudits from Nixon, who in 1970 appointed him deputy director of the Office of Management and Budget. His boss was a University of Chicago academic named George Shultz. They did not get along well.

Consigned to an office in the Old Executive Office Building, Weinberger fretted that Shultz, who enjoyed sumptuous quarters in the White House, was ignoring him and undercutting his authority. In that perception, he was at least partly correct. When seeking advice, Shultz routinely bypassed Weinberger in favor of his other deputy, associate OMB director Arnold K. Weber. It also irked Weinberger that Shultz did not give him authority to hire and frequently made jokes at his expense. At OMB department-head meetings, for instance, Shultz would grinningly annnounce that he was turning over budget-cutting "to Cap, whose mercies are tender." The comment would draw chuckles from everyone but Weinberger.[7]

Even after Shultz moved to Treasury, leaving Weinberger as OMB director, the resentment continued. One sore point was Shultz's habit of calling press conferences to announce the details of new budgets, a task that was ordinarily left to the OMB director. "Cap was devastated," one of his associates said, adding that Weinberger complained to Shultz about the snub.[8] To mollify him, Shultz began inviting him to the press conferences, which, to Weinberger's annoyance, continued to be held at Treasury rather than OMB.

Weinberger's appointment as HEW secretary, in February 1973, improved the situation somewhat, but though his cabinet rank put him on nominally equal footing with Shultz, it was the Treasury secretary who still commanded the headlines. Shultz' departure for Bechtel didn't change matters.

Not long after, Bechtel's Bill Slusser began to court Weinberger for the Bechtel general counsel job. Slusser, who had known Weinberger since the early 1950s and was his campmate at the Bohemian Grove (both were members of the Isle of Aves lodge), was eager to have him, since he was moving over to special counsel status, and enthusiastically recommended his hiring to Steve junior. Despite reservations raised by several of the company's Middle East hands, who worried over how a man named "Weinberger" would go down with the Arabs, and his own reluctance about bringing in another cabinet member so quickly, Bechtel accepted Slusser's recommendation.

The reception accorded Weinberger was considerably cooler than that which had been given George Shultz. In assuming the job as general counsel and vice-president, Weinberger was replacing perhaps the best-liked executive in the company. "I'd been bumming around the world with some of these guys for years," said Slusser. "Jesus, any new kid on the block would have had difficulties being accepted after all we'd been through."[9]

Weinberger was also hurt by the timing of his arrival. As the second outsider to join Bechtel's tight-knit senior management team in less than a year, he became the focus of the resentment that had been building since Shultz' appointment. "Nobody dared go after George Shultz because he had Steve junior and his father behind him," noted one Bechtel executive. "He was always in the eye of the storm. Cap, though, was fair game."[10]

Unlike Shultz, Cap, the native San Franciscan, was also a known quantity, and what was known about him did not endear him to many Bechtel executives. "Weinberger was perceived as a politician and an ex–talk-show host," said one company manager, referring to Cap's part-time stint at San Francisco's public television station. "Consequently, he was regarded as something of a lightweight by a number of the old-timers."[11]

Weinberger did little to help his own cause. Where Shultz had shown himself to be a relaxed, affable, open manager, Weinberger seemed to many to be guarded and unfriendly. In dealing with subordinates, Weinberger, an Anglophile who liked to quote Shakespeare and Churchill, gave the impression of having scant time for lesser mortals. "Cap had people who would funnel him information," said a former Bechtel manager. "He rarely left his office, and, when he did, he'd go directly to whomever he wanted to see without acknowledging or speaking to anyone else."[12]

For all his political experience, Weinberger also showed himself remarkably obtuse about Bechtel's corporate culture. His combativeness, in particular, did not go down well, especially since his primary role was to provide support and legal guidance to the heads of the operating companies and division chiefs. "The average guy at Bechtel thinks of himself as a worker, not a fighter," explained Slusser. "That's because Bechtel is a service company which succeeds because it keeps its customers happy. The client is supreme; he's buying and we're selling. Cap, though, was a fighter. He was a lot more definite about things than most people at Bechtel."[13]

One thing about which Cap was particularly definite was collecting on outstanding balances—a subject that struck close to his fiscal puritan heart. Accordingly, when he reviewed Bechtel's books and saw that some accounts were in arrears, he took it upon himself to issue ultimatums to the offending parties—some of whom were among Bechtel's "sweetheart" clients. "Cap took a pretty adamant position with clients with whom we'd been doing business for years," said Bechtel director

Bob Bridges. "We had to induce him not to issue ultimatums."[14]

Weinberger ruffled feelings even more by hiring a battery of lawyers to augment the Thelan, Marin attorneys who had worked for Bechtel on contract for nearly forty years. When Weinberger called pipeline chief Jack Lynch to inform him of the change, Lynch, who was used to seeking legal counsel from Thelan, Marin attorney David Bridges— son of company director and longtime Steve senior intimate Bob Bridges—immediately called the elder Bridges to tell him what was afoot.

Before long, Weinberger's empire-building became a source of cruel amusement to some of the Bechtel senior staff, who, in a swipe at Weinberger's roots, took to calling the legal department "The Weinberg Company." Smirked one senior Bechtel executive: "Weinberg... Weinberger... what's the difference?"

Either unaware of or unconcerned about what was being said behind his back, Weinberger plunged on. In an effort to tighten up the legal department's hitherto loose operating style, he hired a new, by-the-numbers administrator very much in his own image. Her name was Virginia Duncan, and the fact that she was a woman did not sit well with Weinberger's critics. They were further disquieted that Duncan, like Weinberger, was an "outsider" (prior to joining Bechtel, she had been a vice-president at KQED, the San Francisco public television station) and, even worse, not a lawyer. Groused one Bechtel officer about Weinberger's hiring of Duncan: "He either didn't look or didn't see anyone within the department for the job. His bringing in Duncan meant that people got passed over or pushed aside."

But what really nettled was Duncan's operating style. No less than Weinberger, she ignored the sensitivities of veteran Bechtel staffers as well as the company's longtime relationship with Thelan, Marin. Bechtel executives, accustomed to the personal, drop-everything service provided by Slusser and Bridges, who were given to hopping on airplanes and flying around the world to solve legal problems, were now informed that their needs would be fulfilled on a first-come, first-served basis, regardless of the size or requirements of their projects. "She ran the department like a butcher shop," groused one Bechtel observer. "You took your number and you waited your turn."[15]

Soon, Bechtel lawyers began leaving in droves, even as complaints about Duncan continued to mount. Weinberger, however, refused to intervene. "Cap is not a compromiser," said one frustrated Bechtel executive, after vainly complaining to him about Duncan. "Nor is he a settler of disputes."[16]

Weinberger had complaints—and jealousies—of his own, most of them revolving around his old nemesis, George Shultz, who had trumped him once again. Not only was Shultz Steve Bechtel, Jr.'s, heir apparent and far better liked in the company, he was also a member of Bechtel's powerful executive committee, something Weinberger was not. Even more than Bechtel's board of trustees, the executive committee set company policy, decided on the big deals, charted the course of Bechtel's future. Not being a member of it was a mark of Weinberger's lesser status: he was a functionary, a legal technician, not a shaper of Bechtel's plans. When Shultz tried to buck up his spirits by telling a reporter that Weinberger would be "participating in management decisions, which is the kind of thing Cap likes," Weinberger, who knew the truth only too well, regarded the remark as condescending.

Moreover, if Weinberger had any hopes of keeping a hand in politics, they were dashed by Steve junior's public announcement, shortly after he had been hired, that he would have no "contact with any government agency, local, state or federal"—a stricture that pointedly did not extend to Shultz. Politics was Weinberger's enduring obsession. Now, thanks to Steve Bechtel, Jr., he was reduced to being a sideline player.

The one concession Bechtel had made to Weinberger's political interests was teaming him with Shultz as codirector of the company's well-financed Political Action Committee. But tracking the voting records of state officials and congressmen, important as it might be to Bechtel's corporate interests, did not seem much reward. Weinberger, who adorned his office with autographed pictures of the presidents he had served, wanted more, a chance to once again rub shoulders with the great and powerful.

He got it, if only briefly, when President Gerald Ford visited San Francisco to deliver a speech at the St. Francis Hotel on September 22, 1975. Weinberger attended the speech and later privately met with Ford for a few minutes, congratulating him on his remarks and letting the President know that he was able and most eager to begin moonlighting for the White House. Though Ford was noncommittal about Weinberger's offer, he seemed glad to see him and promised to keep in touch.

A few minutes after Weinberger left the hotel, Ford himself emerged, and was nearly assassinated by Sarah Jane Moore, a deranged 45-year-old member of a local prisoners'-rights group. Horrified by the incident, Weinberger on October 9 wrote Ford praising him for his courage—"I marvel at your calmness and ability to press on after such an event"—and repeating his offer of assistance. Stating that he would soon be traveling to the Middle East and Europe, Weinberger said, "If you think there is anything I can do to be useful on that trip, I would be most honored and happy to try to accomplish it." He added:

> The work here is very interesting and quite new to a real non-engineer such as myself. Also, there is the problem of trying to remember how to be a lawyer again, but the company is very big and has widespread activities, and that certainly adds greatly to the interst.
>
> However, I must confess I do miss working with you in the Department with all of its multiple problems and frustrations and the opportunity to work closely with you. That was a great experience and one for which I will always be grateful. I am only sorry that it was not possible for me to stay on with you.
>
> It was good to see you again, and I really hope that if you think there is anything I can do to be useful either abroad or here at home, you will be sure to let me know.[17]

The President had only to read between the lines to realize that after two months with Bechtel, Cap was already aching to get back to Washington. As the 1976 elections neared and Weinberger became increasingly disenchanted with his new job, that ache would become even more pronounced.

CHAPTER 17

THE ARAB BOYCOTT

The trials of Caspar Weinberger, painful as they might be for Cap himself, did not loom large for the company he served. Just then, Bechtel had more important worries, and none more pressing than its dealing with the Arabs, which, after thirty-five years of profit, were suddenly at risk.

What threatened them was Bechtel's longtime, unquestioning adherence to a policy few outside the Middle East had ever heard of. It was called the Arab Boycott.

Established in 1948, by Saudi Arabia and the other members of the Arab League, in response to the partitioning of Palestine and the creation of Israel, the boycott prohibited Arabs from trading with Israel directly or from doing business with firms which themselves dealt with Israel or were owned or controlled by Jewish interests. The names of these firms—more than 1,500 in all, and including such companies as Ford, Xerox and Coca-Cola—were maintained on a "blacklist" administered and kept current at the Central Arab Boycott headquarters in Damascus, Syria.

Until the middle 1970s, complying with the boycott had never caused Bechtel any notable trouble—nor had Bechtel ever complained about its discriminatory provisions. The company, in the words of its former personnel manager, "ran deep with Aryan blood,"[1] and according to its critics, just as deep with country-club–style anti-Semitism. Steve senior, for one, habitually identified friends and associates who were Jewish—"He's a Jewish fellow, you know,"[2] he would say, as if they required special categorization—while his company employed few Jews generally and even fewer in supervisory positions. Not wanting to offend Arab clients like Saudi King Faisal, who repeatedly harangued Steve senior about the alleged perfidy of "Zionists," the Bechtel Corporation had also resisted numerous invitations to do business in Israel. Its stated reason for doing so was Israel's "unstable conditions"— a stricture that did not apply to countries like Libya.*

Bechtel might have continued in these policies, unquestioned and undisturbed, but for its Arab friends who, emboldened by their growing economic might, decided to extend the boycott's provisions beyond their own borders. Their first attempt came in February 1975, when Arab moneymen, working through the Kuwait International Investment Company, threatened to withdraw from a syndication deal put together by Merrill Lynch unless Lazard Frères & Company and two other Jewish-owned banking concerns were barred from participating.

The Lazard Frères incident raised an immediate public furor. Merrill Lynch chairman Donald T. Regan, who had refused to drop Lazard from the syndicate, assailed the Arab demands as "economic blackmail,"[3] while New York senator Jacob Javits asserted that the Arabs were using their oil wealth to drive "a wedge of religious and ethnic differences into U.S. society."[4] When it was learned that some financial concerns had submitted to similar Arab pressures in other transactions, Martin Leventhal, Jr., the executive director of the Anti-Defamation League, deplored the willingness of these institutions "to be bullied by Arab demands" and called on "Jews and their allies to fight the boycott."[5]

Responding to the controversy, President Gerald Ford told a press conference on February 27 that the boycott was "totally contrary to American tradition and repugnant to American principles" that he was instructing the Justice Department to conduct a full investigation of "all foreign attempts to promote discrimination in U.S. business."[6]

---

* Jewish leaders saw Bechtel's posturing over Israel for what it was, and over the years repeatedly tried to expose Bechtel's anti-Semitism by offering the company attractive business deals with Israel. No less determinedly, Bechtel refused to be ensnared. According to one well-placed company executive, Bechtel's response to such initiatives was to foot-drag, asserting all manner of excuses why it could not do business in Israel except the actual one—namely, the Arab Boycott. When delaying tactics failed, the executive added, Bechtel would attach so many conditions to its participation as to make the deal impossible. "We knew they were waltzing us around, trying to set us up," said the executive. "We waltzed them right back."

What shape the investigation would take, and how vigorous it would be, was left to Attorney General Edward Levi, a former president of the University of Chicago and Ford's first cabinet appointee. A renowned legal scholar, the 64-year-old Levi had a reputation for being tough, tenacious and independent. He proved it when one week after Ford's announcement, he called a press conference of his own to denounce the boycott as "the purest form of conspiracy in restraint of trade." As such, Levi went on, the boycott represented a "violation of Section I of the Sherman Antitrust Act and a crime under U.S. law."[7] Since Levi was powerless to prosecute the Arabs, he settled on going after a major U.S. firm that had complied with their boycott. That firm was Bechtel.

The Bechtel Corporation and its principal officers were no strangers to Levi. Only two months before, an investigation spearheaded by the attorney general had resulted in the indictment of six Bechtel employees engaged in building a nuclear plant at Calvert Cliffs, Maryland, on charges of extorting $240,000, plus several automobiles and a yacht, from several subcontractors.[*] As president of the University of Chicago, Levi had also had a run-in with Bechtel's Shultz. That had occurred in 1968, when Shultz, then dean of the university's business school, had barred Vietnam protestors from using bullhorns on the business-school campus. On his installation as president, Levi had overturned the edict, infuriating Shultz, who angrily resigned.

In deciding to single out Bechtel, though, Levi was motivated not so much by past history as by the company's extensive ties with the Arabs, ties which included strict observance of the anti-Jewish boycott. Probing through Commerce Department records, Levi and his assistants discovered that Bechtel's contracts and manifests in Arab countries reflected the boycott's terms almost verbatim. Typical was a July 18, 1974, agreement between International Bechtel Incorporated and the Egyptian government, which stipulated:

> Bechtel International does not possess any plant, firm or branch in Israel . . . does not have any agreement for manufacturing, assembly, license or technical assistance with any firm or person or resident of Israel . . . has never participated in the boosting of Israeli products . . . does not use David's Star in connection with its products or trademark . . . has no board members [who are] members of the Joint American-Israeli Chamber of Commerce.

---

[*] Bechtel states it uncovered the employees' alleged misdoings itself and turned the case over to government authorities.

Though Levi's attorneys found at least eleven other firms that routinely incorporated similar restrictions in their contracts, Bechtel was the only one of them privately owned—an important consideration in targeting the boycott suit. As one Justice Department attorney put it: "The fact that Bechtel wasn't a publicly traded company meant that no little old ladies were going to get up at stockholder meetings and claim they were being deprived of their dividend checks because of our action."[8]

Another factor in deciding to go after Bechtel was its visibility: with George Shultz at the helm, it had a far higher profile than any other firm complying with the boycott. But what clinched Levi's decision was information the Justice Department had received from Jewish groups charging that Bechtel was discriminating against its Jewish employees. Characteristic of the complaints was one forwarded by the Houston office of the Anti-Defamation League, which reported that a Bechtel procurement manager named Peter Fischer had been dismissed from the company just as his division was about to take on a big job in Saudi Arabia. Wrote Fischer:

> It was common knowledge within the procurement area that purchase orders on this job were to be limited to companies that had no Jewish or Israeli participation. Those companies invited to bid could have no direct dealings with Israel or Jewish founding presidents or Jewish members of the board.
>
> As for my personal predicament, my present work load dictated that my next logical assignment [would be] to the [Saudi Arabia] job. . . . I feel that my termination served the best interests of [the Arab Boycott and] Bechtel's face-saving. I fear that this kind of supine weakness in the Bechtels of this country foments anti-Semitism. It seems economics dictates morality.[9]

Similar allegations were later made by other Jewish Bechtel employees, including a member of the company's New York staff named Rita Cheren. In a complaint filed with the ADL, Cheren, a college graduate who had worked for the Republican majority leader of the New York Senate before going to work for Bechtel in 1969, claimed that Bechtel had hired her not realizing she was Jewish. "I think they simply assumed I was not Jewish because my name doesn't sound Jewish, I came from upstate New York and had been associated with the Republican party," she stated. "However, the first year I worked there, I asked to take the Jewish holidays off."[10] Specifically, Cheren alleged that because of her religion she had been denied a managerial title even though she held managerial responsibilities and trained men for managerial positions above her own. Moreover, she went on, two of her women coworkers, both Gentile, had been promoted despite the fact that neither was a college graduate. In the New York office where she worked, Cheren said, only 25 to 30 members of the 600-person staff were Jewish, and they were kept in low-level positions so "they were not visible when Arabs came into the office."

Despite the stories told by employees like Cheren and Fischer, the documentation of Bechtel's compliance with the boycott in Commerce Department records and Levi's own enthusiasm for the case, a number of Justice Department officials were uneasy about prosecuting Bechtel, especially on antitrust grounds. Whatever Bechtel's sins, the case was clearly political. Moreover, it involved alleged violations that had occurred overseas, an area where the Sherman Antitrust Act had never before been applied. "A lot of people in the department were skeptical," recalled one Justice Department official. "We were breaking new ground here. And frankly, it didn't seem so much a legal issue as a public-policy one."[11]

Levi's determination to prosecute also unsettled many members of the administration, including Gerald Ford, who hadn't expected his attorney general to go so far. Nonetheless, Ford was reluctant to overrule Levi, whom he had installed at Justice to lift department morale, badly shaken by the Watergate scandals; moreover, the Jewish community was watching the case closely, and with a presidential election looming, Ford could hardly afford to alienate such an important voting block. "It was to Ford's advantage politically for the administration to appear to be behind the antitrust action," said a Washington lawyer involved in Bechtel's defense. "The President was smart enough to realize that there was some excellent political mileage to be garnered from this suit."[12]

Ford's silence did not prevent others in the administration from speaking out, most notably Treasury Secretary William Simon. Having worked hard to recycle Arab petrodollars into the still-sagging U.S. economy, Simon, who would later become a consultant to Bechtel and chairman of an investment firm controlled by Bechtel's partner in Saudi Arabia, Suliman Olayan, publicly blasted Levi's plans as a direct threat to the tens of billions the Arabs were expected to invest in the United States.* More criticism came from Deputy Secretary of State

* Upon leaving his post as Treasury secretary in January 1977, Simon became a

for Mideast Affairs Sidney Sofar as well as from Assistant Secretary of State Arthur Hartman. But by far the most formidable opponent of Levi's plans was Henry Kissinger. The secretary of State held Bechtel and its president in high regard. With its Sumed pipeline deal, Bechtel had helped State open the door to improved relations with the Sadat government. Of Shultz, who would later ask the Secretary of State to join Bechtel's Bohemian Grove lodge, Kissinger was unaccustomedly admiring, proclaiming him "the one man whom I would readily entrust with the future of my country."

Beyond these considerations, Kissinger feared that Levi's suit would jeopardize the Mideast peace offensive he had launched in November 1973. As a result of this offensive, the United States had been able to disengage Israel and Syria on the Golan Heights, bring Egypt out from under Soviet influence, lift the oil embargo and restore relations with Saudi Arabia, the world's largest oil supplier. That Levi should now jeopardize all of this by bringing suit against Bechtel was, Kissinger believed, reckless and ill-advised.

In early October, when Ford raised the boycott issue at a cabinet meeting, Kissinger gave vent to his concerns about the contemplated suit against Bechtel. Just as forthrightly, Levi countered that the suit was necessary as a means of ending the boycott. The argument that ensued between the two of them became so heated that Ford finally ordered them to iron out their differences at a private conference. Later, they did meet, but to no avail. The more Kissinger opposed the suit, the more insistent Levi became. "He was like a bulldog on the boycott issue," a former associate of the attorney general's recalled. "And politically, he was untouchable. He wouldn't back down an inch."[13]

Determined as he was, Levi nonetheless took the precaution of drawing up a memorandum summarizing his case against Bechtel and asking Solicitor General Robert L. Bork, a renowned politically conser-

consultant to Bechtel as well as to Saudi businessman Suliman Olayan, a close associate of the Saudi royal family. Olayan, who had begun his business career as a teenage roustabout for Aramco, was also well connected to Bechtel. Self-taught in the English language, he originally served as an interpreter for Steve senior during the latter's trips to the Middle East, and later joined with Bechtel in a number of business ventures, including helping the company secure the contract for Jubail. As a result of these enterprises, Olayan became one of the richest and most powerful businessmen in Saudi Arabia. In 1980, Olayan hired Simon to be chairman of two investment firms owned by himself and Saudi Prince Khaled bin Abdullah bin Abdel-Rahman al Saud, one of the most influential members of the Saudi royal household. Simon remained in that position for two years.

vative legal scholar, to review it. When Bork gave the memorandum his blessing, despite what he noted were the stiff political implications of the case, Levi was ready to make his move. To avoid possible additional interference from the State Department, though, he held off filing suit until the first week of December, when Ford and Kissinger were safely out of Washington on a state visit to the People's Republic of China. Kissinger, however, learned of the filing only hours before Justice lawyers were to present the case in Federal court in San Francisco. Firing off a telegram to Levi, Kissinger requested a delay until he returned to the United States and reviewed the foreign-policy implications of the case. Unwilling to defy the secretary of State, Levi complied, but struck back by leaking word of Kissinger's interference to the press, which gave the story front-page treatment. In Congress, there was outrage. "Such pressure tactics," New York Congressman James Scheuer wrote Ford, "constitute a flagrant violation of your declared policy and that of the Congress of the United States. . . . If we are to combat the Arab economic boycott effectively, the Department of Justice must be unimpeded in its ability to properly enforce the laws of our nation."[14]

When Kissinger returned to the United States, he repeated to Levi all the arguments he had been making for weeks. Still unmoved, and with public opinion now solidly behind him, Levi filed suit against Bechtel on January 16, two weeks into the election year.

Bechtel, meanwhile, had been making moves of its own. One of its first was to head off charges of employing political influence by assigning the case not to Caspar Weinberger but to Lee Loevinger, a lead counsel with the well-connected Washington firm of Hogan and Hartson. A former chief of the Justice Department's antitrust division, Loevinger in turn had met with Levi in early January, in a last-ditch attempt to head off the filing. The meeting had been friendly—at one point, Levi had even offered to remove himself from the suit if Bechtel thought his Jewishness made him biased—but it had produced no alteration of Levi's position. However, Levi had told Loevinger that Justice was not so much interested in punishing Bechtel as it was in ending the boycott. Indeed, Levi went on, Bechtel could avoid a court appearance altogether if the company agreed to sign a consent decree promising to ignore the Arab Boycott in the future. To sweeten his offer further, Levi invited Bechtel to help draw up the terms of the decree, which, he made clear, would be applied to other companies just as soon as the Bechtel case was resolved.

While Loevinger mulled Levi's offer, the company launched a public relations campaign to defend itself. In a statement released to the press, Bechtel did not dispute that it had complied with the boycott, but stressed that "at no time in history has the Sherman Antitrust Act been held to apply to foreign, politically inspired boycotts." The company also contended that the Justice Department was unjustly persecuting it for activities that had been sanctioned—and in some cases, actively pursued—by various agencies of the U.S. government. As evidence, Bechtel noted that for the previous ten years the U.S. Army Corps of Engineers had operated within the constraints of the boycott provisions, under a 1965 treaty with the Saudis which gave the Arabs the right to reject any contractor used by the corps on the basis of the blacklist.* Bechtel complained that it was being unfairly targeted for prosecution. "Why the hell should we be singled out?" John O'Connell groused to a reporter. "We obey the laws of Saudi Arabia and other countries in which we do business just like everyone else."

In fact, Bechtel appeared to have a strong case, as even members of the Justice Department were privately ready to concede. Trying to win the case, however, would subject the company to a long, embarrassing legal proceeding, one that would put its operations, and those of its publicity-shy Arab clients, under unwelcome scrutiny. Moreover, the company was chary of antagonizing the Ford administration, with which it continued to enjoy warm relations (Steve junior continued to receive invitations to the White House), and from which it was still seeking a number of important business favors, most notably help on its various nuclear-energy projects. But what weighed perhaps most heavily against deciding to fight was the fact that at that moment, the company was under siege from several other quarters.

There was, first of all, the press, which, in the person of the *Washington Star*, had in October 1975 been running a series of articles questioning how it was that Bechtel had been able to secure without competitive bidding a $413,000 contract from the Energy Research and Development Administration to study the economics of coal-slurry technology at the same time the company was lobbying Congress for approval to build a $750 million coal-slurry pipeline. The articles had further revealed that the contract had been awarded Bechtel on the

---

* Besides adhering to the terms of the Arab Boycott, the contract between the Saudis and the U.S. Army Corps of Engineers also committed the United States to pay for all military facilities the corps built in Saudi Arabia. The contract was negotiated by U.S. Ambassador to Saudi Arabia Parker T. "Pete" Hart, who subsequently went on to hold a variety of senior posts at the State Department. In 1973, Hart was hired by Bechtel to serve as its representative to Saudi Arabia and North Africa.

basis of a recommendation by an ERDA staff economist named A. Howard Smith, whom Bechtel had flown to San Francisco and wined and dined at company expense. The *Star* series also alleged that a Washington law firm employed by Bechtel had persuaded the National Science Foundation to take the unprecedented step of requiring a scholar whom it had commissioned to study coal-slurry technology to disclaim any NSF connection with the study, which was highly critical. The articles had caused an uproar in Washington and touched off a congressional investigation as to whether Bechtel had violated conflict-of-interest laws. Though the probe had found no criminality, it had raised serious questions about the ethics of Bechtel's business practices and its ties to various federal agencies.

Nor was that the end of Bechtel's woes. The company was also under attack from a number of its female and black employees. Groups of both had filed noisy lawsuits against the company, charging Bechtel with discrimination in hiring, pay and promotion practices.

The women's suit, which had been joined by 6,400 female Bechtel employees—nearly 80 percent of the home office's female work force—alleged that Bechtel functioned "like a men's club" where women served essentially as corporate handmaidens. By the plaintiff's estimates, fewer than 10 percent of the company's managerial and professional-level jobs were held by women, who received significantly smaller paychecks than their male counterparts. The women further complained that of the 4,000 women college graduates at Bechtel, nearly 75 percent were in low-paying secretarial, clerical or technical jobs.

Similar allegations were made in a suit filed against Bechtel by 400 black employees, joined by another 600 blacks who had left the company. They charged that they too had been victims of discrimination, and also of harassment and, in some cases, physical abuse. Bechtel vociferously denied the charges, as it did those filed by the women, but the blacks found support from the NAACP, which made its lawyers available to press the suit. The NAACP also petitioned the governments of Saudi Arabia, Nigeria and other African nations in which Bechtel did business to take a stand against what NAACP officials termed the company's "home office racism."*

While the suits made their way through the courts, Bechtel also

---

* Bechtel settled the sex-discrimination case in April 1979 by paying its suing female employees $1.3 million. A year earlier, the company settled the racial-bias case by paying $700,000.

found itself being pilloried for work it was doing on three major projects: the $3 billion Alaska pipeline, where it was under attack from a consortium of environmentalists; the $1.6 billion Bay Area Rapid Transit System (BART), where delays and assorted construction snafus had resulted in a $500 million lawsuit by the State of California,* and the Washington, D.C., Metro, where local black leaders were complaining that Bechtel had hired only a handful of black workers in a city where 70 percent of the population was black.

The combination of these troubles had resulted in ruinous publicity for Bechtel and put the company in an uncommonly defensive mood. Realizing that more controversy was the last thing the company needed, Steves senior and junior reluctantly decided to settle the boycott suit, and in the spring of 1976 they instructed Loevinger to open negotiations with Justice on the wording of a consent decree.

While Loevinger and company officials worked out peace terms in Washington, Steve junior and Shultz flew to the Middle East to secure the approval of the Arabs. They did not come away empty-handed. "They urged the Arabs to ease the boycott restrictions," said Aramco's former chairman Frank Jungers of their mission. "And with the exception of Iraq and Syria, neither of which did any real trading with the West, most of the Arab League nations were agreeable to it. After all,

---

* Dedicated by President Richard Nixon in September 1972, the $1.6 billion BART system had from its very beginnings been a special project for Bechtel—and one of the most troublesome in the history of the company. The idea for a subway system linking San Francisco, Berkeley and Oakland began with the Bay Area Council, a group of San Francisco–area businessmen, who as early as 1950 had begun plumping for the line as a means of helping make San Francisco the gateway to the Pacific Basin. BAC, in turn, was dominated by Bechtel family members, officials and friends, including company chairman Bill Waste, who served as BAC's chairman, and Steve Bechtel, Sr., a member of BAC's board of governors. In 1957, BAC hired the Stanford Research Institute to prepare a study detailing the benefits that would accrue to the region from mass transit. On the basis of this study, and a lavish public relations campaign heavily funded by Bechtel and its corporate allies, Bay Area residents narrowly approved a $792 million bond issue for the project in 1962. The project itself, however, did not get under way until 1966. With Bechtel as head of engineering construction (a chore for which it was paid $150 million), the job suffered numerous delays. There were more problems with BART's railway cars (half of those delivered malfunctioned so severely they couldn't be used even after extensive repairs); its state-of-the-art traffic-control system (often, cars wouldn't start; equally often, cars that did start wouldn't stop), and not least, with the Bechtel-constructed tunnel beneath San Francisco Bay, which the State of California refused to certify as safe. To complicate matters even further, there were also whopping cost overruns and numerous accusations of fraud, several of them directed against Bechtel.

they needed us as much as we needed them."[15]

By mid-1976, it appeared that Bechtel's decision to cooperate was beginning to pay off. After weeks of intense line-by-line, word-by-word negotiations, Loevinger and Douglas E. Rosenthal, deputy chief of the Justice Department's foreign-commerce division, had forged the first draft of an agreement that allowed Bechtel and other companies doing business in the Mideast considerable latitude in dealing with the boycott. Under the draft agreement's terms, U.S. companies could, for instance, still sign contracts that contained boycott clauses, enforce boycott provisions against foreign companies on the Arab blacklist and allow the Arabs to reject individual subcontractors and suppliers recommended by companies like Bechtel, even if the subcontractors and suppliers were American-owned. So lenient were the terms that several Jewish groups, including the ADL and the American Jewish Congress, argued that the agreement should not be accepted by the court. *

Of far larger concern to Bechtel were two pieces of legislation pending before Congress designed to blunt the boycott's impact. The more moderate of these measures, an amendment to the Export Administraton Act introduced by Connecticut Democratic Senator Abraham Ribicoff, specified that any corporation which complied with the boycott could lose its foreign tax credits, its foreign tax deferrals and its export subsidies. This would significantly reduce the profitability of companies like Bechtel, and as a result, would put them at a substantial disadvantage in competing for Arab business with Japanese and European firms. Harsher still was a measure introduced in the House, which flatly prohibited U.S. companies from cooperating with the boycott. This measure, the so-called "Rosenthal Amendment," put forth by New York Democratic Congressman Benjamin Rosenthal, would impose fines and/or prison terms on executives whose firms heeded the provisions of the boycott, and would provide for the suspension of their export licenses as well. If enacted, either of these amendments would cause severe financial hardship to Bechtel or any U.S.

---

* Jewish resentment of the consent decree continued under the Carter administration, and under mounting pressure, Attorney General Griffin Bell significantly tightened the Justice Department's interpretation of its terms. Bechtel responded by filing suit in June 1977, demanding to be freed from the consent decree altogether. Eighteen months later, U.S. District Judge William Ingram ruled against the company, which then appealed to the U.S. Supreme Court. On November 30, 1981, the High Court sustained Ingram's decision, ruling that Justice had correctly interpreted the consent agreement. The agreement itself remains in force, though to date, Bechtel has yet to undertake any business in Israel.

company atempting to do business in the Mideast. Taken together, they effectively shut the door to virtually all significant U.S. trade with the Arabs for as long as the boycott remained in place.

Alarmed that antiboycott sentiment was getting out of hand, the administration dispatched Kissinger and Simon to Capitol Hill to cool tempers and head off passage of either measure. Simon warned darkly that if either the Ribicoff or Rosenthal amendment were passed, Arab attitudes would "harden" and, as the Treasury secretary put it, "destroy the progress we have already made." No less ominously, Kissinger predicted that enactment of either measure would wreak incalculable harm on U.S. foreign relations and assist the Soviets in creating mischief in the area.

Bechtel, for its part, was frantic at the prospect of congressional intervention, and willing to try anything to head it off, including so unlikely a course as appealing to the ADL.

The idea of asking the ADL to intercede with Congress had originated with Shultz, who had been working closely with his former administration colleagues since the beginning of the crisis. Frustrated with the administration's lack of success, Shultz had called ADL chairman Seymour Graubard and arranged a meeting at Graubard's Park Avenue law offices in early July. Though nothing substantive had come of the conference—Graubard arguing that congressional action was necessary if the boycott was to be broken—the ADL leader had shown a willingness to listen further, and Shultz arranged another meeting for September 1.

By then, Shultz had bolstered Bechtel's position by hiring a Washington lobbyist named Charls Edward Walker. A former deputy secretary of the Treasury during the waning days of the Nixon administration, the strapping, Texas-born Walker was counted as one of the most effective special pleaders in the capital, with a blue-chip client list that included such corporate-giants as General Electric, U.S. Steel and Ford. Folksy in manner, self-deprecating in style (he lampooned his whopping fees by writing a parody of "Amazing Grace" entitled "Amazing Greed"), bluntly direct in approach ("There's no bullshit about him," said one of the many whose arms he tried to twist. "He comes right to the point.") Walker, who held a doctorate in economics and had taught at the Wharton Business School, had been one of the prime movers in creating the Business Roundtable, an association of business leaders which included Steve Bechtel, Jr., and George Shultz among its members and was even more powerful than the old Business Council. His contacts with the Roundtable members, a number of whom he enlisted in Bechtel's cause, along with those on the Hill, made him, in the estimation of *The New York Times*, the strongest lobbying ally a businessman could have.

On September 1, Walker and Shultz, accompanied by Du Pont chairman and Business Roundtable member Irving Shapiro and San Francisco real estate magnate Walter Shorenstein, Bechtel's partner in a number of real estate ventures, traveled to New York to meet with Graubard, who was accompanied by several friends of his own, among them the ADL's president, Benjamin R. Epstein, and its general counsel, Arnold Forster. Graubard opened the meeting by repeating what he had told Shultz in July—notably, that while the ADL did not endorse the attempt by Congress to block the boycott, neither would it do anything to oppose it. Shultz followed by saying that thanks largely to Simon's behind-the-scenes efforts, some of the heat engendered by the boycott issue appeared to be dissipating. From his recent travels in the Middle East, Shultz added, it seemed that the Arabs were softening as well, especially in regard to those provisions of the boycott which barred U.S. firms from employing Jews in Arab lands. "Besides," Shultz added, "Jews assigned to these places by Bechtel mostly don't want to go there anyway."[17] In light of this progress, Shultz urged Graubard to use the ADL's influence to tone down, if not eliminate altogether, the punitive provisions of the riders attached to the Export Administration Act, whose renewal was then before Congress. If the legislation passed with the antiboycott language intact, Shultz warned, it could "well cause a major confrontation between the Saudis and other Arab countries and their American suppliers."[18] The Saudis didn't need the United States, Shultz went on, and, "while they like us," they might, if pushed by Congress, turn to the Japanese and Europeans for services and facilities the United States was currently providing. The ADL, and American Jews generally, Shultz concluded, should be "deeply concerned" about that possibility and "do what is necessary to head it off."[19]

Picking up from what Shultz had said, Walker conceded to Graubard that it was "very late in the day"[20] for the ADL to do anything. Nonetheless, he emphasized, the effort was necessary, and had to be made soon, since Congress would shortly be voting on the bill prior to its scheduled adjournment September 30.

Despite Shultz and Walker's entreaties, and their endorsement by Shapiro and Shorenstein, Graubard remained unmoved. The ADL, he said, was not budging.

Walker shrugged; then, in his Texas drawl, he offered offhandedly,

"Well, the bill's not going to get through Congress anyway. At least, not in its present form it isn't."[21]

"What exactly do you mean, the bill won't pass?" asked Graubard, who had been assured that Ribicoff had ample votes to ensure his amendment's enactment.

Walker confidently smiled. "On the last day of the session, someone in the Senate is going to get up and object to the bill. He's going to get up and talk and talk and talk and the bill's just not going to get through. Not this year."[22]

It took a moment or two for the full impact of Walker's statement to register. Finally, Graubard realized that Walker had already arranged some sort of deal. The bill would fail, whatever the ADL did, but if only for public relations purposes, Bechtel was offering the organization a chance to get on board. Graubard was impressed—and chilled. A few moments later, he brought the meeting to an end.

There turned out to be good reason for Walker's confidence: the fix was indeed in. As a result of what Walker later called "plain old vanilla lobbying,"[23] Walker had recruited Texas Senator John Tower to the Bechtel cause. His role, however, was not evident until September 28, when the bill, of which one version had been passed by the House, another by the Senate, came to the Senate floor, in the form of a motion to name a conference committee. Without such a committee to resolve differences between the Senate and House versions, the bill could not become law. Under ordinary circumstances, however, the naming of a committee was routine. Not, however, this time. Tower rose to object, citing obscure parliamentary points of procedure. Supporters of the Ribicoff amendment, like Illinois Democrat Adlai Stevenson III, were furious. "The will of the Congress," Stevenson declared, "is being frustrated by a parliamentary ploy aimed at keeping this legislation from being brought to a final vote in the Senate. That effort is being supported by the Administration."[24] Stevenson was right, but with Congress anxious to adjourn, there was nothing he could do. Tower's point was sustained, and, with that, the bill—and the threat to Bechtel's interests in the Middle East—died.

"What Charls Walker said would happen, happened, exactly as he said it would," Sy Graubard noted later. "He was worth every dollar Bechtel paid him."[25]

CHAPTER 18

NUCLEAR ECLIPSE

In beating back the controversy over the Arab Boycott, Bechtel had provided a graphic demonstration of its political muscle and legislative clout. The company was a power in Washington, one whose influence reached to the very highest levels of government. But there were some issues on which connections, however gilded and glittering, were not enough. One such issue was nuclear power.

The nuclear industry, and Bechtel with it, had prospered greatly during the late 1960s and 1970s, thanks in no small measure to Richard Nixon, who made the expansion of nuclear power a centerpiece of his plans to combat the Arab oil cartel. Responding to a presidential call to build a thousand nuclear power plants by the year 2000, U.S. utilities in 1973 had ordered a record thirty-one nuclear plants, of which Bechtel, by now the largest builder of nuclear power stations in the world, was scheduled to build more than half. For Bechtel, the orders were only the beginning of the good news—or of the billions that were expected to flow in.

In 1969, the company, working in concert with Union Carbide, had persuaded Nixon to reverse two decades plus of U.S. policy by allowing commercial concerns to produce and sell enriched nuclear fuel, including plutonium, which could be used to power nuclear power plants and build H-bombs as well. It was a historic—and according to its critics, profoundly dangerous—decision; but at the time, the announcement did not receive much notice. Quietly, a Bechtel executive and former Atomic Energy Commission official named Ashton O'Donnell began drawing up marketing plans for a nuclear-fuel development project. By early 1972, the plans were sufficiently advanced for O'Donnell to pay a sales call on the Japanese, who were expected to be major customers for enriched uranium fuel. Flying to Tokyo, O'Donnell met with officials from several Japanese utilities, along with executives from Union Carbide, which had already agreed to join Bechtel in producing and marketing the power-plant fuel. During several days of talks, the Japanese, Bechtel and Carbide committed themselves to jointly spending $6 million on a study that would lay out the whys, wherefores and details of a nuclear-enrichment plant.

In Washington, meanwhile, Bechtel representatives were making a similar pitch to the administration, which, still reeling from the Arab oil "shocks," did not require much persuading. All that remained, aside from getting the approval of Congress, was for the United States and Japan to sign a formal agreement. That, in turn, was accomplished, in July 1972, when Nixon, accompanied by National Security Advisor Henry Kissinger and Secretary of State William P. Rogers, flew to Honolulu for a two-day summit meeting at the Kuilima Hotel with Japan's new 52-year-old prime minister, Kakuei Tanaka. Known by his admirers as the "computerized bulldozer," Tanaka was no less enthusiastic about buying nuclear fuel than Nixon was in peddling it. Using the Bechtel–Union Carbide proposal as a basis for their discussion, Tanaka and Nixon drew up an agreement for a study to be made by the United States and Japan. The document that resulted was, almost word for word, identical with the O'Donnell paper.[1]

In November, with presidential elections over and the study in hand, Nixon gave Bechtel and Union Carbide—and their Japanese partners—tentative approval to build the world's first privately owned nuclear-fuel plant, a $5.7 billion facility at Dothan, Alabama. Financing for the plant, which was to be operated by Carbide and a specially created Bechtel subsidiary, Uranium Enrichment Associates (UEA), was to come largely from the federal government. When, the following June, Nixon provided Bechtel and six other members of the nuclear fraternity with access to the previously classified secrets of uranium-enrichment technology, *The Wall Street Journal* hailed the beginning of "what may be the largest commercial undertaking in history."[2]

Bechtel was no less enthusiastic. Once the Dothan plant was built and private uranium enrichment a reality, the company could function as a veritable one-stop supermarket for the nuclear industry—not to mention the emerging countries that wanted one. As John A. Damm, UEA's business-development manager, glowingly put it in a letter to the Brazilian minister of mining and energy, the company's product line would soon run "the gamut from the development of uranium mines, reprocessing, enrichment fuel processing . . . through the design of nuclear plants themselves."[3]

The confident expectations began going awry when W. Kenneth Davis, Bechtel's vice-president for nuclear development (and later, deputy secretary of Energy for Ronald Reagan) attended a nuclear-energy conference in Washington in September 1973. During a panel discussion, Davis was startled to hear Dr. Stephen Hanauer, an Atomic Energy Commission official, remark offhandedly that "there is likely to be a major nuclear disaster in the world, and the prime candidate is Tarapur." Hanauer went on to charge that "the reactor suppliers and the architect engineer are acting irresponsibly and to the detriment of the best interests of the United States in that they've failed to offer assistance in dealing with Tarapur's problems."[4]

The Tarapur to which Hanauer referred was a nuclear plant in India, located on the Arabian Sea, some 60 miles north of Bombay. It was the first major commercial atomic power station in India, the largest nuclear facility in Asia and a showcase for exporting nuclear technology to developing nations. All of which would have been cause for alarm. But there was one fact more: Tarapur had been built by Bechtel.

Still disbelieving what he had heard, Davis accosted Hanauer afterward to ask if it was true, and in reply, received another jolt. Not only was it true, Hanauer told him: the situation was, if anything, even worse than he had described. Recently, he recounted, an AEC official named Clifford Beck had visited Tarapur and, among other horrors, found Indian laborers perched above the plant's "radwaste" facility, trying to disperse radioactive debris with long bamboo poles. So ineffective was Tarapur's waste-disposal procedure, Hanauer went on, that extremely high levels of radioactivity had been found in the nearby waters of the Arabian Sea. This in turn had led the Indian government recently to ban all fishing in the area, which traditionally supplied fish and mollusks to the markets of Bombay. Moreover, according to Hanauer, Beck had also found large quantities of radioactive material and drums of radioactive waste, many of them open, strewn around the plant like uncollected garbage. Under existing conditions, Hanauer quoted Beck as saying, Tarapur was a disaster waiting to happen.

Davis hurried back to San Francisco and apprised his superiors of what he had heard, adding a recommendation that Bechtel talk to Beck, as Davis put it, "to find out how much of what Steve [Hanauer] said was exaggeration and how much is true."[5] Bechtel did talk to Beck, who confirmed everything Hanauer had said. Now truly worried, the company immediately dispatched one of its senior nuclear engineers, John G. Walker, to inspect Tarapur personally.

On arrival in Bombay, Walker spent several days conferring with Indian officials and also with executives of General Electric, the supplier of Tarapur's reactor. He then traveled to Tarapur, where his findings essentially confirmed those of Beck.[6] As Beck had observed, the radwaste facility wasn't functioning properly, primarily because the amount of waste being processed, some 50,000 gallons per day, was more than the system's capacity. In addition, Walker discovered that the plant's complex network of pipes, valves, pumps and condensers was leaking like a large and extremely dangerous sieve. One area alone, the so-called drywell section of the plant, was experiencing the leakage of between 3,000 and 4,000 gallons a day of radioactive fuel. As a result, Walker told company officials when he returned to San Francisco, "all of the personnel directly involved in the plant's operations (more than 500 employees)" had received "a large radiation dose." The same, he added, was true of many of the hundreds of temporary workers employed by the plant, including local natives who were hired as "valve twisters." Summarizing the growing health risks, Walker noted that in 1969, 399 Tarapur workers had received "substantial exposure" to radiation; a year after that, the number had grown to 550, and was on its way to a total of 1,500 workers by the end of 1972. Nor was that all. During one recent incident, a refueling outage that had occurred in May 1973, the radiation exposure had been so severe that, as Walker put it, "it was the equivalent of 'burning out' 400 people for a year."

In a memo to Bechtel officials, Davis tried to put the best face on Walker's findings, asserting that they did "not quite substantiate Steve Hanauer's stated opinion with respect to 'a major nuclear disaster.'" Nonetheless, Davis could not conceal his unease. "I found it far from reassuring and indeed it is most disturbing," he wrote, referring to

Walker's report. "I am concerned that some incident or other may arise out of this situation which might have international publicity and repercussions. It doesn't sound good."[7]

As Davis and his colleagues in San Francisco would soon discover, Bechtel's nuclear problems weren't restricted to India. Even as Walker was inspecting the Tarapur plant, another Bechtel nuclear official had learned from an executive at Chicago's Commonwealth Edison that Dresden I, the prototype nuclear plant built by Bechtel and General Electric in 1959, was experiencing the same kind of problems as Tarapur.[8] Already, the utility had spent $700,000 to commission a study on how to clean up Dresden I's radioactive wastes and was estimating that the costs of an actual clean up would run as high as $30 million. Without such a cleanup, Dresden I would not meet AEC standards. Even with it, Dresden I might have to be retired far earlier than had been expected. By far the worst news, though, was contained in a memo from a Bechtel executive who, noting the problems with Tarapur and Dresden I, predicted that the same fate would probably befall "all BWR [boiling-water reactors] which went into operation before 'the lowest practicable release' designs were required." In short, the entire generation of BWR plants Bechtel and GE had begun building during the late 1950s were not—if the Dresden and Tarapur situations were any indications—in compliance with minimum AEC safety requirements.*

---

* The alleged construction defects in Bechtel-built nuclear plants were also a source of concern for a number of Bechtel employees, few of whom fared well for complaining.

A case in point was that of E. Earl Kent, a senior quality-control engineer, who in 1982 was told that he had to take an oral welding test after he complained—first to his Bechtel superiors, later to the Nuclear Regulatory Commission—that Bechtel was using substandard building materials and faulty welding techniques in the Midland, Michigan, and San Onofre, California, nuclear power plants. Kent, a master welder who had passed previous written welding tests with flying colors, was told he had failed the oral exam—itself a highly unusual procedure in the construction industry—and was subsequently discharged. He later filed suit against Bechtel, but after nearly four years was forced to drop the litigation because he hadn't the funding to pay legal and court costs.

Bechtel also allegedly moved to silence Richard Parks, a senior start-up engineer involved in the Three Mile Island cleanup operation. After Parks and several of his colleagues claimed that the salvage operation was fraught with safety violations and excessive waste, they were, or so they claimed, harassed and in Parks's case, stripped of his responsibilities and ultimately fired. Parks later filed a fifty-six-page affidavit detailing his charges, claiming that after his discharge, his apartment was broken into and his papers rifled. Though nothing was taken during the alleged break-in, Parks was suffi-

FRIENDS IN HIGH PLACES

While Bechtel was sorting out what to do about Tarapur and Dresden, it was also facing unexpected problems on another front. Hoping to drive up the price of uranium, and thus make commercial enrichment development more appealing, the AEC in 1973 had announced it was going to limit the amount of enrichment supplies that U.S. and foreign utilities could obtain. The immediate beneficiaries of the decision, however, were not the Americans, but the Europeans, who, with the U.S. stranglehold on nuclear supplies broken, began enticing Third World customers with offers not only to build nuclear plants, but to supply the fuel that would run them.

By 1974, European concerns were taking away business from American suppliers in half a dozen countries, including Iran, where European manufacturers were awarded contracts for two nuclear reactors GE and Westinghouse had counted on supplying. A similar situation developed in Brazil, where Bechtel and Westinghouse had been assiduously wooing the government for three years in anticipation of building that country's first nuclear plants. So eager was Bechtel for the Brazilian business that the company had even arranged financing for the project from the Export-Import Bank, a triumph much hailed by Henry Kearns at the 1971 Decatur House press conference. But in the final stages of negotiation, the Brazilians, frustrated that they could no longer look to the United States for nuclear supplies, began to back-pedal, threatening to give the business to a German firm. What good were its nuclear plants, a Brazilian official complained to Bechtel, if the Americans couldn't supply the fuel to run them?

After all its effort, Bechtel had no intention of losing out to the Germans, especially not with an estimated $8 billion in nuclear work pending. The trouble was that Bechtel couldn't ensure nuclear-fuel delivery until its planned enrichment plant at Dothan, Alabama, was in operation. In March 1974, Bechtel, at a critical impasse, devised what turned out to be a disastrous solution: it offered to build Brazil a nuclear-enrichment plant of its very own.

The Brazilians were still mulling Bechtel's proposal when, on May 18, the Indian government, using plutonium produced by the Tarapur reactor and heavy water obligingly provided by the Nixon administra-

---

ciently unsettled by the incident to take his family into hiding. As a result of the suit against Bechtel, Parks received a settlement from the company in 1987. Throughout the incident, Bechtel maintained that the harassment of Parks consisted of the company's not allowing him to use Bechtel's office equipment and support staff to run his own outside company in violation of Bechtel's rules and common business practices.

tion, detonated an atomic bomb at the bottom of a 107-meter-deep shaft in the Rayartham Desert.

As nuclear explosions went, the Indian bomb was hardly more than a firecracker. All the same, it had a megaton impact. "A psychological barrier had been broken," wrote one nuclear historian. "The Indian test appeared to be the first step toward a new age of nuclear chaos. It now seemed that anyone might build a bomb: desperately poor nations, mad dictators, even political terrorists."⁹

Nowhere were the repercussions more severe than in Washington, where Henry Kissinger tried unsuccessfully to conceal American involvement by claiming that it was the Canadians who had supplied the Indians with heavy water, not the United States. Kissinger's clumsy attempt at deception succeeded only in enraging Congress, which thereupon temporarily shelved the administration's proposal for commercial nuclear-fuel enrichment. In August came another blow when the nuclear industry's chief cheerleader, Richard Nixon, was forced from office. By the end of the year, U.S. utilities had cancelled or deferred 60 percent of the nuclear capacity they had ordered only twelve months before.

Staggered by the sudden turnabout in events, but not deterred by them, Bechtel switched its nuclear lobbying efforts to Nixon's successor, Gerald Ford. At first, the company's prospects seemed promising. In late September, at the behest of Steve junior, the new president flew to Detroit to address the Bechtel-organized "World Energy Conference." In his speech to two thousand delegates from eighty countries, Ford announced the creation of "Project Interdependence," a sort of reverse OPEC in which the United States and other oil-importing nations would band together to conserve and share their energy resources. Later the same month, Ford, who had already sought Bechtel's views on overcoming inflation, appointed Steve junior as one of eight management representatives on the newly formed White House Labor–Management Committee, "whose counsel and recommendations," said Ford, "will not only be sought but given to me face-to-face."¹⁰ To no one's great surprise, Bechtel's counsel was for the United States to begin a crash program of building domestic nuclear power plants. He also recommended that Ford continue his predecessor's policy of backing the commercialization of nuclear-fuel enrichment.

Before long, a stream of communications, boosting Bechtel's nuclear plans, was flowing back and forth between San Francisco and the White House. Typical was a telegram fired off to William Seidman,

Ford's special assistant for economic affairs, by Bechtel vice-president Cordell Hull, a distant cousin of Franklin Roosevelt's secretary of State who bore the same name, in late 1975, protesting a rumored cut in funding for the Export-Import Bank, which had financed many of Bechtel's nuclear projects.[11] Almost apologetically, Seidman wrote back to tell Hull that Bechtel could "feel assured that necessary financial support—direct loans, discount loans and guarantees and insurance—will be available in order to maintain U.S. competitiveness in foreign markets."[12]

Bechtel also enlisted Ford, as it had Nixon, in the cause of privatizing nuclear-fuel enrichment. On May 30, 1975, UEA submitted to White House domestic assistant James Cannon a proposal outlining the terms and conditions under which it would proceed with the building of the Dothan plant, which had yet to be given congressional authorization. Written by the ubiquitous Ash O'Donnell, the proposal, which covered the cost of building Dothan plus two adjacent nuclear power stations, called for the U.S. government to put up a total of $8 billion in loan guarantees. It was a staggering amount, one that rendered the federal bailouts of Chrysler and Lockheed minuscule by comparison. Despite his calls for fiscal restraint, and his recent turndown of New York City's plea for $1 billion in loan guarantees to avoid bankruptcy, Ford did not blanch. On June 26, three weeks after the Bechtel proposal reached the White House, Ford called on Congress to pass the Nuclear Fuel Assurances Act.

"Today," he proclaimed, "I am asking the Congress to join me in embarking this Nation on an exciting new course which will help assure energy independence. I am referring to the establishment of an entirely new private industry in America to provide fuel for nuclear power reactors—the energy resource of the future. I am referring to uranium enrichment which is presently a government monopoly."[13]

The administration's proposal—a virtually verbatim duplication of the Bechtel plan—called for the federal government to grant UEA a number of extremely generous technical and financial concessions. Among them, the government was to: ensure that its financial guarantees would remain in effect until the plant had been in operation for a year; grant UEA access to the government's stockpile of enriched uranium to meet its contracts, in the event the plant was unfinished or working below capacity during the first five years of its operation; purchase up to two-thirds of the plant's output during the first five years of operation, if UEA couldn't sell it elsewhere; agree to buy the domestic owners' interest in the plant and assume all their liabilities if the plant failed—and finally, in what was the most attractive assurance from UEA's standpoint, guarantee the domestic participants in UEA a 25 percent profit on their investment in case the Dothan plant went bankrupt. The total potential liability in this deal to UEA was a small fraction of the potential $8 billion liability to the U.S. taxpayers.

In laying out NFAA to Congress, Ford never mentioned any of these concessions, noting only that "contract authority in the amount of $8 billion will be needed." To take the sting out of that figure—the largest-ever federal commitment for any private project of any kind—he hastened to add, "We expect almost no actual government expenditures to be involved. In fact, creation of a private enrichment industry will generate substantial revenues for the United States Treasury through payment of federal income taxes and compensation of use of government-owned technology."[14]

Ford was similarly upbeat in describing the role foreigners would play. While acknowledging that "under the proposed arrangements there will be an opportunity for foreign investments in these plants" (indeed, Bechtel had already lined up tentative participation from Japan as well as West Germany, France and Iran), Ford assured the lawmakers that "the plants will remain firmly under U.S. control. There will be no sharing of technology," the president went on. "Foreign investors and customers will not have access to sensitive, classified technology."[15] In fact, the United States, under Nixon, had already entered into an enrichment-technology agreement with one of UEA's proposed investors: namely, Japan.

This too Ford failed to mention. Instead, he urged Congress to pass NFAA with all possible speed, so that, as he put it, the United States could count on "continued availability of reliable energy."

Given Ford's timing, the bill's whopping concessions and not least, Congress' worries over nuclear proliferation, the chances of authorization were at best remote. They diminished even further when, one day after the president's message, West Germany announced its intention to sell enrichment technology to the Brazilians, despite U.S. efforts to block the sale. When the State Department demanded an explanation, the Germans said they were merely countering an offer from a U.S. firm, Bechtel Power Corporation, to build an enrichment plant in Brazil.

Confronted with the West Germans' revelation, the State Department professed both ignorance and righteous indignation. Various department officials told the press that Bechtel's Brazilian gambit was "totally unauthorized" and "way out of line." In San Francisco, meanwhile, a Bechtel spokesperson asserted that the offer to build the multibillion-dollar plant had been made by an "overzealous salesman" without authorization from headquarters. The company maintained that Bechtel's senior management, including Shultz and the Bechtels themselves, had been totally unaware of what had been going on.

Such, at least, was the corporate line. Not long afterward, though, an unnamed senior Bechtel executive told a reporter from *Science* magazine that Bechtel wasn't as ignorant as it claimed. "These guys aren't selling used cars, you know," said the executive. "They're very, very cautious. Bechtel headquarters was kept fully informed." The executive added: "The State Department knew what we were doing every step of the way. My impression is that Dixie Lee Ray [AEC chairperson and a former member of Steve junior's World Energy Conference organizing committee] was [also] kept apprised, totally."[16]

Though Bechtel continued to maintain its innocence, the executive's assertions were largely borne out by a confidential Bechtel working paper obtained by California Public Utilities commissioner Leonard Ross in August 1976. The documents, not made public until now, indicate that Bechtel based its offer to Brazil on a statement made by Secretary of State Henry Kissinger to the Washington Energy Conference on February 11, 1974. "Within a framework of broad cooperation," Kissinger told the Energy Conference delegates, "the United States is prepared to examine the sharing of enrichment technology, diffusion and centrifuge."

With the explosion of the Indian nuclear device in May, however, the plans Kissinger spoke of were shelved. Apparently less concerned by the policies of its own government than it was by competition from the Germans, Bechtel nonetheless pressed on, and in February 1975, offered to build Brazil an enrichment plant. According to the documents obtained by Ross, the offer was "authorized" by Bechtel's corporate chiefs, and included a promise to build the plant *whether or not* the U. S. government endorsed the proposal. The papers further reveal that the State Department was informed of Bechtel's proposal some time in late February of early March 1975—four months before the Germans' disclosures. According to the papers, the State Department raised no objections.

Despite this evidence, Bechtel continued to protest its innocence, as did Shultz, who, in his 1982 confirmation hearings for secretary of

State, told the Senate Foreign Relations Committee that he had "heard about the incident long after the fact." As for the offer itself, Shultz dismissed it as the unauthorized act of "an over-enthusiastic business development person."[17]

By then, however, the damage was long since done. Infuriated by the revelation that Bechtel was casually marketing the most dangerous technology in the world, Congress failed to pass NFAA, and the dream of producing a profit from nuclear fuel was dead.

In its press releases, and in the pronouncements of executives, Bechtel would remain optimistic about the value of nuclear power, both to the world and to the company's bottom line. All the same, an era had come to an end. Once confident it could build anything anywhere, the company was hunkering down, turning inward, growing more cautious. It was an appropriate posture, for there were more problems still ahead.

CHAPTER 19

COMPANY TROUBLES

On a sweltering day in March 1977, at a tiny Saudi Arabian fishing village on the shores of the Red Sea, Bechtel began work on the largest project in construction history: the creation of the industrial city of Jubail.

It was a daunting undertaking by any standard, from its cost—an estimated $30 billion—to the number of men involved in its construction—41,000 laborers from thirty-nine countries, plus 1,600 Bechtel project managers, civil and mechanical engineers, architects and draftsmen—to the sheer amount of sand to be moved—370 million cubic meters of it, and that merely to prepare the ground for Jubail's industrial park. Surveying the site where a city with the population of Minneapolis would rise, *Time* magazine enthused: "In their short-sleeved shirts and wide ties, toting clip boards and pocket calculators, the Bechtel brigade seems the very embodiment of American technological know-how. In all the expansive sweep of civil engineering from the pyramids of the Nile to the construction of the Suez Canal, nothing so huge or costly as Jubail has been attempted."[1]

For Bechtel, which had not been a major presence in Saudi Arabia for nearly a decade, the project came at an especially welcome moment. After the embarrassment of the Arab Boycott, the near-collapse of the nuclear power industry and the recent loss of several major projects, most notable among them the Alaskan pipeline, the company badly needed a winner just then, and in Jubail—which would bring in an estimated $200 million in profits every year for the next two decades—Bechtel clearly had found one. Moreover, there was other good fortune in the offing, in the form of contracts to build another Saudi Arabian industrial city (the $1 billion Yanbu), the $3.4 billion Riyadh International Airport and assorted other projects growing out of the Saudi government's decision to commit $145 billion to industrial and civic development between 1975 and 1980.

But with the windfall would also come problems, both in Saudi Arabia and in Bechtel's own corporate headquarters. The first and most immediate of those problems was certain members of the Saudi royal household, whose greed was growing in direct proportion to the funds being paid Bechtel.

Meeting the demands of various Saudi princes was nothing new to Bechtel, which, in the years it had been operating in the kingdom, had paid out millions in so-called "business commissions." Legally, there was nothing in either Saudi or American law to prohibit this practice, as long as the commissions on a particular project did not exceed 5 percent. During the boom days of the 1970s, however, royal profiteering began to get out of hand. According to an investigation of Saudi corruption by *The New York Times*, at least a dozen members of the leading branches of the royal family were routinely demanding commissions in excess of the 5 percent legal limit. "Billions of dollars have been spent on corrupt payments over the last decade, often in violation of Saudi and American laws," the *Times* reported. "The payment of multimillion-dollar commissions to Saudi business agents, many of whom offer only influence in exchange, is frequently a requirement for companies trying to enter the Saudi market. Businessmen say they consider these payments thinly veiled bribes."[2]

Whatever they were called—bribes, *baksheesh* or plain payoffs—few Saudis were better at extorting them than Mohammad ibn-Fahd al-Saud, the American-educated son of Crown Prince (and later king) Fahd. Operating through a company called Al Bilad ("the nation," in Arabic), Prince Mohammad had received fat "commissions" from a number of foreign companies doing business in Saudi Arabia, including Hyundai Construction of South Korea, Philips Electronics of Holland and Ente Nazionale Indocarburi (ENI) of Italy.[3] In one transaction, a $4 billion communications contract, Al Bilad reportedly demanded and received a commission of $500 million. "Mohammad operated extremely aggressively and he was very greedy," recalled one American businessman who dealt with him during the 1970s. "He threw his weight around and used henchmen to get his way."[4]

Until the mid-1970s, however, Prince Mohammad had refrained from trying to put the bite on Bechtel, partly out of friendship—he'd discussed doing business several times with Steve senior and had been entertained in California by John O'Connell—but mostly because of Bechtel's business relationship with Suliman Olayan, one of the wealthiest and most powerful members of the Saudi merchant class, and himself a close business associate of Prince Khaled bin Abdullah bin Abdel-Rahman.

The equation altered after the assassination of King Faisal in 1975. Alarmed by Faisal's murder (he had been murdered by a deranged nephew), Khaled moved to England the following year, taking with him Suliman Olayan's entrée to the Saudi royal family. That development alone might have provided Prince Mohammad with the opportunity to begin to pressure Bechtel. But there was one thing more: an increasingly nasty dispute between Bechtel and Olayan over profits Olayan claimed were his due.

The argument revolved around Olayan's partnership arrangement with Bechtel, which guaranteed the Saudi businessman a set percentage of the profits from Bechtel's Saudi Arabian work, once the company's costs had been deducted. The arrangement had worked well, as long as Bechtel's costs were kept in line. According to a senior Bechtel official, the problems began when several longtime Bechtel executives, resentful at what they considered Olayan's overly close relationship with the company, began systematically increasing Bechtel's stated costs, reducing Olayan's profits to close to zero.[5] After unsuccessfully complaining to Bechtel's London office, Olayan took the matter to Steve junior.

In appealing to Bechtel's chairman, Olayan had every reason to believe that the dispute would soon be resolved. For one thing, he and Bechtel had enjoyed a long and mutually profitable relationship and had a number of major joint ventures in the works, including the proposed acquisition of a huge tract of land in Al Khubar, just outside Dhahran. Since under Saudi law it was illegal for foreigners to own land, the title to the property was to be in Olayan's name with a side letter stipulating that Bechtel owned 50 percent of the property. With this acquisition pending (it was apparently completed in 1976), Bechtel could ill afford to alienate Olayan. As one of the company's executives in Saudi Arabia put it, "Bechtel needed Olayan much more than Olayan needed Bechtel."[6]

Even so, at the urging of John O'Connell, Bechtel held firm, informing Olayan that O'Connell's men in Saudi Arabia had checked and double-checked their books and had found the accounting to be correct. Astonished and angered, Olayan vowed to keep pressing for a new and complete accounting. Press he did, and Bechtel finally reached a settlement.

In the interval, O'Connell, who privately scorned Olayan as "a rug merchant," began reasserting his influence on the Saudi scene. His most important—and for Bechtel, expensive—move was courting Prince Mohammad Fahd.

Convinced that the prince possessed influence with the Saudi court, and unaware, apparently, of his history with other companies, O'Connell asked Fahd to intercede with the Saudi government to secure final approval for the Riyadh job, which had been stalled since 1974. "O'Connell was anxious to push the project through, particularly since Olayan hadn't had any luck with Riyadh and this was John's chance to show him up," noted a Bechtel officer. "Mohammad informed him that the only way for Bechtel to get the contract was for the company to give him the same deal it had cut with Olayan. In other words, no Mohammad, no Riyadh."[7]

Having Mohammad, though, was not cheap. He was already Bechtel's partner in Saudi Arabia. By 1978, however, he wanted nothing less than a 10 percent interest in the soon-to-be created Arabian Bechtel Company, Ltd., the Bechtel subsidiary which would manage both Jubail and Riyadh.[8] In addition, published reports indicate that the prince also insisted on having a major say in selecting the subcontractors to be hired by Bechtel.[9] When Bechtel's financial executives totaled up the tab of the prince's demands over the expected life of the project, they came to more than $200 million.[10]

O'Connell was prepared to agree. The final decision on whether to bring Mohammad in as an actual shareholder, though, rested with the Bechtel executive committee, a group consisting of Steve junior, Shultz, Jerry Komes and four other senior company officials. Some committee members were concerned that meeting Mohammad's terms could violate Saudi law and the Foreign Corrupt Practices Act. However, "The choice was clear-cut," a Bechtel vice-president explained afterward. "Either give in or get out; and the executive committee decided to approve giving Mohammad a 10 percent interest." (A year later, according to Bechtel, the company obtained an opinion letter from an outside law firm stating that the arrangement did not violate the Act.) According to Olayan's associates, Suliman was furious when he found out. He hadn't even been consulted about what was going on.[11]

For all of Olayan's outrage, there was nothing he could do, and in late 1978, the well-connected, avaricious prince became a legitimate shareholder in Arabian Bechtel Company, Ltd. Five months later, on April 7, 1979, the Bechtel Corporation announced that Arabian Bechtel Company, Ltd. had been awarded the contract to manage the construction of the Riyadh International Airport.

The decision to give in to Mohammad Fahd's demands embittered many Bechtel executives, including Caspar Weinberger. For all of his faults, Cap had scruples about this sort of business. He especially didn't like paying princes in the Middle East, an area he had visited frequently on Bechtel business and on which he considered himself an expert. But what seemed to nettle Cap most was the fact that the decision had been reached without any input from him. Like the hapless Suliman Olayan, he had not been consulted.

The slight was one of many suffered by Weinberger, whose career at Bechtel had not been going well. On several occasions, legal advice he had provided on important cases had been ignored or overridden. One such instance involved a 1977 suit that had been filed against Bechtel by the U.S. Labor Department, seeking, in the words of the complaint, "to enjoin the firm from violating the overtime provisions of the Fair Labor Standards Act and to recover unpaid back wages for Alaska pipeline workers." The suit had grown out of a complaint filed with the department by a thousand quality-control engineers, who claimed that Bechtel had failed to pay them overtime for their work on the pipeline in 1974 and 1975. Most company executives, including Shultz, wanted to settle, if only to avoid bad publicity. Bechtel had already been embarrassed by its connection with the pipeline, which was substantially over budget and from which the company had been fired. Weinberger, however, was in a fighting mood. Arguing that Bechtel had a strong legal case, he claimed that he could beat the Labor Department's complaint, provided management backed him up. This management, in the person of Shultz, was unwilling to do. Instead, at Shultz' recommendation, Bechtel agreed to settle with the government for $3 million—the largest such settlement in U.S. labor history.

Cap was overruled again, six months later, in connection with the sex-discrimination suit brought by Bechtel's female employees. Once more, Weinberger wanted to fight, just as much as Shultz wanted to settle. The argument climaxed in the spring of 1979 when Shultz ultimately overruled Bechtel's intransigent general counsel and ordered the litigation settled.[12]

Shultz, whose star was continuing to rise, made matters worse by taunting Weinberger—a not altogether difficult task, given Weinberger's penchant for delivering long-winded corporate perorations. Recalled former Bechtel treasurer Raynal Mayman, "At directors' meetings, Cap would launch into these flights of rhetoric and Shultz would come down on him or contradict him very abruptly. He really pricked Cap's balloon."[13] Now and again, Shultz even twitted Weinberger publicly. In an interview with a reporter, Shultz cracked, "San Francisco, Cambridge and Harvard—that's what Cap likes. And there's London and the countryside. He likes that, too."[14]

A far bigger problem than Shultz, though, was Cap himself. Executives were wearying of what one Bechtel vice-president described as his "all or nothing" approach, his habit, as the vice-president put it, of "staking out extreme positions on legal matters and absolutely refusing to back down."[15] Even more troubling than Weinberger's beliefs was his temperament, some of his former colleagues asserted. "Cap had an enormous temper," said an ex-Bechtel personnel manager. "He'd direct his anger at whoever happened to be bypassing his office—often secretaries and clerks. He was impossible to deal with."[16]

At the very least, Weinberger appeared to be deeply unhappy. Despite the perks, the big house in the San Francisco suburbs, the salary that topped a quarter-million per year, he conceded to friends that coming to Bechtel had been a mistake. His heart remained in Washington, where he had hoped to return, following Ford's reelection, in a senior cabinet-level position. Jimmy Carter, of course, had put an end to that, and according to friends, Weinberger's disappointment showed. "After the first couple of years he lost all interest in the job," said his predecessor as general counsel, Bill Slusser. "He was just biding his time."[17]

With the approach of the 1980 presidential election, however, Weinberger's mood perked up. The leading contender for the Republican nomination was Ronald Reagan, the former California governor who had appointed Weinberger his finance chief and who, as president, could be expected to reward him again. Around the office, Weinberger started talking up the Reagan cause—and soon found that his enthusiasm for the former movie actor was not shared. Instead, the favored candidate of the Bechtel executive suite—as he was in boardrooms across Americia—was former Treasury secretary and Texas governor John Connally.

In the early going, Connally appeared to be a formidable candidate. By November 1979, he had already raised $10 million, the overwhelming bulk of it from corporate givers, including Steve Bechtel, Jr., and his father, who, with their wives, had attended a $1,000-a-plate dinner for Connally in California earlier that fall. As far as the Bechtels were concerned, Connally had a number of things to recommend him, not least of them his position on the Middle East. Connally spelled out that position on October 13, a month before Reagan's declaration of candidacy, in a forceful speech at the National Press Club in Washington. Raising the specter of "the economic upheaval that would ensue if the flow of Arab oil, the lifeblood of Western civilization for decades" were disrupted, Connally called on Israel to abandon the West Bank, return the strategic Golan Heights to Syria and give up its exclusive sovereignty in Jerusalem. The Bechtels, who had been lobbying in behalf of the Arabs for decades, were delighted—so much so that they hired the speech's ghostwriter, a former CIA analyst and National Security Council staffer named Samuel Hoskinson. Israel's supporters, though, reacted with fury. In *The New York Times*, columnist William Safire blasted Connally's address as "designed to disturb and dismay every American supporter of Israel."[18] As other publications echoed the refrain, Connally's support began to wither, and by the time of Reagan's upset win in the New Hampshire primary, his campaign was functionally at an end.

With Connally out, and George Bush showing signs of sputtering, it appeared increasingly likely that the nomination would go to Reagan. Since the onetime actor's election as governor of California, he and members of the Bechtel family had enjoyed warm personal relations. Steve and his brother Ken had contributed heavily to Reagan's first gubernatorial campaign, and applauded his tough stand against student demonstrations at Berkeley, where both Bechtels had gone to school. Candidate Reagan's stock soared even higher with the Bechtels after he promised to name a committee headed by former CIA director and onetime Bechtel partner John McCone to "investigate the charges of

Communism and blatant sexual behavior on the Berkeley campus,"
which, according to Reagan, was the site of "sexual orgies so vile I
cannot describe them to you."

As governor Reagan proved most helpful to the Bechtels' corporate
interests, particularly in the area of nuclear power. Prior to Reagan's
election, nuclear-plant construction in California had been moving
relatively slowly, largely because of the failure of the state Public Utilities Commission to raise electric rates significantly. That all began to
change when, after intense lobbying by Bechtel and the state's two
largest utilities, PG&E and Southern California Edison, Reagan appointed board members to the PUC who hiked rates by a total of more
than $2 billion per year. Flush with the proceeds of this windfall,
PG&E and Southern California Edison hired Bechtel to build several
major nuclear plants.

In 1974, Reagan assisted Bechtel again, this time by extending a
state-tax surcharge for an additional two years. The revenue gained—a
total of $82.2 million—went entirely to the support of the financially
beleaguered Bay Area Rapid Transit system (BART), which Bechtel
was building. The financing allowed BART to remain afloat until
Bechtel and the project's other sponsors could find additional federal
funding.

Despite its long-standing ties with Reagan, however, Bechtel was still
lukewarm about the Californian's candidacy, largely because of his
"supply-side" economic views. As Bechtel lobbyist Charls Walker,
who had served as Connally's chief economic advisor, put it: " (Reagan's) plan was based on the premise that there was such a thing as a
free lunch. You could have welfare *and* tax cuts."[19]

The situation began to change after the appointment of William
Casey as Reagan's campaign manager, following the New Hampshire
primary. A self-made millionaire Wall Street lawyer, Casey had become a good friend of George Shultz' while chairman of the Securities
and Exchange Commission under Nixon and, later, as head of the
Export-Import Bank under Ford. Worried by the continuing opposition
to Reagan's economic proposals, Casey asked Shultz to meet with the
candidate and hear his views. Shultz agreed and flew to Los Angeles in
mid-March.

The meeting did not go well. Reagan, Shultz later told a friend,
seemed confused about the economic proposals he was espousing, and
in setting out their details, was vague in the extreme. All in all, said
Shultz, "Things were in a worse mess than I thought."[20] The one glim-

mer of hope was that Reagan appeared open to new ideas. Given a prod in the right direction, Shultz told Casey, Reagan might yet be salvageable. For the moment, though, Shultz added, Reagan left him with "deep concern."

Casey was concerned as well, and two weeks later he asked Shultz to head a new coordinating committee to advise Reagan on economic matters. Shultz accepted, as, in short order, did economist Alan Greenspan and Citibank chairman Walter Wriston, both of whom Shultz had gotten to know through the Business Roundtable. Other recruits included Charls Walker, who continued to serve as one of Bechtel's lobbyists, and Cap Weinberger.

Through the spring and summer, Shultz and the coordinating-committee members met with Reagan during campaign breaks at Reagan's Santa Barbara ranch. Slowly, the candidate began to come around— not entirely, but sufficiently to make Shultz an admirer. "I believe in what Ronald Reagan stands for," he told Walker after one session at the ranch. "Limited government, low taxes and a strong defense. I look at him and I see a man who is secure in himself. I look at his record and I see that ninety-five percent of the time, Ronald Reagan has surrounded himself with highly competent people."[21] After Reagan captured the Republican nomination in late July, Shultz also began boosting the candidate with his fellow CEOs on the Business Council and the Business Roundtable. "George used to sing Reagan's praises at our meetings," said one Roundtable member. "He was Reagan's most convincing emissary to the business community."[22]

News of Shultz' missionary work reached Reagan, who, according to Walker, was so gladdened "that his eyes misted over." He expressed his appreciation September 9, when, during an address to the International Business Council in Chicago, he announced the appointment of Shultz as chief of a council of economic advisors. Walker was named to the council as well, with responsibility for devising tax reforms, as, in a decidedly minor role, was Cap Weinberger, who, following a stream of flattering letters and offers of help, was quietly active during the Reagan campaign.

Despite his relegations to bit-player status, Weinberger still had hope. Appointment as a Reagan advisor, he told friends, meant he was in the running for the cabinet slot of his dreams, notably, secretary of State. The only trouble was that his old nemesis George Shultz wanted the same job, and was being actively promoted for it by, among others, former Federal Reserve chairman Arthur Burns and former Defense secretary

Melvin Laird. Though the election was still a month off, the press too was plumping for Shultz' nomination—much to the distress of Steve Bechtel, Sr., and his son, who intended to make Shultz president of the Bechtel Group, a newly formed holding company that would oversee all of Bechtel's operations. The fate of Shultz, who was being closemouthed about his plans, was, accordingly, on the minds of both Bechtels when they attended a Business Council meeting at Hot Springs, Virginia, in mid-October. During a break in the proceedings, Steve senior pulled Walker aside and asked him for a reading of Shultz' intentions.[23]

"My feeling is he'll go," Walker responded, "but only as secretary of State."

Steve senior frowned. "I think you're right."

Caspar Weinberger too was keeping tabs on Shultz' ambitions, and after Reagan's election, doing his best to thwart them. Early on in the transition period, Cap had accepted an offer from Reagan to become secretary of Defense, a job second only in foreign-policy clout to the one at State. Pleased with his new role, and apparently unwilling to share his status with the likes of Shultz, Weinberger, some of Shultz's allies later asserted, passed along word to Reagan that it would be unwise politically to appoint two senior Bechtel executives to top national-security positions, and that Shultz had already committed himself to stay on at Bechtel.

Shultz, who had done nothing of the sort, was, as a result, stunned when, shortly thereafter, he received a call from Reagan, who told him he had talked to a "friend of yours" and understood completely his desire to remain at Bechtel. Perhaps, Reagan added, he could help the administration in other ways. Before Shultz could protest or explain, the conversation was over, and with it, seemingly, his hopes of being secretary of State. "I was never invited to join the administration," a dazed Shultz later told a reporter. "And I never turned it down—I never had a chance to."[24]

The immediate beneficiary of this apparent misunderstanding was Bechtel, which retained Shultz—whose pain was assuaged with an increase in salary to almost $600,000 and added stock in the company, making him one of the best-paid executives in the country—and at the same time, got rid of Weinberger. "Ronald Reagan did Bechtel a huge favor by saving the company the embarrassment of having to let Cap go," said a company executive, one of several who disliked Weinberger. "They [Steves senior and junior] weren't going to fire Weinberger. That wasn't Bechtel's style. They were just dancing him around and pointing him at the door. When it finally happened, there was an almost audible sigh of relief."[25]

Ray Mayman, Bechtel's treasurer, put it more kindly. "Cap's being at Bechtel," he said, "was like a heart transplant that just didn't take. The system rejected him."[26]

CHAPTER 20

POWERHOUSE

With Caspar Weinberger's departure for Washington, a momentary calm fell over Bechtel headquarters—a calm that was very much a reflection of the personality of the man the *San Francisco Examiner* referred to as "Bechtel's superstar," George Shultz.

In the six years he had been at Bechtel, Shultz had wrought a number of profound changes, not least of them the way he was perceived. Originally, he had been seen as the outsider, the avuncular nonengineer parachuted into the corporate ranks as much for his political influence as for his financial acumen. Now there was little doubt about his expertise—or of his clout. Subordinate only to company chairman Steve junior, he was the *primus inter pares*, the boss in fact as well as title. "George was clearly in charge," said a Bechtel executive admiringly. "At the weekly interdepartmental meetings he chaired, the construction people and the engineers were frequently at each other's throats. George would let them chew away at each other for a few minutes and then step in and say, 'Now, here's the way we are going to proceed on this, gentlemen.' "[1]

Under Shultz' leadership, Bechtel was proceeding as never before.

One notable example was diversification. Believing the company too narrowly focused on construction and engineering, Shultz, beginning in 1977, had initiated a program to give Bechtel equity participation in a number of other businesses, many of them energy-related. His first plunge, undertaken in partnership with Williams Brothers, Fluor and three other corporations, was to acquire the nation's largest coal producer, the Peabody Coal Company, from Kennecott Copper for $1.2 billion—$800 million of it in cash. That acquisition was followed in short order by several others, including WellTech, a Houston, Texas-based oil-and-gas-field services company in which Bechtel obtained half interest in 1979 for almost $100 million; the Dual Drilling Company of Wichita Falls, Texas, purchased in 1980 for an undisclosed sum, and the Becon Construction Company of Houston, bought for $9 million the same year. There were also investments in the oil industry, including a $39 million, 25 percent stake in Lear Petroleum's undeveloped oil and gas leases, and for $60 million, a limited partnership with T. Boone Pickens' Mesa Petroleum to explore for oil and gas on 1.9 million acres spread across fifteen Southern and Western states.

Through Sequoia Ventures, a firm that had been created to handle the Bechtel family portfolio, Shultz was investing his employers' personal funds as well. Much of their assets went for real estate and oil deals, but the most significant purchase, made in April 1981 for $18 million and a commitment to pump tens of millions of dollars more into the business, was of Dillon, Read & Company, the "white shoes" Wall Street investment house long presided over by Kennedy administration Treasury secretary C. Douglas Dillon. "We observe that people who have reached out from the stream of their experience," Shultz told a reporter, explaining his investment strategy, "have not done well." He added, "We can afford as a private company to make investments we can be patient with."[2]

Besides diversifying and investing, Shultz was also helping the company by drawing on the contacts he had made while in government. Perhaps the most important of them was John Turner, a politically well-connected Toronto lawyer, who would become Canada's prime minister in 1984. Shultz had met Turner in the early 1970s, when the latter was serving in the short-lived Conservative Canadian government as finance minister. A friendship had developed, and when Shultz went to Bechtel, he invited Turner to become a director of Bechtel's Canadian subsidiary, Bechtel Canada, Ltd. In that capacity, Turner was instrumental in cementing a number of critical deals, including lining up $350 million in Canadian government financing for Bechtel's Algerian oil and gas customer, Sonatrach.[3]

By 1982, Shultz had made himself all but indispensable to Bechtel's operations. Though now and again he would slip off to Washington or a foreign capital to advise on economic policy, he seemed content at Bechtel, which kept him on the road as often as he would have been as secretary of State. He was a company man, and he seemed to relish the role—nearly as much as Steve junior relished having him play it. It might have continued that way—the affable, clubbable George Shultz a permanent fixture of the Bechtel executive suite—but for the peculiar personality of Alexander Haig.

Since becoming Ronald Reagan's secretary of State, the former general and Nixon chief of staff had been engaged in turf and policy battles with virtually every important member of the administration, from the vice-president to the national security advisor to the secretaries of Defense, Treasury and Agriculture. He had blustered; he had bullied; he had threatened, more than once, to resign; and Reagan's patience was wearing thin. It snapped, finally, in June 1982, when Haig blasted the White House for issuing a statement calling on Israeli Prime Minister Menachem Begin not to attack Beirut and to resume talks on west bank autonomy as soon as possible. Summoning Haig into the Oval Office early in the afternoon of June 25, Reagan reached into his desk, pulled out a piece of paper and handed it to Haig. It was a statement accepting his resignation.

Within the hour, Reagan was on the phone to George Shultz, then in London on a business trip, offering the Bechtel president Haig's job. Shultz asked for half an hour to think it over, then accepted.*

Richard Nixon, who was among the first to hear the news, congratulated Reagan on selecting Shultz. "I happen to be one of the few who know both Shultz and Haig, perhaps better than anyone else," the

---

* The incident that spelled Haig's downfall as secretary of State—his public anger at the White House's criticism of Israeli moves on Beirut—came as the climax of a long-simmering war between Haig and Caspar Weinberger over U. S. policy vis-à-vis the Middle East. As it happened, Shultz also played a role in Haig's demise, when, in an effort to head off a threatened Haig trip to Israel to demonstrate U. S. support, he recommended to the State Department the appointment of retired diplomat Philip Habib as a special presidential emissary. The fact that Habib, not Haig, went to Israel, was among the numerous straws that, for Haig, finally broke the camel's back. Shultz was gratified on two counts: not only did he win the government post he sought, but Philip Habib was, then as now, a consultant to Bechtel.

former president told reporters. "Secretary Shultz will carry on. He will have his differences from Haig's policy, perhaps a shade of difference in the Middle East, although not nearly as great as some have indicated. But he's going to carry on and be a very effective secretary of State. If there has been any sniping or guerrilla warfare against the secretary of State, as Secretary Haig has indicated, let me tell you, you're not going to see anything publicly about it from Secretary Shultz. He will not tolerate it. That will stop."

Not so sanguine over Shultz' appointment was Steve Bechtel, Jr. He had been at the company's Alaska fishing camp when Reagan made the call to London, and though Shultz had frantically tried to reach him, Steve had been informed only when he heard news of Shultz' appointment on the radio. "I was shocked," Bechtel said later. "I just didn't think it would happen. [But] I knew George well enough that I felt that if the president really wanted him, put the arm on him, George would go."[4]

Bechtel hurried back to San Francisco. En route, he drafted the outline of a corporate reorganization plan he would present to an emergency meeting of the Bechtel executive committee he had called for that weekend. The plan, dubbed Management Memo Vol. 14, No. 7, called for Steve junior to reassume the responsibilities of Bechtel group president while continuing as chairman, with Shultz' ancillary responsibilities to be divided among other Bechtel executives. "I am very confident that everyone will cooperate in helping make these transitions work as smoothly as possible," Steve junior wrote in a note accompanying his memo. "There can be no question that we will personally feel George's loss to the company. But Bechtel is a strong organization, financially very sound and well-positioned in the industries we serve. I look forward to our future with great optimism."

While Bechtel was reorganizing itself, Shultz was being asked to sort out some matters of his own. In confirmation hearings before the Foreign Relations Committee, senator after senator bored in on Bechtel's various dealings and the role Shultz had played in them. Republican Larry Pressler of South Dakota, who pronounced himself worried that "there are too many people from Bechtel in this administration,"[5] pressed Shultz for details of Bechtel's lobbying efforts to sell AWACS aircraft to Saudi Arabia, where the company had a total of $40 billion in contracts.* He also questioned how Shultz could deal objectively

---

* Under George Shultz' directions, Bechtel's government-relations department had mounted an aggressive lobbying campaign to secure the controversial $8.5 billion

with the issue of nuclear nonproliferation, given Bechtel's extensive involvement in building nuclear power plants and waste-disposal facilities around the world. A testy Shultz shot back: "If I'm not qualified to take part in discussions of nuclear nonproliferation, then I'm not qualified to be secretary of State and you want somebody else in the job."[6]

Taking up where Pressler had left off, Maryland Democrat Paul Sarbanes asked Shultz to explain Bechtel's adherence to the Arab Boycott. Again Shultz took a hard line, denying Bechtel had violated U.S. law, despite the fact that the company had been the subject of an antitrust suit brought by Gerald Ford's Justice Department.

Yet another sensitive topic was raised by Alan Cranston of California, who pointedly wanted to know whether Shultz was involved in Bechtel's promise to sell Brazil advanced nuclear technology with potential weapons application, despite U.S. policy restricting such exports. "I resent what I regard as a kind of smear on Bechtel," Shultz bridled. "I think it is a marvelous, honorable, law-abiding company that does credit to our country here and all over the world."[7]

Shultz was soon confirmed, but the media coverage of his appointment and the hearings had made Bechtel a household word—and the stuff of jokes on the Johnny Carson show. Publicly, Bechtel's chairman professed distress at the publicity, and at the leave-taking that had occasioned it. With Shultz and Weinberger in Washington, he complained to a reporter that "government officials have to bend so far over backwards [in dealing with Bechtel] to be sure there's nobody who can say there's any favoritism at all."[8]

In fact, the addition of George Shultz to the Reagan cabinet did nothing at all to hurt Bechtel's business, or its increasingly powerful presence in Washington, where the company was now being represented by no fewer than thirteen paid lobbyists. Much of their work was focused on persuading Congress to fund what was becoming for Bechtel a new—and highly profitable—growth industry, one it had inadvertently helped create: the cleaning up of chemical and nuclear wastes. Already, Bechtel had secured a $320 million contract from the

AWACS sale, which was bitterly opposed by Israel and its supporters in Congress. Meeting frequently at the Business Roundtable's Washington office during the late summer and early fall of 1981, a Bechtel-led coalition of major U.S. corporations had mapped out a congressional lobbying strategy. In addition, Bechtel itself had sent out letters to every member of Congress, stating that "the AWACS deal is vital to the national interest as well as to the stability of the Persian Gulf." Despite heated opposition from Secretary of State Alexander Haig, the strategy had paid off when, on October 28, 1981, the Senate voted to authorize the sale.

department of Energy to tidy up 32 sites in 13 states that used radioactive materials as part of the Manhattan Project. By the time of Shultz' nomination as secretary of State, it was also taking in several hundred million dollars in federal funds to store nuclear wastes, making it the largest such operator in the industry. It was also one that required—and got—extraordinary help from the Reagan administration, particularly after the accident at Pennsylvania's Three Mile Island.

Though Bechtel had not been involved in Three Mile Island's design, construction or operation, the March 28, 1979, accident was to prove a decisive event for the company (which initially profited by winning the $1.5 billion contract for the plant's cleanup) and for its chairman. "After Three Mile Island went down," explained one senior Bechtel executive, "Steve junior became obsessed with proving that nuclear power really was safe and with keeping the industry viable. He was absolutely determined that Bechtel should devote its full resources to keeping atomic energy alive."[9]

His enthusiasm was not shared by many of his own executives, who privately thought that in the aftermath of the accident, the company should be scaling back its nuclear plans, not expanding them. No one, however, was willing to challenge him. "Junior managed by counterpunch," said a Bechtel official. "He'd listen to what you said and then take your block off if he didn't like what he'd heard. After Three Mile Island, interveners were shutting down nuclear plants left and right, but Steve wanted us to return to the wondrous days of yesteryear when nuclear power was in its glory. Nobody was going to tell him that we shouldn't be riding off into the sunset shouting a hearty 'Hi-Ho Silver.'"[10]

Mounting up, Bechtel, on May 20, 1979, summoned to San Francisco the representatives of thirteen of the country's leading nuclear suppliers and utilities whom he had chosen to play the role of Tonto. Their job, as Bechtel Power president Harry Reinsch explained it to them, was to form a lobbying group—the United States Committee for Energy Awareness—and through it, pressure Congress for a renewed commitment to nuclear power. In addition, USCEA was to mount a $40 million–a–year advertising campaign — a campaign that would be financed by the utilities through rate hikes— aimed at relieving public concern about the dangers of nuclear power. According to a memorandum prepared by a Bechtel staffer, the campaign was to stress four main themes: that "the nuclear industry is making an all-out effort to increase nuclear safety as a result of the lessons learned at Three Mile Island"; that "the nation cannot meet the growing demand for electricity if it abandons nuclear energy"; that people will "suffer economically and environmentally if [the United States] abandons nuclear energy" and that the nuclear industry was trying to find "ways to minimize potential exposure to radiation and to develop acceptable ways to transport and store the nuclear waste."[11]

At Reinsch's suggestion, each of those present at the meeting secured from his company an initial $100,000 to get the campaign off the ground. A few weeks later, they saw the first result of their contributions in a full-page ad in *The Wall Street Journal*, featuring an ominous prediction by Dr. Edward Teller, the father of the hydrogen bomb.[12] Referring to the protests triggered by the Three Mile Island accident, Teller declared, "I believe we have reached a turning point in history. The antinuclear propaganda we are hearing puts democracy to a severe test. Unless the political trend toward energy development in this country changes rapidly, there will not be a United States of America in the twenty-first century."

The ad, and the ones that followed it, found at least one believer, and a most important one: Ronald Reagan.

Reagan had been an outspoken proponent of nuclear power ever since his days as a spokesman and speech-giver for General Electric, the nation's foremost builder of reactors. He reemphasized his commitment shortly after his election as president. "I believe in nuclear power," Reagan declared at a news conference, announcing his intention to speed along the government's nuclear licensing procedures. "And I think it has been unnecessarily obstructed by some anti–nuclear-power activists. We think that by changing some cumbersome and useless regulations . . . and in removing those obstacles that enable activists to interfere . . . we can encourage continued development of nuclear power."[13]

The man Reagan charged to carry out that task was W. Kenneth Davis, a former AEC official who for the last 20 years had been head of Bechtel's nuclear-developmental operations.* Davis' association with Reagan had begun during the 1980 presidential campaign, when the

---

* When Davis left Bechtel to become Reagan's deputy secretary of Energy, he was compelled by government regulations to file a financial-disclosure statement. The data he provided are a vivid demonstration of Bechtel's generosity and a prime reason why the company is able to recruit extraordinary executive talent.

During his last fourteen months at Bechtel, Davis, then vice-president for planning

then-candidate appointed him a member of his energy advisory committee, a group that included James Quenon, president of the partly Bechtel-owned Peabody Coal, and Harold Haynes, soon to be appointed a Bechtel director, and then chairman of Bechtel's oldest and best customer, Standard Oil of California. In its forty-one-page report, the committee recommended that the government move to revitalize the anemic U.S. coal industry—a direct benefit to Bechtel—and that it streamline nuclear regulatory procedures, another benefit for Bechtel that Davis and the other committee members deemed "absolutely essential."

By the time of the committees' recommendations, Davis was in an excellent position to implement them; in January 1981, he had been appointed by Reagan as deputy secretary of Energy. Though the department was nominally under the control of James Edwards, a former South Carolina governor and ex-dentist, around Washington it was an open secret that Davis actually called the shots—and call them he did.

In 1981, for instance, Davis led a high-level U.S. delegation to Mexico in an effort to win contracts for U.S. firms—Bechtel among them—to build the first two of twenty nuclear plants Mexico planned to erect by the end of the decade. That same autumn, in a move that Davis supported, the White House ordered the U.S. Export-Import Bank,* which had recently provided an additional $1.1 billion in financing for U.S.-built nuclear plants overseas, to offer Taiwan especially generous financing for the construction of two nuclear plants, both of which were eventually built by a Bechtel joint venture for $340 million.

During the same period, Reagan—again on Davis' recommendations—directed the Nuclear Regulatory Agency, as the president put it, to "take steps to facilitate the licensing of [nuclear] plants under construction." Of the 35 plants that fell under Reagan's order, 15 had been or were being built by Bechtel. A month later, the administration

---

and advanced development, received a salary of $240,000. Through stock option plans, Davis also owned a minimum of $250,000 in each of four separate Bechtel stocks. Additionally, he had between $100,000 and $250,000 in the Bechtel savings plan and was owed another $120,000 in deferred company bonuses. When everything was totaled together, Davis, a high-ranking middle-manager, was receiving more than $500,000 annually in salary, bonuses and stock benefits—well beyond what a manager in his position would have been paid at one of Bechtel's competitors.

* Like Henry Kearns, his predecessor as the bank's chairman, John L. Moore would wind up working for Bechtel. He joined the firm in 1982 as vice-president for financial development.

helped Bechtel's nuclear efforts overseas by lifting U.S. restrictions against the sale of nuclear fuel to South Africa and by informing Brazil, which, like South Africa, had not signed the Nuclear Non-Proliferation Treaty, that it was now free to acquire nuclear fuel from U.S. sources.

In January 1982, there was still more good news for Bechtel when the Energy Department secretly authorized the export to Argentina of a sophisticated computer system needed to operate a "heavy water" plant capable of manufacturing nuclear-weapons-grade materials. Davis, who talked regularly by telephone with his former colleagues in San Francisco, also pressed to allow foreign partners to participate in commercial reprocessing ventures with the U.S. His enthusiasm was shared by Richard T. Kennedy, a former consultant for an energy concern that counted Bechtel among its clients, whom Reagan had named the U.S. representative to the International Atomic Energy Agency.

Summing up all the activities of recent months, Davis told the IAEA in April 1982, "The Reagan administration is trying to deal with the proliferation issue in a more realistic manner. . .We are now seeking to build bridges in our nuclear relations with close friends and allies. Our nation also is seeking to resume its traditional and historical role as a leader in international affairs and as a stable and reliable nuclear partner." At the time, Bechtel was eagerly trying to sell sensitive nuclear technology to Japan.

Davis himself seemed destined to go far. In June, his boss at Energy, James Edwards, told him he would soon be resigning to return to South Carolina. He added that he would recommend Davis as his successor and predicted that his nomination would be a shoe-in. Delighted, Davis returned to California for a long-overdue vacation. On June 25, he was sitting in his cabin on Lake Tahoe when the news came over the radio that George Shultz had replaced Alexander Haig as secretary of State. "That sure ended that," Davis mourned later. "There was no way the administration was going to have three cabinet members from the same company."[14]

Even without Davis in the cabinet, Bechtel was doing quite nicely. When a $2.7 billion nuclear plant it was building in Mississippi ran into licensing trouble—brought on largely by the 74 percent boost in electric rates that would be required to pay for its completion—Edwards' successor at Energy, Donald Hodel, personally flew to Mississippi to testify before the state's Public Services Commission. As a result of Hodel's intervention, the first ever by an Energy secretary, the plant was saved, and with it, millions for Bechtel.

Although he had recused himself from participation in particular matters involving Bechtel, George Shultz's official actions happened to prove most helpful to the company. Within a few weeks of being sworn in as Secretary of State, Shultz persuaded Reagan and then National Security Advisor William Clark to relax their hitherto fierce opposition to the building of a natural-gas pipeline between Soviet Siberia and Western Europe. Though Bechtel was not involved in the Siberian project, it was quick to capitalize on the thaw in U.S.–Soviet relations Shultz had initiated. In early October, with State Department approval, two representatives from Bechtel and Occidental Petroleum chairman Armand Hammer arrived in Moscow to pitch the construction of yet another pipeline, this one to transport coal slurry. Even while that deal was still pending, Shultz himself flew off to China, a market Bechtel had unsuccessfully been trying to crack for years, with an offer to provide U.S. technology in exchange for China's allowing U.S. companies to share in an estimated $20 billion of nuclear-plant construction. A State Department sponsored nuclear cooperation agreement enabling U.S. firms to sell nuclear technology to China cleared Congress on July 23, 1985. That same week, a Chinese delegation visited the United States for a firsthand look at American nuclear plants, as well as Bechtel's first showplace, Hoover Dam.

Shultz' official actions were also helpful in India, where the company had been in bad odor since the leaks at its Tarapur nuclear plant had led to the radioactive exposure of thousands of Indian workers. The problem was a serious one for U.S. nuclear exporters, including Bechtel, made all the more so by the Carter administration's refusal to sell the Indians parts needed for the plant's repair, because of the Indian government's unwillingness to abide by the provisions of the Nuclear Non-Proliferation Treaty. While on a May 1983 visit to New Delhi, however, Shultz quietly assured the Indians that treaty signature or no, the United States would soon authorize the sale of the needed parts.

Taken together, the efforts of Shultz, Weinberger, Davis and the other members of the Reagan administration were cause for good cheer at Bechtel, which, despite having given them up, appeared to be booming. "We're preeminent in the field now," a company executive boasted, referring to Bechtel's nuclear operations. "When people get in trouble, they come to us."[15]

They were coming, and thanks to them, profits were up. For the moment, at least, Steve junior's ride as the Lone Ranger had been a smooth, untroubled one. The question was how long it could last.

CHAPTER 21

THE NEXT GENERATION

T he course Steve Bechtel, Jr., had charted for his company was a bold and single-minded one. It rested on a belief that nuclear energy was the power source of the future and that in the meantime oil would continue to command the same high prices as in the last decade. The strategy was high-risk, higher than anything the Bechtel organization had attempted in the last half-century, and for it to succeed, the world economy had to keep churning along, undisturbed, undiminished. Buoyed by the billions in contracts that had flowed in from places like Saudi Arabia and Algeria, Indonesia and Mexico, Steve junior was confident that that would be the case. As events soon demonstrated, his assumption was mistaken; nearly fatally so.

The problem, in a nutshell, was that the world economy, contrary to his expectations, headed into deep recession. As oil prices plunged and Third World debt mounted, American construction companies, already burdened by a strong U.S. dollar, which made it possible for foreign competitors to undercut their prices, began to feel the pinch. It grew more painful as the number of cancelled projects multiplied, until by 1984, the industry, once seemingly invulnerable, was in its worst economic straits since the Great Depression.

As the biggest company, and the one with the heaviest foreign exposure and commitment to energy, Bechtel was particularly hard hit. The first blow landed in January 1984, when Bechtel received word that the owners of the troubled Zimmer nuclear plant in Ohio—a long-delayed facility Bechtel had hoped to finish building—had, despite eighteen months of intense pressure from Bechtel and the Reagan administration, decided to convert to coal. The news staggered Bechtel, which had been so confident of winning the $700 million job that it had already assigned nearly five hundred engineers to begin planning the project.

Two months later, the company was rocked again, when Saudi Oil Minister Ahmed Yamani, alarmed by his country's sharply dwindling oil revenues, abruptly cancelled a $1 billion oil refinery Bechtel had been building at Qasim. With the loss of the project, hundreds more engineers were thrown out of work. "It happened literally overnight," shuddered one Bechtel executive. "We came in one morning and they were gone. Their desks were clean. A billion dollars had gone out the window just like that."[1] Nor were Bechtel's troubles over. Four months after the cancellation of the Qasim refinery, the Consumers Power Company informed Bechtel executives that it was abandoning construction of a massive nuclear plant at Midland, Michigan, a project that had been bringing Betchel hundreds of millions of dollars each year.*

---

* The Midland shutdown, which, among other things, cost 3,352 Bechtel employees their jobs, loosed a torrent of outrage within the company, much of it directed at antinuclear activists. Reflecting the depth of Bechtel's anger was a message sent to all company managers by Harry Reinsch, president of the Bechtel Power Corporation. Wrote Reinsch: "The demise of Midland ultimately was brought about by a virulent no-growth anti-power lobby seeking to weaken the very society in which it lives. That group has taken upon itself the responsibility to decide that the power that supplied growth is not needed. Under the current system it can be frivolous, deceitful and even malicious yet never held accountable for the impact and monumental cost it causes. The no-growth, anti-power lobby must be accountable for its actions."

The same day Reinsch fired off his letter, he also instructed Bechtel's manager of government relations to seek a meeting with President Reagan. The purpose was to enlist the White House in drawing up a plan to, as Reinsch put it, "lay the foundation for a financially healthy electric utility industry . . . so that we can . . . avoid a national electricity crisis." In plain words, Bechtel was seeking a financial bailout. Though the White House did appoint a cabinet-level "Council on Economic Affairs" working group to study the problem, nothing came of the bailout proposal, largely because so many of the nuclear industry's problems were of its own making. The same day that Steve Bechtel, Jr., received word of the Midland shutdown, for instance, he was meet-

With three major projects out the door in six months, and numerous other smaller ones delayed or cancelled, Bechtel's revenues, which had reached a record $14.1 billion in 1983, plummeted the next year to $8.2 billion, a drop-off of more than 40 percent. Even more worrisome was the decline in new work being booked, down from $11 billion in 1983 to $6 billion in 1984. For the first time in more than a decade, Bechtel had lost its rating as the world's largest construction and engineering firm.

No one took the news harder than 84-year-old Steve senior, who, despite a bad heart, continued to come into the office every day in his role as senior director. As the empire he had built began to crumble, he fretted to a reporter, "Like a savings account, when withdrawals begin to exceed deposits year after year, we know eventually there will be a day of reckoning."[2]

Steve junior, whose aggressive nuclear and oil undertakings had, according to a number of Bechtel executives, deepened the company's predicament, was even gloomier. "Our market fell apart on us," he confessed to an interviewer, shortly after losing the Midland contract.[3] "The power business went on its nose; in the petroleum business, the price of oil came down and consumption leveled off. We got a little less sure of what the future held, where the opportunities lay and what the problems were. We feel the slack market is going to continue for a year or two," he added. "You can't hold your breath for that long."

To make matters worse, a number of real estate and oil-drilling investments made during the Shultz era also suddenly soured. According to a former company financial executive, the losses from these deals, when combined, totaled upward of $250 million.

Under pressure on all fronts, Bechtel began going after costs with a meat-ax. Some trims—like selling off two of the company's three corporate jets, ordering all but the most senior executives to fly coach and installing reflector panels behind the fluorescent lights in each office (a measure that saved $400,000 in electricity bills per year)—were comparatively easy. Others, such as scrapping Steve junior's cherished plans to build a $100 million office complex in downtown Oakland, and along with it, closing down several of the company's outlying offices,

---

ing with Arizona governor Bruce Babbitt. The topic of their discussion was the Bechtel-built Palo Verde, Arizona, nuclear plant, which at the time was three years behind schedule and, at $5 billion and mounting, was the costliest nuclear facility in the United States.

were more painful. But the biggest wrench came in paring down the work force. Between 1982 and 1987, some 22,000 employees—almost half of the Bechtel "family"—were lopped off the company payroll, the majority of them in two mass firings that occurred just before Christmas 1984 and 1985. Company executives too felt the pinch: in 1982, 58 had been employed at the senior corporate vice-presidential level or higher; by 1987, that number had dwindled to 37. Those who remained had their salaries frozen, their yearly bonuses stripped back by as much as 80 percent and the majority of their corporate perquisites eliminated.

The cutbacks and the firings, and the manner in which they were accomplished, engendered enormous bitterness, especially among the large number of discharged middle managers, many of them in their mid-50s "It's like the military," one fired executive told a reporter. "If you've been a major too long, forget it."[4] "The fast-trackers, the Harvard MBAs, are the ones Bechtel is keeping," added a fired cost engineer with sixteen years at the company. "I don't think that Bechtel will ever be thought of as a 'family' again."[5] "They tend to act like God," said still another executive, as he contemplated the prospect of unemployment, "but not with nearly the compassion."[6]

As the belt-tightening continued, the survivors began fixing blame, with many tracing the company's woes to the departure of George Shultz. "Shultz' leaving nearly proved the death knell of the company," said Raynal Mayman, Bechtel's former treasurer. "Without his financial expertise, Bechtel really got caught with its pants down when the recession hit."[7] "Shultz was one of the few people in the company who could—and would—bring Steve junior the bad news, when there was bad news to be delivered," added another senior-level Bechtel executive. "Most of the corporate vice-presidents were afraid of upsetting the chairman. The upshot was, if you had a problem, you simply swept it under the rug. At Bechtel, the downside risk in telling the emperor he wasn't wearing any clothes was enormous. You had nothing to gain and your career to lose."[8]

Belatedly, Steve junior began to realize that at least some of what his critics were saying was right, and began putting together what he called "a board of special counselors." Composed of retired corporate heavyweights like Citibank's Walter Wriston, IBM's Frank Cary, Du Pont's Irving Shapiro, Utah Construction's Ed Littlefield and Socal's Harold Haynes, this board of "special counselors," Bechtel told an interviewer, "is our answer to an outside board of directors. These were people whom I personally knew," Bechtel went on. "I wanted them to help us digest some of the big experiences and advise us on future conditions in the economic, political, social and technological fields."[9]

Meeting with Bechtel every few months, the counselors advised Steve junior to take various cost-cutting measures—most notably, to unload Dillon, Read, which Bechtel sold off in 1986. They also urged Bechtel's chairman to diversify and scale down the company's executive hierarchy, so that the firm would be more responsive and better able to pursue new customers. Another important piece of advice was for Bechtel to pursue jobs that only a few years before would have been brushed off as too small. That Bechtel was taking the suggestions seriously was apparent from the jobs the company began to go after, and win—from a $900,000 concrete-pouring project in Michigan to a $3.5 million waste-energy plant in Florida to a $25 million highway project in Turkey.

Under prodding from the counselors, Bechtel also began capitalizing on resources it already owned. A leading case in point was a $150 million micrographic facility in Gaithersburg, Maryland, erected by Bechtel Power to store and process records for nuclear plants. With the collapse of the nuclear power industry, the facility seemed in jeopardy, and with it, Bechtel's entire investment. Instead, Bechtel made the best of a bad situation by winning a contract from the Securities and Exchange Commission to use Gaithersburg to process all the SEC's documents. Estimated yearly income to Bechtel: $23 million. Proclaiming the company leaner, meaner and hungrier, a Bechtel executive told *The Wall Street Journal*: "If there's no project, we'll try to find one. If there's no client, we'll try to assemble one. If there's no money, we'll get them some."[10]

By the end of 1986, when the company reported income of $6.5 billion, it appeared that the worst for Bechtel was over. Though revenues hadn't yet begun to turn around, they had a least stabilized at their 1985 levels. "Our business has had its ups and downs," Steve junior told a gathering of company employees on St. Patrick's Day 1987. "But don't be disillusioned. We are operating in the black— many of our competitors aren't—and we are financially sound. I am confident that we will come out of these tough times stronger than before."[11] Looking uncharacteristically drawn and tired, the Bechtel chairman added a cautionary note. "We've got to put more emphasis on marketing, on strategic planning, on business management," he said. "We need to get back to the attitudes and work practices of twenty years ago. That means less formality, more flexibility, more of a 'can-do' attitude, more speed and responsiveness, more teamwork."[12]

Managing a smile, Steve junior then called for questions. "Is the Bechtel family thinking of getting out of the business?" an employee asked, referring to rumors that the Bechtels were considering selling the company.

"That's the last thing in our minds," Steve junior answered emphatically. "My first love is the engineering and construction business, and even when the time comes for me to step out of the line—a few years from now, when I'm sixty-five—I plan to still be around and active and helpful to the extent that I can be. At the age of eight-six, my dad still comes into the office every day, and I intend to do likewise."[13]

A final question: "Is 1987 the bottom?"

"I hope so and I think so," said the chairman, the tightness showing in his voice. "I'm more confident than I have been in recent years."[14]

With his company seemingly righted, Steve junior increasingly began looking to the future. As he had noted to his employees, he was nearing Bechtel's mandatory retirement age, and though there was no question of his vigor—lately, he had been part of an expedition that had climbed partway up Mount Everest—come 1990, someone else would have to lead.

The most obvious candidate, if only in terms of experience, was Alden Yates, whom Steve junior had installed as company president after Shultz' departure. The son of Bechtel energy chief Perry Yates, Alden, as one of his fellow executives put it, "was born with a Bechtel spoon in his mouth."[15] In addition, Yates, who had spent his entire career at the company, was counted as a solid construction boss and an excellent manager. But there was one thing Yates lacked: the Bechtel name. "Blood is blood," said one senior executive. "There's no way the Bechtels are going to turn over the company to a non–family member."[16]

There were five children in the Bechtel brood—daughters Shana, Lauren and Nonie; sons Gary and Riley—and with one exception, Steve junior, who tended to be as remote as he was demanding, had had troubles with all of them.

The exception was the oldest girl, Shana, who had been born in 1947. Described by one of her cousins as "Miss Goody Goody," Shana had pleased her parents by marrying a hardworking, if lackluster, former middle manager at Gates Tire named Clint Johnstone. They were pleased even more when, immediately following the marriage, Johnstone went to work for Bechtel, while Shana retired to the suburbs to begin having babies.

Nonie, the youngest daughter, was not so conventional. She had first irritated her father by going off to Paris for a year to improve her French, an undertaking viewed by Steve junior as irredeemably dilettantish. Better, he told friends, that she remain at home and study something practical like nursing, as her aunt Barbara Davies had before her. When Nonie did return home, she further offended her father by marrying Sheldon Ramsay, the scion of a socially prominent California family. Chary of bluebloods, Steve and Betty opposed the marriage, but to no avail.

They had even more difficulty dealing with their middle daughter, Lauren. A contemporary of Patty Hearst's, "Laurie" was a strong-willed, idealistic young woman who rebelled early on against what she termed her parent's "bourgeois values." By her late teens, she had adopted a countercultural lifestyle, espousing views that Steve and Betty regarded as dangerously radical. Nor was she shy about making those views known. At a 1973 family party given by Steve and Betty to celebrate Steve senior and Laura's fiftieth wedding anniversary, Laurie startled guests—and enraged her parents—by rising in the midst of the congratulatory toasts to deliver an impassioned speech on the need to aid Bangladesh refugees. "It was as though she had doused ice water on everyone in the room," said a family friend. "For weeks afterward, all the Bechtel women could talk about was Laurie's scandalous behavior."[17]

The friction between Laurie and her parents intensified when she fell in love with Alan Dachs, a college student from Great Neck, New York, who'd come out to California on a visit. Dachs was not at all what the Bechtels had in mind for their daughter. Not only was he an outspoken left-wing activist, he also was Jewish. Neither fact, though, deterred Laurie, who announced that she was moving back east with Dachs, who attended Connecticut's liberal Wesleyan University. In a fury, Bechtel, according to one family member, told his daughter that unless she broke off with Dachs, he would cut her off financially. When Laurie held firm, Steve enlisted his father, with whom Laurie had always been close, in hopes that he could change her mind. Steve senior, however, had no better luck than his son. In reply to her grandfather's entreaties, Laurie revealed she was marrying Dachs. If the family didn't accept the union, Laurie threatened she would sever all ties with them. Faced with Laurie's ultimatum, Steve junior gave in and Laurie and Alan Dachs were married in Steve and Betty Bechtel's garden in Piedmont by the Presbyterian pastor of the Piedmont Community Church.[18]

Steve's problems with Gary, his older boy, were of an altogether different sort. A striking look-alike of his father, Gary, according to family members, had all of Steve junior's mannerisms, but little of his shrewdness and his aptitude for hard work. After graduating from the University of the Pacific in the late 1960s, Gary, at Steve junior's urging, joined Bechtel. There, under the supervision of executive vice-president Ed Gabarini, he was placed on the company fast track. He performed competently enough and was well liked by his colleagues. The troubles began after Gary secured an annulment of a brief first marriage and married a second time. Gary's actions created a rift with his father, who was a stickler for keeping marriages intact, however unhappy, and resulted in Gary's quitting Bechtel to take a job as an ironworker. Later he returned to the fold and was given a job with Bechtel-owned Becon Construction, where he recently was made a vice-president.

Riley Bechtel, by all accounts the ablest of Steve junior's children, had become estranged from his father in still another way. After picking up an undergraduate degree from the University of California at Davis, and an MBA and law degree from Stanford, he had embarked on a law career—not for Bechtel, but for Thelan, Marin. "Riley was the white hope, the brains of the family," said a Bechtel family member. "When he decided to go into law rather than join the company, it broke his father's heart."

Through the 1960s and for most of the 1970s, the relations between Steve junior and his children remained tense. They began to change after the first of his grandchildren were born, an event which, according to a family friend, "mellowed Steve, made him warmer and more approachable." With the passage of time, the children too had mellowed, especially Laurie, whose radicalism began to wane as her husband's business career progressed. After their marriage, she and Dachs had moved to New York, where, following graduate business studies at New York University, he had obtained a job as a trainee at the Chemical Bank. Eventually Dachs took a job with Bechtel and, after working in Houston in a field capacity, returned to San Francisco with Laurie. There Dachs took a financial job at Bechtel, and Steve junior, who was selling the family home in Piedmont, offered it to the couple if they were willing to match an offer that had been made by another party, which they did.

At Bechtel, Dachs quickly proved an able executive, and by 1983 he had become vice-president of Bechtel International. "Alan could be abrasive at times, but he was very sharp, a quick study and a zealous worker," said Ray Mayman, who supervised his work. "There was no question he was going places in the company—and not simply because he was the chairman's son-in-law."[19]

One of the effects of Dachs's rapid rise was to stir other family members from their lethargy. That was especially true of Shana's husband, Clint Johnstone, whose early career at Bechtel had, in the words of one associate, been marked by an attitude of "Why should I bust my ass? I've got it made." With Dachs impressing the Bechtel hierarchy, Johnstone now began to catch fire as well, working late hours and taking on additional responsibilities. His efforts paid off in 1984, when he was named a group vice-president and charged with turning around Bechtel's troubled Minerals and Mining Group.

Though remaining in North Carolina, Gary too came back into his father's good graces, not so much because of his professional brilliance —"He's never going to be a world-beater," conceded one sympathetic cousin—as for the way he was conducting his second marriage, which had thus far produced three children.

But it was young Riley who was making the most accelerated push for power. Bright, ambitious and like his father, a workaholic, he had, in 1981, abandoned a promising career at Thelan, Marin and, at the age of 30, joined Bechtel, where he was given a crash course in running the family store. His first assignment was to handle the legal chores on a coal-fired power plant Bechtel was building outside Detroit. After that, he had been posted to Indonesia to work on a liquid-natural-gas plant Bechtel was building for Pertamina. When that job was over, he moved to New Zealand, where Bechtel was building a huge synthetic-fuels plant. His arrival did not sit well with the project manager, a hard-nosed Bechtel veteran named Donald Hassler. "I already had someone perfectly capable," Hassler recalled. "I told San Francisco the last thing I needed was another goddam attorney."[20] San Francisco took a different view: Hassler was fired and Riley named his replacement. A year later, in 1984, young Bechtel was on the move again, this time to London, where he was promoted to Managing Director of Bechtel, Ltd., a post that in the view of company insiders signaled his grooming for Bechtel's top slot.

By 1986 it was clear that one way or another, command of Bechtel would remain inside the family however the succession worked out. It was becoming equally clear that the worst of Bechtel's financial troubles were, if not completely over, at least well on their way to resolution. Heartened by both developments, Steve junior that spring flew to Washington for a gathering of the powerful friends who had done so much to make Bechtel the company that it was.

The occasion was a black-tie dinner given by the University of Chicago in honor of George Shultz, for whom a chair was being named at the university's business school. Bechtel was in an excellent mood, made all the more so by Ronald Reagan's recent appointment of yet another Bechtel executive—civil engineering and mining chief Richard Godwin—to a newly created post of almost unimaginable power: under-secretary of Defense for Acquisition. Among Godwin's other chores would be awarding contracts for the Strategic Defense Initiative, a multibillion-dollar program in which Bechtel already had an active interest.

As Steve Bechtel, Jr., gazed about the ballroom of the Hay-Adams House, his smile widened. He was in good company here, with friends like David Rockefeller and William Simon, Henry Kissenger and Milton Friedman, Charles Percy and David Packard. And, of course, there was Shultz, who one day might be coming back to Bechtel.

The dinner was a longish, self-congratulatory affair, with the usual cigars and brandy and talk of business deals to come. After the hellish last few years, Bechtel was glad to be with such friends again, and gladder still that several of them would be sending business his way. The company, he privately confided, had turned an important corner. It was on its way again, back toward the heights it had climbed once before. Indeed, even now his son Riley was preparing to leave for the Middle East sheikdom of Qatar to arrange a deal for developing what geologists claimed could be the largest natural-gas reserve in the world. Potentially, billions were at stake, and Bechtel had few doubts that his company would claim the lion's share of them.

The next morning, Steve returned to San Francisco, where there were smiles on his employees' faces as well. The annual survey of the world's leading engineering firms conducted by *Engineering News Record*, the bible of the construction industry, was out, and after a three-year absence, the Bechtel Group once again topped the list. It was cause for celebration, and to mark the occasion, Stephen D.

Bechtel, Jr., boss of this most private of companies, did something quite unusual. He ordered the lights in the skyscraper he had built to be lit that night in a pattern, a twenty-three story announcement the world could not help noticing. It spelled out a single numeral: the number "1."

NOTES

CHAPTER ONE

The account of Stephen Bechtel, Jr.'s, visit to the Bohemian Grove in July 1982 is based on interviews with Bohemian Club members and their guests who were present at the 1982 encampment. Also useful was the 1982 Bohemian Club list of the lodges and their members and guests.

Numerous accounts of The Grove have appeared in a variety of publications, including *The New York Times* (8/14/77), *The Christian Science Monitor* (8/22/81), *The San Francisco Chronicle* (9/16/81) and *Newsweek* (8/2/82). At least two books have been done on The Grove as well: *The Bohemian Grove and Other Delights: A Study in Ruling Class Cohesiveness*, G. William Domhoff, and *The Greatest Men's Party in the World*, John van der Zee.

1. Off-the-record interviews with Bechtel family members.

2. The Reagan-Nixon meeting has been well chronicled in such publications as the *San Francisco Chronicle*, 7/16/81.

3. Interview, John D. Erhlichman, July 1982.

CHAPTER TWO

The account of Warren A. Bechtel's career and the Bechtel family's origins is based on interviews with surviving family members, including Warren's middle son, Stephen D. Bechtel. In addition, I have relied on the privately published story of W. A. Bechtel, *A Builder and His Family* (1948) by Robert L. Ingram, as well as other company records. Warren Bechtel's achievements and background were also chronicled at some length by the Oakland *Tribune* and the *San Francisco Chronicle* (both 8/29/33) after his death.

1. *A Builder*, Ingram, 3.

2. Ibid., 5.

3. Ibid., 9

4. Ibid.

5. Ibid., 11.

6. Ibid., 13.

7. Interview, Stephen D. Bechtel, July 1984.

8. *Fortune*, "The Earth Movers," August 1943.

9. SDB interview.

10. *Fortune*, op. cit.

CHAPTER THREE

1. *The Kaiser Story*, privately printed, 1968, 18.

2. *Fortune*, August 1943.

3. Ibid.

4. Interview, Stephen D. Bechtel, July 1984.

5. *Fortune*, op. cit.

6. Ibid.

7. *Bechtel News*, January 1982.

8. *New York Times*, 8/10/31.

9. *New York Times*, 8/19/31.

10. *New York Times*, 4/11/32.

11. *Annual Report*, Smithsonian Institution, 1935, 449.

12. *Harold Ickes of the New Deal: His Private Life and Public Career*, Graham White and John Maze, Harvard University Press, 1985.

13. *The Secret Diary of Harold L. Ickes*, Library of Congress, 445.

CHAPTER FOUR

The account of W. A. Bechtel's death and Stephen D. Bechtel's early career and rise to power is based primarily on many of the same sources that were used in Chapters Two and Three. In addition, the privately printed *The Bechtel Story* by Robert L. Ingram, 1968, provides an account of the Bechtel company's history under Stephen D. Bechtel and his son, Stephen D. Bechtel, Jr.

1. *Fortune*, September 1943.

2. *A Builder and His Family*, 36.

3. *San Francisco Chronicle*, 8/29/33.

4. Interview, Robert L. Bridges, July 1984.

5. Oral history of John L. Simpson, Bancroft Library, University of California, Berkeley.

6. *A Builder*, 42.

7. Interview, Stephen D. Bechtel, July 1984.

8. Bridges interview.

9. Off-the-record interview with Bechtel family member.

10. SDB interview.

11. Ibid.

12. *Fortune*, August 1958.

13. SDB interview.

14. Ibid.

15. *Fortune*, March 1951.

CHAPTER FIVE

The account of Bechtel's far-flung activities during World War II is derived from interviews with a number of the principals involved, including Robert L. Bridges, who negotiated many of the wartime contracts for Bechtel; Jerome W. Komes, who worked under John McCone at Calship, and Stephen D. Bechtel, Sr.

For an overview of the efforts of Bechtel and its Six Companies partners during the war, I also relied on a number of newspaper and magazine accounts, the most comprehensive of which is the aforementioned *Fortune* series "The Earth Movers."

Details on the Canol Project were obtained from the papers of Harold L. Ickes on file at the Library of Congress in Washington, D.C., and from a series of columns Ickes wrote in July 1946 for a New York Post Syndicate. In addition, Ickes and other government and military figures such as Lieutenant General Brehon Somervell testified at length before the U.S. Special Committee Investigating the National Defense Program in November 1943. Records of these hearings are on file at the Library of Congress.

The library also has on file a seven-volume history of the Canol project, *The Canol Project and the History of the U.S. Army Eastern Defense Command During World War II*, and *The Canol Project*, 1945, a declassified report that was prepared by a Committee Representing the Central Division, Office of the Chief of Engineers, Office of the Quartermaster General and Commanding General Northwest Service Council.

Commissioned by Stephen D. Bechtel, Sr., *The Canol Project* by Richard Finnie (printed privately in 1946) also provides a perspective of the project from the builder's viewpoint.

Bechtel's involvement with the war effort in the Pacific is best chronicled in *Builders for Battle: How the Pacific Naval Air Bases Were Constructed* by David O. Woodbury (E. P. Dutton, 1946). The privately published company history *A Builder and His Family* is also a useful guide to Bechtel's activities in the Pacific and elsewhere in the war effort.

Records of the Birmingham project are available in the transcripts of the civil suit (*U.S. of America* ex rel. *George B. Alexander* v. *Bechtel-McCone-Parsons*) on file at the General Services Administration, Region 4, Federal Archives and Records Center, East Point, Georgia.

Detailed records of Bechtel's activities at Calship and Marinship appear in the transcripts of the Hearings before the Committee on the Merchant Marine and Fisheries, House of Representatives, in Investigation of the National Defense Program. These hearings were conducted during the last week of September 1946.

1. *Fortune*, September 1943.

2. Interview, Stephen D. Bechtel, July 1984.

3. *Fortune*, op. cit.

4. Investigation of the National Defense Program.

5. A *Builder and His Family*, 64.

6. Ibid., 67.

7. Ibid.

8. Interview, Robert L. Bridges, July 1984.

9. SDB interview

10. U.S. Special Committee Investigating the National Defense Program, October 1943.

11. *The Canol Project*, Finnie.

12. New York Post Syndicate, 7/22/46.

13. New York Post Syndicate, 7/26/46.

14. Ibid.

15. SDB interview.

16. Bridges interview.

17. J. McEany interview with John McCone, 4/28/43.

18. Ibid.

19. Letter, Marguerite Johnston to Mr. Johnson, 3/5/44.

20. Interview, George P. Alexander, February 1987.

21. McEany McCone interview.

22. *Alexander v. Bechtel-McCone-Parsons.*

23. National Defense Program investigations.

CHAPTER SIX

The account of Stephen Bechtel's hiatus after World War II, the formation of Bechtel Brothers–McCone and his reemergence as the head of the newly formed Bechtel Corporation is based largely on an interview with Robert L. Bridges and company records.

John L. Simpson's involvement with the J. Henry Schroder Bank, his initial meeting with John Foster Dulles, his wartime activities and his coming to work for Bechtel are detailed in the John L. Simpson oral history at the Bancroft Library at Berkeley and in Federal Bureau of Investigation files obtained through the Freedom of Information Act.

Steve Bechtel's postwar business philosophy and his dealings with James Black and Jack Horton are based on interviews with Bechtel, Jerome Komes and Robert Bridges. Details of the Transmountain Pipeline Deal were obtained largely from the letters and papers of C. Stribling Snodgrass which are on file at the University of Wyoming. Bechtel's role in helping to found the Stanford Research Institution (SRI) and his company's extensive support of that organization are based on SRI papers and annual reports.

1. Interview, Robert L. Bridges, July 1984.

2. Ibid.

3. Ibid.

4. John L. Simpson oral history.

5. Ibid.

6. Letter, Stevenson to Simpson, 8/25/45.

7. Interview, Jerome Komes, July 1984.

8. Interview, Stephen D. Bechtel, July 1984.

9. Komes interview.

10. Bridges interview.

11. SDB interview.

12. Letter from Sid Blair, president Bechtel Canada Ltd., to SDB, 12/28/50.

13. *Fortune,* May 1958.

CHAPTER SEVEN

The account of Bechtel's activities in Saudi Arabia from 1943 through 1951 is based largely upon State Department files in the National Archives.

1. *The Kingdom: Arabia & the House of Saud,* Robert Lacey, Harcourt Brace Jovanovich, 1981, 233–34.

2. *Arabia, the Gulf and the West,* J. B. Kelly, Basic Books, 1980, 255.

3. Dispatch, J. Rives Childs to secretary of State, 12/3/47.

4. Dispatch, Childs to secretary of State, 2/17/47.

5. *Bechtel Briefs,* May 1947.

6. Dispatch, Francis E. Meloy to Division of Near Eastern Affairs, 9/29/48.

7. Memorandum, American Consulate in Dharan to American Delegation at Jeddah, 6/28/47.

8. Dispatch, Parker T. Hart to secretary of State, 4/13/49.

9. Dispatch, Childs to secretary of State, 2/21/49.

10. Ibid.

11. Dispatch, Childs to secretary of State, 8/4/49.

12. Ibid.

13. Dispatch, Childs to secretary of State, 3/5/49.

14. Letters, Childs to SDB, 12/9/49; to John Rodgers, 12/19/49.

15. Dispatch, Childs to secretary of State, 9/7/49.

16. Ibid.

NOTES

CHAPTER EIGHT

1. Interview, Stephen D. Bechtel, July 1984.
2. *Fortune,* May 1958.
3. *I.F. Stone's Weekly,* 11/7/60.
4. Interview, Jerome Komes, July 1984.
5. Ibid.
6. John L. Simpson oral history.
7. *Life,* July 28, 1958.
8. John A. McCone oral history, Dwight D. Eisenhower Library.
9. Ibid.

CHAPTER NINE

1. Interview, W. Kenneth Davis, August 1984.
2. Ibid.
3. Ibid.
4. *Bechtel News,* February 1950.
5. *Fortune,* August 1958.
6. Speech given before the U.N. General Assembly, 12/8/53.
7. Interview, Stephen D. Bechtel, July 1984.
8. Interview, Robert L. Bridges, July 1984.
9. Interview, Jerome Komes, July 1984.
10. Ibid.
11. Ibid.
12. *U.S. News & World Report,* 10/9/53.
13. *Dun's Business Month,* February 1972.
14. SDB interview.

15. *Fortune*, August 1958.

16. Drew Pearson, *Washington Post*, 1/11/62.

17. Pearson, *Washington Post*, 1/10/62.

18. McCone oral history.

19. *Eisenhower: The President*, Stephen E. Ambrose, Simon and Schuster, 1984, 479.

20. Eisenhower to Bechtel, 11/5/58.

21. John L. Simpson oral history.

CHAPTER TEN

The account of Bechtel's involvement with the intelligence community is based on papers in the National Archives and the Library of Congress, many of which were recently declassified. It also draws upon the papers of Allen Dulles at the Princeton University Library; the papers of John L. Simpson at the Bancroft Library, University of California, Berkeley, and the papers of C. Stribling Snodgrass at the University of Wyoming. Of immense help too were interviews, some of them off the record, with former Bechtel and U.S. government officials who are familiar with Bechtel's intelligence links.

1. Dispatch, Captain E. E. Roth, USN, to Leonard Parker, State Department, Near East Division, 7/14/45.

2. Catlin to Meloy, 5/18/48.

3. Ibid.

4. Borman to Meloy, 10/14/47.

5. Memorandum for Files, Subject: Demolition of U.S.-owned Refineries in Saudi Arabia and Bahrain, 7/19/48.

6. *Big Oil Man from Arabia*, Ballantine, 1958.

7. Simpson to Dulles, 12/16/52.

8. Dulles to Simpson, 2/27/51.

9. Simpson to Dulles, 6/4/54.

10. Simpson oral history.

11. Interview, Frank Jungers, May 1985.

12. Dulles to Simpson, 1/15/62.

13. *New York Times*, 3/22/67.

14. Messersmith to secretary of State, 8/27/42.

15. Bechtel to Suleiman, 10/1/50.

16. Snodgrass to Sanger, 10/28/46.

17. Snodgrass to Bechtel, 7/6/51.

18. Bechtel to Snodgrass, 10/24/50.

CHAPTER ELEVEN

This account of the Bechtels' family life and Steve junior's rise to power is drawn from an interview with Steve junior as well as numerous off-the-record interviews with members of the Bechtel family.

1. Interview, Stephen D. Bechtel, Sr.

2. Interview, Stephen D. Bechtel, Jr., July 1984.

3. Ibid.

4. Ibid.

5. Interview, Robert L. Bridges, July 1984.

6. *Fortune*, November 1955.

CHAPTER TWELVE

1. Interview, Frank Jungers, May 1985.

2. *Strategy and Negotiation for the International Corporation: Guidelines and Cases*, John Fayerweather and Ashok Kupoor, Ballinger Publishing Co., 1976, 89–120.

3. *Ambassador's Journal*, John Kenneth Galbraith, Houghton Mifflin, 1969, 544.

4. *Financial Express*, 3/3/65.

5. Off-the-record interview.

6. Off-the-record interview.

CHAPTER THIRTEEN

1. *Making Democracy Safe for Oil*, Christopher T. Rand, Atlantic–Little, Brown, 1975, 253–54.

2. Off-the-record interview.

3. Interview, William C. Eveland, August 1984.

4. Interview, John L. Lynch, January 1986.

5. Ibid.

6. *Making Democracy Safe*, 273.

7. *Libyan Sandstorm: The Complete Account of Qaddafi's Revolution*, John K. Cooley, Holt, Rinehart and Winston, 1982, 13–14.

CHAPTER FOURTEEN

This account of Henry Kearns's activities at the Export-Import Bank and those of Stephen D. Bechtel, Sr., and the bank's advisory committee is based in part on the Minutes of the Meeting of the Advisory Committee to the Export–Import Bank of the United States (1969–1974). These minutes were obtained through the Freedom of Information Act.

Also useful were interviews with Henry Kearns and other former bank officials, including Rosemary Marzon, the bank's public affairs officer during the Nixon administration.

Many of the details of the Yakutsk project were made public during hearings of the U.S. Senate Subcommittee on Multinational Corporations during the summer of 1974.

1. *Engineering News Record*, 2/21/74.

2. Interview, John L. Lynch, January 1986.

3. Interview, Forbes Wilson, January 1985.

4. Ibid.

5. The payments were first reported to me by a former McKinsey & Company management consultant who traveled extensively in Indonesia. They were corroborated by senior-level officers of both Pertamina and Bechtel.

6. Minutes, MAC, September 1969.

7. Minutes, MAC, February 1970.

8. *Engineering News Record*, 3/31/74.

9. *Washington Post*, 2/26/74.

10. Ibid. The reporter was William Clairburn.

11. Kearns's lobbying efforts for Sonatrach were uncovered by the Anti-Defamation League of B'nai B'rith.

CHAPTER FIFTEEN

1. *Memoirs*, Richard M. Nixon, Grosset & Dunlap, 1978, 438.

2. *Fortune*, January 1975.

3. Interview, Willis Slusser, July 1985.

4. Interview, John L. Lynch, January 1986.

5. Interview, John Ehrlichman, July 1982.

6. *Time*, 7/5/82.

7. Interview, Fred Jacobs, January 1985.

8. Off-the-record interview.

9. Interview, John Haggard, February 1986.

10. Lynch interview.

11. Slusser interview.

CHAPTER SIXTEEN

1. Oral history interview with Caspar W. Weinberger, Governmental History Documentation Project, The Bancroft Library, University of California, Berkeley, 1980.

2. *New York Times*, 2/14/85.

3. Weinberger oral history.

4. Ibid.

5. Ibid.

6. *Reagan's Ruling Class*, Ronald Brownstein and Nina Easton, The Political Accountability Group, Washington, D.C., 1982, 435.

7. *New York Times*, 2/14/85.

8. Ibid.

9. Interview, Willis Slusser, August 1984.

10. Off-the-record interview.

11. Interview, John L. Lynch, January 1986.

12. Interview, Fred Jacobs, February 1985.

13. Slusser interview.

14. Interview, Robert L. Bridges, July 1984.

15. Ibid.

16. Slusser interview.

17. Weinberger to Ford, 10/9/75.

CHAPTER SEVENTEEN

1. Interview with Margaret Lucas Montgomery, February 1984.

2. Off-the-record interview with Bechtel family member.

3. *New York Times*, 2/13/75.

4. *New York Times*, 3/5/75.

5. *New York Times*, 2/24/75.

6. *New York Times*, 2/27/75.

7. *New York Times*, 3/3/75.

8. Off-the-record interview.

9. Letter, Fischer to Tom Neuman, Houston office, ADL, 2/20/75.

10. Cheren's charges were detailed in the *American Examiner–Jewish Week*, 3/4/83.

11. Off-the-record interview.

12. Interview, Lee Loevinger, September 1985.

13. Off-the-record interview.

14. Letter, James Scheuer to Gerald Ford, 12/17/75.

15. Interview, Frank Jungers, August 1985.

16. *Forbes*, 10/1/76.

17. ADL memorandum, 9/14/76.

18. Ibid.

19. Ibid.

20. Interview, Charls Walker, March 1987.

21. Interview, Seymour Graubard, April 1987.

22. Ibid.

23. Walker interview.

24. *Congressional Quarterly Almanac*, 1976, 257.

25. Graubard interview.

CHAPTER EIGHTEEN

The Bechtel company memos regarding the problems at the Tarapur nuclear plant were originally obtained by the late Paul Jacobs. The material relating to Bechtel's involvement with the Ford Administration was obtained in large measure from the presidential papers of Gerald R. Ford through the cooperation of the Gerald R. Ford Library, Ann Arbor, Michigan.

1. Many of the details of the Japanese–U.S. enrichment agreement and Bechtel's role in it were first reported by J. Kwitny in *The Wall Street Journal*, 11/2/75.

2. Ibid.

3. Damm to minister Ueki, 2/25/75.

4. Memo, Davis to H. F. Brush, 9/27/73.

5. Ibid.

6. Bechtel Power Corp. Jobsite Inspection Report Tarapur Project, Job No. 4267, 11/19–23/73.

7. Memo, Davis to Harry O. Reinsch, 12/27/73.

8. H. F. Brush to Reinsch, 12/13/73.

9. Robert L. Beckman, *Nuclear Proliferation: Congress and the Control of Peaceful Nuclear Activities*, Westview Press, 1985.

10. *Engineering News Record*, 2/21/74.

11. Hull to Seidman, 12/24/75.

12. Seidman to Hull, 1/6/76.

13. *Congressional Quarterly Almanac*, 1975, 24-A, 25-A

14. Ibid.

15. Ibid.

16. "A U.S. Firm's Troublesome Flirtation with Brazil," Robert Gillette, *Science*, July 1975.

17. *Washington Post*, 7/14/72.

CHAPTER NINETEEN

1. *Time*, 7/12/82.

2. *New York Times*, 4/16/80.

3. Prince Mohammad's business dealings have been chronicled by a number of reporters, including David Mizrahi in *Mideast Reports*, June 1982, and Michael Field in *The Merchants: The Big Business Families of Saudi Arabia and the Gulf States*, The Overlook Press, 1985, 114–15.

4. Off-the-record interview.

5. Off-the-record interview.

6. Ibid.

7. Off-the-record interview.

8. Prince Mohammad's terms have been reported in *Mideast Reports* and in *Saudi Arabia and Its Royal Family*, William Powell, Lyle Stuart, 1982, 155.

9. *The Merchants*, 115.

10. Off-the-record interview.

11. Off-the-record interview.

12. Interview, Willis Slusser, August 1984.

13. Interview, Raynal Mayman, June 1986.

14. *Miami Herald*, 7/13/82.

15. Off-the-record interview.

16. Off-the-record interview.

17. Slusser interview.

18. *New York Times*, 10/15/79.

19. Interview, Charls Walker, March 1986.

20. Ibid.

21. Ibid.

22. Off-the-record interview.

23. Walker interview.

24. Martin Schram, "The boys from Bechtel may not always see eye to eye," *Miami Herald*, 7/13/82.

25. Off-the-record interview.

26. Mayman interview.

CHAPTER TWENTY

1. Off-the-record interview.

2. *Forbes*, 12/7/81.

3. *Toronto Star*, 6/11/84.

4. *Newsweek*, 7/12/82.

5. *Washington Post*, 12/14/82.

6. Ibid.

7. Ibid.

8. *San Francisco Chronicle*, 9/20/82.

9. Off-the-record interview.

10. Ibid.

11. *San Francisco Chronicle*, 5/31/79.

12. *Wall Street Journal*, 6/15/79.

13. Reagan news conference, 10/18/82.

14. Interview, W. Kenneth Davis, August 1982.

15. *Wall Street Journal*, 7/31/84.

CHAPTER TWENTY-ONE

1. Off-the-record interview, April 1987.

2. *Wall Street Journal*, 6/6/84.

3. Interview, Stephen D. Bechtel, Jr., July 1984.

4. *San Francisco Chronicle*, 1/15/85.

5. Ibid.

6. Ibid.

7. Interview, Raynal Mayman, March 1986.

8. Off-the-record interview.

9. SDB, Jr., interview.

10. *Wall Street Journal*, 6/6/84.

11. *Bechtel Briefs*, May 1987.

12. Ibid.

13. Ibid.

14. Ibid.

15. Interview, John L. Lynch, April 1985.

16. Off-the-record interview.

17. Off-the-record interview.

18. Off-the-record interview.

19. Mayman interview.

20. Interview, Donald Hassler, September 1984.

INDEX